REQUIEM LETTERS

Some Compositions by Ronald Senator

HOLOCAUST REQUIEM
Soloists, narrator, children's and adult choirs, orchestra

INSECT PLAY
Opera in three acts
Libretto by Ursula Vaughan Williams after Karel Capek

FRANCIS AND THE WOLF
Children's opera in two acts
Libretto by Peter Porter

TROTSKY IN NEW YORK
Musical in two acts
Book by Anthony Burgess

ECHOES
Panaroma of the City of London's history
For the City of London Festival 1986
Text by Ursula Vaughan Williams

CONCERTO FOR PIANO, STRINGS AND PERCUSSION

STUDIES IN SYMPHONY

GREENWOOD AND PARADISE
French mediaeval love lyrics translated by Ursula Vaughan Williams

CABARET
Blues, Pop Song and Ballade, for Willard White
Poems by W.H. Auden

SPRING CHANGES
Clarinet and piano, for Stanley Drucker

SHAKESPEARE SONNETS
Reciter with piano, for Miriam Brickman

PIANO MOBILES
for Miriam Brickman

SUN'S IN THE EAST
Classical Chinese lyrics translated by Ezra Pound
Soprano and String Orchestra

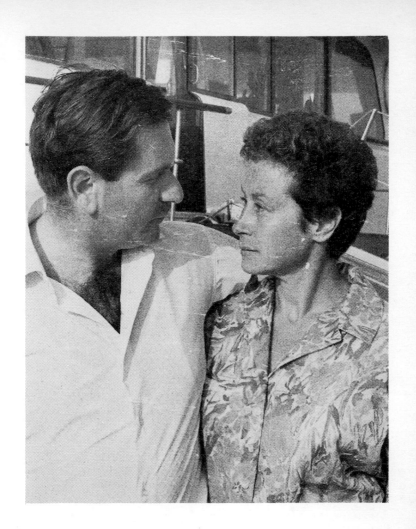

Ronald Senator

REQUIEM LETTERS

Marion Boyars
London • New York

First published in Great Britain and the United States in 1996
by Marion Boyars Publishers
24 Lacy Road, London SW15 1NL
237 East 39th Street, New York, N.Y. 10016

Distributed in Australia and New Zealand by Peribo Pty Ltd
58 Beaumont Road, Mount Kuring-gai, NSW 2080

British Library Cataloguing in Publication Data
Ronald Senator
    Requiem Letters
    I. Title
    941.0820922

Library of Congress Cataloging in Publication Data
Ronald Senator
    Requiem Letters/ Ronald Senator
    1. Senator, Ronald. 2. Composers--Biography. I. Title.
ML410.S4626A3 1995
782.23'092--dc20   95-13119
            ISBN 0-7145-2999-0 Cloth

Typeset in 11/13pt Palm Springs and Erie by
Ann Buchan (Typesetters), Shepperton
Printed on acid-free paper by
Biddles Ltd, Guildford and King's Lynn

Contents

Foreword

This is not a work of fiction.

This is a book based on real events lived through by two real persons. I am one of them. My wife Dita was the other. I shared with her the aftermath of an ill-conceived brain operation called pre-fontal leucotomy. She shared with me the aftermath of an infinitely more shocking trauma, her experiences in Auschwitz and the loss of almost all her family and childhood friends. This biographical reality is important to stress, if only because there are revisionists who dare to claim that there were no gas chambers and so forth. If they were right, Dita would have been an unimaginably cunning and diabolical liar (along with her father, the only other survivor of her family), the number tattooed on her arm which I saw daily for twenty years would have been an illusion, the pain she carried inside herself would have been some kind of phantom, like hysterical pregnancies, and the German courts themselves would have been deluded in awarding her father what they called *Wiedergutmachung*, restitution.

So this book is not *fiction*. But it is *literary* in the telling. The moment we open our mouths to speak, we use devices of speech. The moment we set pen to paper, or finger to keyboard, we use devices of literature. Language and literature are devices, both collective and personal. Facts are cast within the literary devices, as a human subject is cast in a sculpture. The facts are not changed by the devices, any more than is the human subject of a sculpture. But the telling provides a view of the facts. It puts facts in changing perspectives. It arouses feelings about the facts. There can be an infinite number of views of the same facts, as there can be an infinity of sculptures of the same human subject.

The central device I invent or imagine here is an exchange of letters with a person now dead. In this way she can write in the first person.

The person who actually lived through the events is the indispensable witness. These things actually happened, however incredible, however gruesome. No telling, no matter whose, can ever replace the realities. The witness gives the witness's account, of the experiences which must forever remain his or hers: the rest of us can never stand in the same shoes. On the other hand, its 'authenticity' does not guarantee it to be the most telling, the most effective, the most comprehensive account: anymore than there is any guarantee that the human subject may have the gifts and training to mold the best sculpture of himself or herself. 'Authenticity' in itself cannot dispense with the devices of language and literature once it opens it mouth to speak, or sits down to write.

Tolstoy wrote *War and Peace* a generation after the Napoleonic War, to which he could have been no firsthand witness. Yet it remains a classic exposition of that War, in spite of its blend of fictional and real characters.

In this book, none of the characters are fictional, though their names are changed. There really was (and is) a Jacob's Palace in Kosice where my wife grew up, and President Benes lived overhead. The communities of different kinds I lived in — monastic, artistic, therapeutic — all existed and some still do. Much of what is said here about the community where Dita and I lived out our marriage is taken from public papers by its leading therapists, and most of what the therapist Kay says is taken from her own words and writings.

The devices of this book are designed to recreate the events, feelings and relationships which the characters experienced. The reader, for his or her part, is assigned the role of an eavesdropper or an intruder into an intimate exchange of letters which, nevertheless, are devised for that end: to make the eavesdropping irresistible and unforgettable. Think of it, then, as a very original kind of biography. A bi-biography. Two biographies which converged into a common life, a confluence of two rivers. But not for a second as fiction, rather a reality seen through subjective eyes. And our personal chronology is woven inevitably into the tapestry of world events without which it could not have existed.

Prelude
Ronald to Dita

The ancient Egyptians, Ditukam, had an easy commerce between the dead and the living. It seems clumsy to us nowadays, the way they inscribed their letters laboriously on papyrus or on earthenware dishes. Modern e-mail, of course, can imprint our letters like magic on the phosphorus of the computer screen.

Not that it's exactly instantaneous, however. I am sighing out my feelings all over the Mac keyboard, searching for the right words. Can you really know how much I've been aching to write to you? Ever since you died. Died, actually while I held you in my arms, these same arms which now hold my head hunched over the computer. The words have too much to carry, that's the real trouble. So they stumble and get bottlenecked.

Do you remember that horror film we saw together called *Dead of Night*? Michael Redgrave as the ventriloquist whose dummy came to life? The dummy, who seemed to know all the secrets of his life, took over his life and tormented him. Sometimes I think of my Mac like that. It seems to take over and find my words for me.

It squats there in front of me like a god from some newly erupted island, ogling me with its single rectangular eye, Cyclopean and huge. Gawking through and behind my own eyeballs, scanning all those slivers and splinters which form the prism of my soul. With its own secret scanning program, its Optical Character Recognition, which translates what it scans into an intelligible program. The program of my life, that is. The program of the lives we lived together, you and I . . . Secretly, I used to envy the computer one capacity which is lacking in our human minds: to forget. That is, to erase completely, not suppress temporarily. I was wrong: Mac does not do that. Sometimes I think it has a kind of mission to set the record straight. Like that other recently unearthed god-like creature the Unconscious, whose role is to hoard truths which are painful to us, all the while bursting to reveal them, and forced by us to resort to codes which we then have to decipher. Codes, as every programmer knows, are also the very lifeblood of a computer.

I know you, my darling. You're going to belittle my Mac's power. But the fact is, I wouldn't be able to hear from you at all without it. Often it wakes me up with its clang! clang! clang! and there's your letter to me on the screen. A metallic clang penetrating right into my sleep, like a ship's bell in the fog muffled by the yellow eiderdown which covers the sea-bed. And, ah! how the Mac bell uncovers half-forgotten voices like apparitions out of the ocean's cradle, as the tolling of a church bell once rallied a village community out of their beds to call them to mourn or to celebrate their lives together, just as we are being summoned to mourn and celebrate ours . . . Imagine! The bell of a private *Cathédrale Engloutie* swallowed up inside my own Mac!

You know the Greek and Roman world was inhabited by sprites. When you came across them unexpectedly they looked just like dancing fauns. You saw them in the tangled branches of forests. That's where they lived. That's where they worked, spirits both good and evil.

So I'm thinking there must be a twentieth-century breed of sprites in my computer, dancing and doing their work among the intertwined branches of its circuits. Maybe they've mutated to adapt to this new kind of complex circuit-board forest, with its tendrils of wires and its gnarled synaptic knots. Still good or evil. The good ones bring to light, the fluorescent moonlight of the Macscreen, those half-truths and all kinds of fraction-truths buried along with the dead, all needing to be converted into whole-truths. There should be a new command in the Mac menu, to mobilize these good sprites — 'DEFRAG', meaning 'defragment': collect together the fragments of files, the pieces of scattered lives, and integrate them.

Is it, after all, so surprising that the Mac should let me enter into you and your world again, just as I used to when you were alive? The latest programs take us out of this world right through the screen, through the Galactic Frontiers, through nets of polygonal graphics, while being transformed by scaling, zooming, and rotoscope like a passage through Purgatory. No wonder, after so many magical computer maneuvers, that your words, my darling, which girate in the endless dark space of the universe behind the screen, can be reached and brought back into the light of phosphorescence. Like a re-entry into this world's — my world's — atmosphere. So that those words, your words, glow red-hot, and sometimes even burst into flame.

LETTER ONE
Ronald to Dita

Canterbury Cathedral

It's over five years since your death from cancer, and I've wanted to write you very often. The thought unnerves me, I don't know really where to begin, I've put it off time and again. But I have to write now, because I'm bursting to tell you about this week's amazing event. It took place in the great Gothic Cathedral of Canterbury, no less, and it's an event which concerns you very intimately. And I don't want all the external fuss and publicity to obscure a maze of feelings within me spinning around the hub of that event, around that Cathedral nave — chaotic and painful feelings which have to be shared with you and you alone.

The musical oratorio performed at Canterbury Cathedral today I wrote in your memory. I mourned your death and I mourned that terrible trauma in your life, Auschwitz, through this music. What use are the blank and bald words, if I tell you that I poured into it love, and also misery? Anger, and also compassion? For only the music knows the real words to speak, and its voice is heard only by those who have ears to hear. The agony inside myself, by a kind of alchemy, gave birth to a musical star. A pulsating sun, bitter and magnificent. A white giant.

Perhaps to become a red dwarf one day, waning beyond the night horizon. But today it glowed fiercely, and I was burned by its radiation, along with many thousands of other listeners.

My oratorio commemorates the million and a half children who suffered and died under the Nazis. That seems appropriate to me, although I know you were already a teenager when they took you to Auschwitz. That was our private joke, wasn't it? That Auschwitz was your University, as Oxford was mine? That the blue-black number tattooed on your arm was your graduation certificate! Your diploma. Well, actually, your entrance exam. You weren't unlike those raw children taken to the Terezin Camp, whose unsophisticated poems and diaries were sung today at Canterbury in my settings. You too were still a girl just ripening, naive and terrified as you passed under the motto on those now infamous gates: *Arbeit Macht Frei.* What school, what professors, could have prepared you — or any freshman — for such an Admission? (Or any of us, half a century later, still unbelieving novices before those horrors.) You graduated in one of history's most special schools, a school whose purpose was to manufacture human cruelty and human degradation. You earned your *maturitas* by shock and terror, by lessons in survival, stripped of everything and clutching at straws of humanity; by learning to believe the unbelievable, that Maria your younger sister was gassed immediately, then burned to bone and ash, along with your mother, your grandmother, your aunts and uncles, cousins, all your family, so many friends, an entire childhood universe, a whole culture, a complex web of life, everything vanishing into veils of black smoke within hours of arrival at those gates.

So I took for my texts the poems and diaries written by children in the Nazi Camp Terezin, that fortress town north of Prague in your own country, Czechoslovakia; the Camp advertised as a Resettlement Home, deceiving the world because the world wanted to be deceived. I chose those children's words because they are tender and vulnerable and, with an irony which is unbearably poignant, sometimes even playful. That really gets under my skin, you know. That puppy friskiness which outdoes all the filth and all the brutality! Nature's gift of heroism, but oh, with so small an *h*. What a beautiful, heart-tearing *h*! That miniscule *h* of a child which has the power to make mountains skip like rams, and dried-up tear ducts to flow again.

Not that those exterminators could weep, of course. Isn't it a refrain of history?

Innocence defeating its tormentors. The victims becoming the victors. In spite of itself, our non-believing age has given birth to a newly sacred book of psalms, the Holocaust psalms. The modern Psalter, like the old, is a cauldron of cries of anguish and of disbelief and of longing for belief; but its screams are specific to our own epoch, which closes its ears to them. And among so many, the simplest, the most acid-sweet voice is of the child betrayed.

> *Somewhere, far away out there, childhood sweetly*
> *sleeps.*
> *Along that path among the trees,*
> *There o'er that house*
> *which was once my pride and joy.*
> *There my mother gave me birth into this world*
> *So I could weep . . .*

And the child still plays, even in the valley of death's shadow.

> *A mousie sat upon a shelf*
> *catching fleas in his coat of fur.*
> *But he couldn't catch her . . .*
> *He turned and wriggled,*
> *knew no rest,*
> *that flea was such a nasty pest!*
>
> *His daddy came and searched his coat*

he caught the flea and off he ran
to cook her in the frying pan.
The little mousie cried,
'Come and see!
For lunch we've got a nice fat flea!'

My settings are, of course, for children's voices. I build them of simple musical blocks, like children's toy blocks, for innocence: I make them of musical glass, fragile and transparent, for vulnerability. Through the long narrow nave of the Cathedral, weaving in and out of its flowering Gothic arches, high among its hidden galleries into the vaulted roof itself, they glisten like jewels of sound. But the jewels are embedded into a heavy gold. I frame the children's poems with adult lamentation and with a history-laden liturgy for the adult choir and orchestra.

You couldn't know, could you, that our friend Rabbi Albert Friedlander and I projected this text in my study even as you lay dying in the bedroom. He suggested poems by Paul Celan and Nelly Sachs, and liturgical texts which are meaningful for both Jews and Christians, usually direct translations from Hebrew into Latin or English, the heritage taken from the mother religion by the daughter. *Eli, lama azavtani — Lord, why have you forsaken me? Requiem aeternam — El mole rachamim — Lord, have mercy. Kadosh, kadosh, kadosh — Holy, holy, holy. Meloh kol ha-eretz k'vohdecha — Earth is full of your glory. Aveenu shebashamayim yitkadash shemecha — Our Father in Heaven, hallowed be your name.* The work concludes with the *Kaddish,* a cousin of the Christian *Our Father in Heaven,* the Jewish prayer for the dead. With a musical sixth which rises relentlessly, beseechingly, the voices overlay each other to form a Jacob's ladder of sound which climbed today into the winged vaults of the Cathedral.

But surely you must have *heard* all this from where you are? Did you recognize your name inscribed into so many great waves of sound? Did you recognize my signature there? My heart beating? My love and mourning for you? To tell the truth, I'm astonished what a big social event it all turned out to be, there in the Cathedral. A religious event, even, like the burnt offering of primitive religions: a two-way journey between heaven and the rest of us, flesh and spirit of music offered in flames, and something received back in flames, a communion.

A *Kaddish* in Canterbury Cathedral! After two millenia, after a Holocaust, a mixed assembly, a coming together of Jews and Christians! In the orchestra I even use a *shofar* — the sacred Jewish ram's horn, the awesome symbol for over four millenia of the convention before their God of the entire scattered Jewish community. The *shofar* is four times as old as these august and polished Cathedral stones off which its rough sound resonates: stones which once echoed with the swords of Becket's murderers, or with the fervent prayers of the mediaeval Christians to expel the cursed Jews from their land! Never before has a Jewish *Kaddish* or *shofar* penetrated these godly, guarded precincts. A Holocaust has been necessary, the murder and smoke of millions, to awaken some Christians to their own role in fomenting it. The Dean of Canterbury publicly acknowledges this role from the pulpit, before the performance of my work. His voice is heard by millions on the live BBC broadcast, or in one of the many repeats; and his exact words are reported worldwide by Reuters. This performance itself is under the auspices of the United Nations, the German Government, the Council of Christians and Jews, the B'nai Brith. There's a TV program. The Cathedral itself invites and blesses the whole occasion. Six centuries ago, in the time of Chaucer, Christian pilgrims walked along the Pilgrim Way, roughing it even in a rough age, jostling to receive the precious blessings from Canterbury, the heart and the queen of the Christian churches in England. The journey which Jews now make to Canterbury, by car, coach and train is, I suppose, a kind of pilgrimage also: to some kind of Reconciliation, to a healing of wounds which have two millenia of history. The modern journey is quicker and more comfortable, but the road is much, much longer. For it has to be built over heaps of skeletal bodies, it is blackened with smoke from the crematoria chimneys, and it has to find its way through mounds of sheared hair, stacks of false teeth and spectacles, and piles of lampshades made of human skin.

I hope you will be able to respond to this letter, because I want to hear your own voice again. *I have to hear your own words.* They fade too easily, they are smelted into the debased currency of the popular media which have now signed up the Holocaust. Entertainment is everything nowadays, and it swallows up personal pain as much as Presidential elections. *I have to hear your own voice again.* In the hands of this new sorceress Media, the Holocaust is the stuff of popular thrills, sentimentality, titillation, trivialization. Like her namesake, sorceress Medea, she destroys her own children — by defiling the rivers of reality from which they drink. And she acknowledges no barriers.

Barriers. You said it often. You had to have been there to know what it was like. You had to have been shaved and branded. You had to have shivered daily in the endless dawn *Appel.* You had to have smelled the smoke. You had to have lived through starvation and sickness. You had to have been destroyed.

To know, you had to have been destroyed. You had to have been destroyed.

We were both destroyed persons, weren't we?

I was destroyed too. But through very different means. *Destroyed.* How can I use the same word to describe the indescribable outrage you suffered, and that which I did? Can there be comparison in weight or scale?

And yet we were, each of us, victims of our times. In a society which is disintegrated, which has destroyed its rites of passage from adolescence to maturity, which has severed the world from its spiritual moorings, I was a victim of that disintegration. Nazism grew out of that disintegration, a political, even a quasi-religious panacea, and you were one of millions of victims caught up in its coils.

And we shared the after-effects of destruction, whatever the causes. We each knew despair, struggle, and hope. The therapist Kay said it at our wedding, in the community where we chose to live. Bruno Bettelheim said it, and other therapists. But we needed none of them to know that we had something special to offer each other, and to share. You were the miracle survivor of the Nazi death-camps. I was the miracle survivor of a crude prefrontal leucotomy from the hands of knife-happy surgeons, a brutal and unnecessary operation which, by any statistical norm, should have left me some kind of vegetable or monster. A different kind of abuse, not on the center stage of European history, and without its lime-lighted trials of Crimes against Humanity.

We each faced a kind of *extinction.* Of *not-existing.* We each had our own watershed of survival, and we had to refer back to it constantly. It was as if we'd been born again, but out of a devil's womb. Aborted, violently, with savage forceps. And thrown crippled into another kind of life, a life we could never have expected, and never have wished for. Like orphaned and adopted children who celebrate a second birthday, the day of their adoption, we too looked back to a second birthday, though hardly one to celebrate. We were like those adopted children who are never to know what persons they *might* have become.

So everyday life, for each of us, had a sense of skating on ice. We each knew that the normal goals of living, possessing, enjoying, were all too flimsy and precarious. If our life became rich and creative, it was because we knew its shadows. Because we never lived far from those backward glances over our shoulders into something dark and monstrous, without which everyday reality was a surface mask, some kind of half-truth, and therefore a lie.

We learned to salve from wreckage. 'Success' for us was never a glossy cover story. It was pain of labor. It was uneven and groping, like a baby's, learning to walk again, to laugh and cry again.

In each of us was sown a second question: *why was I saved?* It heightened the first question: *why was I born?* which is planted in every child.

The last book you were reading, before the cancer reduced you to a mumbling and withered skeleton, was Victor Frankel's *The Search for Meaning.*

LETTER TWO
Dita to Ronald

My dying, and my father's

I'm really glad to have heard from you, bumblebee. I wish you'd written sooner. My dying was for me both terrible and amazing. But of course it was impossible to tell you anything about it at the time.

Yes, the last weeks of the cancer were horribly difficult, as you ebbed further and further away from me, together with the winter sunlight through the skylight over the bed. I'm not sure how much you really knew, at the very end, what was going on inside me. You had no response from me of any kind, as you sat holding me in your arms, sitting on our bed in the panelled room of our attic apartment. But I heard every word you said. You didn't stop talking to me, did you, that it was alright to let go and leave you, that Apu and Anyu, and all my family were waiting for me. I called out, *APU,* because I saw him. Really very clearly. But you were a blur, though your voice was strong, and I was so grateful to you, and so helpless. And June and Anita were even more shadowy. It was impossible for me to speak at all, in that heavy, sticky haze in which I was groping, and sometimes floating.

I struggled partly because I couldn't bear to leave you. There were whirlpools, deep and luminous, which I resisted and longed for at the same time, they held promise of peace and space. In the end, they sucked down my breath, first into quick gasps, then long deep inhalations, separated by silences. Until the final one. They call this the agony of dying, which means a contest literally, as if wrestling with an angel. And I did wrestle. My body, wasted and shrivelled by the cancer, was the arena. How could you have coped with that decay, day after day, hour after hour? How could you have still held me in your arms, a hag without a hair on my head? Through all the haze of the drugs, I felt the pain of decay and I smelt its putrid smell as it invaded my body, relentlessly. And well past my birthday — for at least one timeless week more: that would have been the sensible time to die, after all, if we'd been part of some romantic novel.

That was at the end. I couldn't make real the idea of actually *dying* — to make it *mine.* We did talk about it, you and I, didn't we? Like the time I told you I wanted to be cremated and my ashes scattered in Jerusalem. (That thought gave me some peace. It was like the times of turmoil after the liberation from Camp, when I was also wasted and haggard, a specter haunting the apartment in Kosice where we'd lived: in those days too, the dream of Israel gave me some strength.) I protected you in my dying, as I had often in my living, and I cried alone. At the beginning I fought against taking the morphine pills, in spite of the terrible pain in my belly. I said to the visiting nurse, *I am too young to go to sleep.* Do you remember when I even rolled on the floor of the bedroom with pain — as we'd seen Apu do in Hampstead, from *his* cancer, barely a year before? Till you called up Laura, a nurse, from the end porch — and together you persuaded me to take the pills. First the morphine hung lacy curtains over everything, and then closed its heavy velvety drapes. The great soother. And the destroyer too. In those last days, I fought against the morphine even while I was welcoming it, clogging and dimming the last remains of the world outside me.

But I dreamed endless dreams. Sometimes frightening,

but often reassuring. Freshly painted dreams, usually, in far more vivid colors than the world I saw with open eyelids.

This one, for example.

I am travelling on a bus, very tired after a day's work, going home. The land around is red and yellow, a rocky desert. Nothing grows there, except jade-green prickly cactus. Yet here and there, rosy red buds are peeping from out of these harsh tough-skinned plants. The buds burst into red flowers, and the flowers part their petals. Inside, there are human faces. Cruel, hard, unfriendly faces, leering at me. (But the people in the bus are very warm and friendly. I recognize many from our community: Jan, Daniel and Frank, Karl, Max and Anita, Laura and Frances . . .) We arrive at a bus-stop, which is the one near my home on Mount Carmel in Haifa when I lived in Israel. And sitting there is my cat Susie, waiting to meet me, just as she always used to do. I get off the bus. Then Susie leads me and I follow her, but it isn't into my house, it's down the mountainside. Now the sun is sinking very fast, the hulk of Mount Carmel is jagged with shadows, and the sea beyond is dark purple. Susie leads me to Elijah's cave. She turns around. Her gray-green eyes, unblinking, hypnotize me and suck out my energy like the yolk of an egg from its white. She meows, then disappears into the blackness of the cave. I follow her. I am in a kind of tunnel. I can feel the cold damp rock-walls close on either side, and low over my head. I see Susie's eyes flash green at me somewhere ahead. And then I hear human sounds: a strange collage of moaning, hysterical babbling, laughter, talking, the voices of many people, including children. I see nothing. Gradually some voices separate themselves from the melée. I hear Anyu's soft tones. I hear Apu. And then my younger sister Marika. I know that Marika's skin is still smooth and unscratched, that her flesh is still soft and virgin, although she died in the gas chamber among women and children screaming and clawing each other to reach the metal doors and the unpoisoned air over their

*heads. Now Susie walks straight over to Marika, and purrs
against her legs. Marika picks up the cat she clearly adores
and is gently stroking her. Set deep in the background
darkness, in what I know to be the large open cave itself,
I see glittering and flashing things, like cellophane, or jewels. And my ears feel crushed with sounds of rushing
water . . . Suddenly I feel stabs of anguish in my womb
(the seat of my cancer operation), and in my breasts. My
body begins to tremble. I am sobbing now. I call out to
Maria, again and again . . .'*

Do you realize what a precious thing you gave me? That
I could waste away and finally die in our own home, and
not in the hospital? Do you remember when you took me
for the first weekend of chemical treatment in the Royal
Marsden Hospital? How I broke down and cried uncontrollably (it was only then for the first time that I could),
when I saw the rows of nicotine-colored patients, bed after bed, like sepulchers; and how that plump Irish nurse
(whose own husband had died of cancer) just took me
into her arms and held me, while I shook? A simple act,
worth mountains of words, by someone who *knew* the
reality. And she arranged a private room for me, away
from all the sights and smells of decaying flesh. It was
hard for me to believe, then, that I would look like those
others so soon: and even harder for you.

Yet only two months later I see a similar waxwork grimace back at me, lifelessly, from my own mirror. Hairless
now, pallid and shrunken. A head-hunter's human tro-
phy. Can you imagine how I feel? How I feel as a *woman?*
How I recoil from myself, how I want just to hate everything?

I believe you did imagine. You come to me in bed one
night, after weeks of sleeping separately. And you hold
me, so gently, and you love that skeleton which is *me*,
and you caress what remains of its flesh. Perhaps it is a
love heavy with pity. But oh, I have never so much needed
that embrace, that warm breath, that living smell of your
body, that lifeline . . .

That New Year was my last. It dimmed the world outside to shadows, and it sealed me off from it, deep inside the pain of my own body, deep inside the heavy ocean waves of morphine. But in the last three months of the old year, my last Old Year, I didn't really believe that would happen to me. I couldn't. You remember how weak I was, and how easily I tired: nevertheless, I wanted to *devour* every grain of life carried into that cramped bedroom by everyone who came to visit me. Especially the children of our community, the carriers of so many tomorrows; so *many* children, all of them 'mine' in some family sense, though some closer, like the ones I got to know better teaching them pottery, and a few very close, like Joel and Jacqueline your god-daughter who'd grown up with us since they were born, the two families even sharing the same kitchen and bathroom (Do you remember when Joel, with the innocent sweetness of his six years, asked if we had sex and, if so, could he watch us?). But I was also disturbed to see the children frightened by me, by my color and my withered body.

And the adults too. So many, who have worked and given themselves in order to *belong together,* whatever the different relationships, as one-to-one. Among them the three men with whom I talked Czech, all teenage refugees from my own Czechoslovakia who had escaped the death-camps but lost their parents. And then some who were outside the community: Anna, and Jane from the Richmond pottery (whose husband David had given up the directorship of BBC 2 television channel to make the 'Life on Earth' wildlife films); Albert the Rabbi, in whose temple I'd found some spiritual food, and his wife Evelyn; Gwynneth the pianist and Roger; your close friend Louis the therapist, and Hindle . . .

In those months I believe that the world for me, in spite of my pains and my fears, or perhaps because of them, was richer and more poignant than ever before.

I lay thinking how Apu had died of cancer only a year before. I know that every father is a link with a past that is over and gone. But hardly ever with a past that was destroyed so savagely and so completely as ours. We were the only two, father and one daughter, to come out of the jaws which swallowed up all the rich life of Kosice, Anyu, Marika, all our family and relatives and the lives and futures of the dozens of friends we knew and countless thousands we did not. Apu and I represented to each other all that was lost, beyond recall, and that loss was somewhere even beyond belief. We meant for each other not only love but unspeakable pain; yet the bonds which tied us together were unbreakable. Perhaps, so long as Apu lived, he always nourished some mental stronghold deep inside me which never fully accepted that my mother and sister and all that past was truly annihilated, that I was finally and irrevocably orphaned. True, he had a long fight against cancer, years of it; but the shock of his dying was beyond anything I could imagine.

And it was a terrible death, in a clinic in Germany, among nurses and doctors he mistrusted as former Nazi sympathizers. He died in an atmosphere poisoned by his mistrust, a complete contrast to myself, I thought, being cared for in our community. He would speak to nobody, not to you, not even finally to Rycha his second wife, only to me, and in the Hungarian he'd spoken to me since I was born. But now in a thin, wind-piping voice. It's strange, that strength I found in myself to be with him then, as he lay yellow-faced and bitter, kept alive by a babybottle drip fed into his arm — an arm lacerated from many needles, because he pulled them out ferociously in his half-comatose, half-waking state. As if I had held in reserve a secret power waiting for his last days, as if I alone had a special task to escort him into his death, through his struggles, his despair, as nobody else could. We'd flown to Bad Nauheim together, remember, you and I, through heavy, such heavy black clouds like pall-bearers: but you had to get back quickly to college. Anyhow, Apu's closed face, with its angry and tired eyes, was withdrawn from you and from everybody — except from me.

And this stocky giant of a man was finally beaten down, defeated at last by his own sick and shrunken body. He had been a fighter before Auschwitz. As a boy of twelve he had provided for his mother in Galicia, and once defended her with an axe during a pogrom. In Kosice, he had built from nothing one of the largest timber businesses in Eastern Europe, and bought an apartment in the same building where President Benes also lived. Into Auschwitz itself he had smuggled a diamond in his anus, and bribed the head kapo with it for a job in the kitchens. That meant warmth, scraps of food, survival. And after the war, after his unbearable losses, when it was most difficult to be the fighter, still he'd worked as a garage hand or sweeping floors, in California and in Israel, before he went to Germany to fight his own *Wiedergutmachung* case. The Germans dragged their feet, with heels they had once clicked in Nazi parades, and the Allies now wanted Germany as an ally against Stalin's Soviet Union. You know, don't you, that only three percent of all the surviving half-million slave laborers managed to receive compensation rarely amounting to a thousand dollars. The industrialist Flick never paid one penny, though he left over $1000 million when he died in 1972. (Do you remember Sartre's play *Altona* we saw at the Royal Court, about the tormented son of a German industrialist of the Nazi era? He was played by Kenneth Haig, who used to be part of our community and was at our wedding.)

That is what brought Apu to Germany, to fight for some restitution. (*Restitution!* Of the gassed, the shot, the hanged, the burned, the starved to death? *Wiedergutmachung* — making good! How do you make such evil good?) And in Germany he married the widow Rycha, a Polish woman who had lived through five mole-years of hiding from the Nazis, protected by her Polish lover. (There were many thousands of Anne Franks, all over Nazi Europe, and each one must have had an amazing story of risk and fear and courage, and often betrayal.) And they settled in Germany, the country of their murderers, although they had a house in Israel. As did so many Jewish survivors, who felt at home in the Germanic culture they had been brought up on, in spite of everything. The money he was paid, said Apu, was a bribe by people who would not face their guilt. In the elegant shops and cafés of Bad Nauheim where they lived, in the palatial parks and the ornate formal gardens, he never knew, Apu said, which of these respectable German citizens had the red hands of murderers. *Blut mit Schlagsahne,* blood with whipped cream, he said. But still he went on living there. And he died there, also, filled with mistrust for the haughty German doctors and their prim nurses.

So in that Old Year, my last year, I lay in bed or hobbled round our apartment in the community, and I thought about survivors, and how Apu had the fight in him before Auschwitz, as he did afterwards; and perhaps that I had something of his fighting spirit also, not as great, but enough. . . And yet I was frightened, and I wondered whether, in spite of the fight in me and my driving love for living, and in spite of all the healing trust and care in our community — something Apu never had — still, I wondered whether there were wounds gashed too deep inside me ever to be healed, ever. And sometimes I just cried. Alone. I cried myself to sleep, often. I didn't call you from the study. I tried to protect you, darling. I loved you. That was why I couldn't bear to leave you without my care. I was not ready to die, I couldn't imagine how anybody could be ready to die. I was too young to die.

And I know what a high price you yourself paid for my being able to die at home.

LETTER THREE
Ronald to Dita

Cancer Hospital. Losing your hair

Thank you, *édesem*, thank you. (*Édesem, drágám, drágaságom, majomochkám, veverichkam, békachkam, my sweet, my darling, my treasure, my little monkey, my little squirrel, my little frog*. . . all those silly-magic Hungarian and Czech words of loving you taught me to stake out our own intimate world, and took their meaning from that world. Perhaps other lovers use them too, but then their meaning must be quite different.) It's been so long, but it's your voice alright, as authentic and present for me as my own self.

But do you know that I also have your *real* voice, I mean the voice which vibrated the air and twanged the harp in my ear as well as my heart for twenty years? Yes, really. I have it trapped. In a Panasonic pocket tape-recorder. You see, I used that recorder like a confidante, in the hour-glass months before your death, to whisper or cry into, sometimes even to shout with anger into, alone at night in my study. I trusted those tiny two-inch tapes more than my memory, because they were impersonal. They couldn't hide too much reality or pain, and they couldn't later lose themselves in distractions. I could bury that agonized

present in them like a time-capsule . . . Do you remember
that we wired up an intercom speaker from the bedroom
to the living room, so that the nurse could hear you if you
were in need? On the evening of your last birthday, not
long before you died, I taped your voice through the
speaker. I wanted your voice, I needed to have your voice,
I clutched at this way of keeping your voice, now that
you were leaving me forever. Even though it wasn't the
voice I knew from the past twenty years, laughing, serious, sweet, angry, bubbling, matter-of-fact. It was now a
voice in agony. I took what I could get, then, in the last
days. My last chance. Although it's your voice distorted
by pain. Babbling your native Hungarian, bewildered,
wanting to be reassured, to be held together as your world
dissolved.

I felt helpless, so unbearably helpless. Oh God, your
moaning, your terrible and endless moaning. I can't bear
to hear it.

As if this moaning was the real core of your life, un-
wanted but always returning, in spite of all your sweetness and all your hunger for even the smallest morsels of
living.

And, yes, in the center of all the moaning you are crying out for Marika. Again and again, *Marika! Marika!
Marika!* Marika who looks like you on the photo I have
of you both — you, a sunny sixteen, wearing that scarf
your boyfriend gave you, Marika curling her lip as she
smiles. Marika who died in the gas chambers with your
mother and all the others. My tape is like a sculpture in
sound: an artificial memorial which has forever captured
you crying for your destroyed sister, and with her for your
own destroyed youth, for your own lost life.

That same photo, of yourself and Marika as girls, I once
showed to Apu. It was unthinking and foolish of me. I
didn't realize the ice was so thin, just two or three sec-
onds thin. It cracked, and he collapsed into uncontrolla-
ble sobbing.

I too remember the anguish of Apu's cancer, a year before your own. I remember his groans as he writhed on the floor in Hampstead. His eyes were rolling and his hands clutched his stomach in pain, as he said to me, *Ronnie, look after Rycha, look after Rycha, please, please.* He was the caring one, even in his pain. Before the clang of the ambulance bell, before two men with a stretcher, and the young intern on duty in the Hospital Emergency who announced brazenly he doubted Apu would live through the night. Rycha shrieked. Not with despair at losing her husband, but with anger at the doctor. *What did he know?* *She* had kept Apu alive for ten years with constant, careful dieting. The operation was a fiasco, the artificial segment for his diseased duodenum was inserted the *wrong way round,* and the valve was ineffective. Yes, how strange that he went back to Bad Nauheim to die, to the country which had robbed him and murdered his family . . . Apu loved me as the son he never had, as the future for his daughter who alone had survived the wasteland of his past — and I loved him too.

The other records I have of you are all visual. Photos, home movies. From your past, but also of our rich life together. So many taken in the community, but also in Israel, in Greece, in Italy, in Spain, in America, in Australia . . . Laughing and wet in the Thames by Max's boat; delighted at the spring ducklings behind the church at Bosham; you with that Mona Lisa, serene half-smile that I loved; or serious, with lowered head cocked sideways, eyes upwards and intent, during an after-dinner talk under the skylight of our attic kitchen . . . So many faces, so many gestures, stored in so many boxes of photos and films: but inside me they add up to, and can never add up to, only one person. That's the mystery. Of loving one person. Of losing one person.

You are right, the cost *was* high for me. You wasted away and died at home and not in hospital. We wanted to avoid the strangers, the nurses and doctors, the impersonal priorities of treatments and technical apparatus. We wanted you to struggle for your life and, if need be, to die your own death, close to me, and in the climate of openness and trust which we had created in our community — something few people have. To share your dying as we had shared your living. I remember how, some years before, the Dominican priest and disciple of Jung, Victor White (who had his own quarrels with his God) chose to come to the community to die, away from his monastery, for that very reason: *to have his own death.*

Yet, in the event, once the glow of Christmas had gone, death crept past us into the bedroom and into your body, into both our lives, so stealthily, such a thief in the dark, that it seemed your last moaning delirium arrived before we knew it, or were ready for it.

I'd no experience to imagine how terrible that delirium would be. When we entered together the ward in the cancer hospital at Sutton, that autumn, for your first weekend of the platinum treatment, when we saw the rows of ghostly nicotine faces, their life drained, I was astounded that you burst into tears. You foresaw what I couldn't: a mirror of your own face in theirs. The pudgy Irish nurse also knew. She gave you her chubby warm hug to cry into, without a word. And when I was alone with her, she warned me you would soon be as consumed as the patients in her beds. At that time, I would sooner have believed that chalk was cheese.

And so the winter comes, the treatment has only a limited effect and I watch you shrivel and turn yellow. From my study, where I sleep, I watch the year die and the leaves and the great sun itself waste away daily into yellowness, just as you do, *édesem.* Yet the leaves possess a luxuriant, garish beauty in their dying, unlike human victims of cancer. Their death is beautiful, year after year — and there is no doubt they will be reborn in the spring, as did the ancient gods.

There is one blustering night, and my feelings are stormy to match as I fall asleep in the studio. After a few hours, I get out of bed and open the curtains. I'm surprised to feel brilliant sunlight caressing my face. The garden below has become a sort of parkland. The branches of treetrunks are dripping with springtime blossoms. One bush stands out, a mass of flame-colored flowers. It has grown from the frail sapling we planted together in the community garden, as a kind of ritual, saying the Jewish *Kaddish* for the dead, on the spot where we buried the Nazi soap — you know, the soap you'd hoarded for years, that soap marked *RDF*, for *Reines Jüdisches Fett: Pure Jewish Fat.* But the strangest things in this dream are the animals. Many are prehistoric. Great pterodactyls, wings half-folded, perched on the back walls; even a giant Tyrannosaurus rex in the far corner (where we built the mound, you remember, out of the builders' rubble when the original four houses were joined together). There are large scarab beetles, alligators, a Staffordshire bull-terrier with a single horn in his forehead, like the unicorn of legend, and cats with many-colored stripes and enormous yellow eyes. And your own voice seems to hover over the whole scene, and penetrate it. More precisely, I think your voice is coming from the wooden shed in the No. 6 garden which you made into your pottery, with shelf upon shelf of pots and figurines where you worked at the wheel, where you gave your classes, where you had your periodic firings in the kiln. Your words are very clear but curiously hollow and resonant, *It all depends on the firing. Yes, the clay can be remolded. Even the rotten glazing. It all depends on the firing* ... This might be a very frightening vision, but it isn't at all. The bizarre community of animals all seem to be at peace with one another, and with their surroundings. Nor am I disturbed by the time warps, which have brought together our own familiar garden where you work, with one of the many ancient springtimes in the evolution of the earth.

For this is my own dream, my own version of the myth of the everlasting springtime of life, when the clay will be remolded, the primal clay from the world's first day.

I wake up with a sweet taste. But the darkness of the room creeps back and soon muddies my dream. That heavy weight is lowered again onto my chest. My dream is cut away sharply by the razor-edged reality I must live with.

I'm helped by my composition at the studio, away from the apartment. Strange, some work I do for Thames Television is an encounter with death. Peter Greenaway is making a film called *Lightning.* He is sitting in my studio with the cameras and continuity girl while I am interviewing an Alpine guide in front of my electronic synthesizer — in order to imitate the natural sounds he describes. The guide was trapped in one of those mountain pockets where lightning is born. The electrical charge builds up (I turn up the white noise till it reaches a high pitch, volume, and density) and then (swoosh!) discharges across the valley. The guide's metal braces sing with electricity, as does the match he strikes for his last cigarette . . . He escaped, but his hair turned white.

How can I accept what is happening to you? That your body becomes as cold and as gnarled as the year's dead wood? That your head becomes shriveled and fleshless like the kernel nuts on the freezing ground, stripped bare of their once ripe flesh of fruit?

It is a torture to watch you and be helpless in watching. There was a time when we could have stopped our story from beginning. Now we cannot stop it from ending.

It seems that even the smallest and most commonplace things we did, so many times before now, seem charged and meaningful, like precious gifts stolen from eternity. In *The Idiot*, Dostoevsky describes the condemned man for whom the last remaining minute of life unfolds itself, peeled bare, spread out into 'Nows' beyond numbering. The sort of experience saints are supposed to have, or artists who agonize to capture the transient present. You are right . . . It seems our marriage entered (in between the ticks of the clock, in between the heartbeats) into a new and frightening sphere like Alice through the looking glass. Little things became bigger, big anxieties became smaller, passing pleasures became priceless, everything high-lighted under the lens of a microscope set up by the coming darkness.

Like just eating together. By the New Year you can't eat any more, your intestines are blocked. I think of that anchovy paste, for instance. Max hears you love anchovy and brings you a large box stuffed tight with tubes of paste, like sardines in an oversized tin, and your palate is still sharp enough to savor it. Or watching together the movie of your choice, the last you'll ever see, *Guys and Dolls*, which my nephew Ricky, who works for Warner Bros, brings over and projects. We hold hands watching the trees swelling with the late summer, through the study window. But as the autumn first dyes and then ravages them, so you too lose the strength to walk there from the bedroom.

Do you remember the evening I leave you and go out to meet Samuel Pisar? He is talking about his new book, *Of Blood and Hope.* He is a 'graduate' of Auschwitz like yourself. He might even have been on the very same transport out of Hungary in May 1944. Pisar writes about the impersonal mentality which is able to murder legions of innocent people, in Hiroshima as well as in Auschwitz. The gas chambers were an early warning of this mentality to the entire world, which did not heed it. When I tell him that you are struggling for your life at home, he gives me his book for you, with this inscription:

For Dita Senator
the same blood
the same hope
the same struggle
with best wishes from her brother in the eternal
struggle for survival
Samuel Pisar

I am grateful to you that you can still be busy with me even in your weakness. You insist on hearing every detail of my première at St. John's Church, Smith Square, where I conduct *Sun's in the East*: settings of Chinese

lyrics, which Jane Manning sings with such verve and
finesse. You have to know exactly how she looked in her
glittering Chinese jade costume. You have to know who
was there, and the very words they spoke. You have to
play the recording over and over. And then there's that
fiasco of the lost manuscript, the first act of my opera,
Insect Play which Ursula Vaughan Williams has adapted
for me from the original Karel Capek (your countryman!).
I'm beside myself. Ursula hasn't made a copy. And then
suddenly it turns up. Max finds it in the gutter outside (I
must have dropped it getting out of the car), crumpled
and weather-beaten and looking for all the world like
some venerable manuscript surviving from the Middle
Ages! (Do you remember the other manuscript story with
Ursula? How as a student I'd borrowed from the Oxford
Press one of the few copies of Ralph Vaughan Williams'
Tuba Concerto and it had got badly burned in the fire in
my Maida Vale apartment — that Ash Wednesday — *Yes!
Ash Wednesday!* — just before I met you. And they
thought that some student disliked the work enough to
set fire to it!)

Sometimes we pass in and out of different worlds
abruptly. A cancer hospital is a different kind of world,
a frightening one from which you mightn't get out
alive. Solzenitzhyn once described an everyday Soviet
Russian world which existed side by side with another,
unsuspected world of prisoners: and, quite suddenly,
on a street with a passing car, or on the Metro escal-
ator, a person was arrested and transported from one
world into the other. It is like that when I first take you
to the modern Royal Marsden hospital. Set in serene
suburbia, near Sutton, I've driven past it often on the
way to college. Once inside, we are actors and victims
of another universe. Though for the doctors, nurses, ra-
diologists, registrars, even the transport drivers, cancer
is their daily bread. Chemical feeds, amputations,
scannings and radiation therapy, the decay of tissue,
organs and bones; husbands, wives, children, support-

ing (or resenting) each other during the drudgery of treatments; the large foyer, like a hotel lobby or an airport lounge, always crowded with patients waiting wearily, hopefully, desperately, for their scan, for their diagnosis, like a verdict. For all the reassurance of small-talk, of comfortable armchairs and magazines and of the cafeteria, it seems to be a great antechamber to a Court of Life and Death, to a Kafkaesque Trial where people aren't sure who the Judge is, how you can get to him, or on what grounds the verdict is finally made. The staff knows this scene from every hour of their working life in that institution, but for us it is new and shocking. Over there, drinking tea, sits a middle-aged man, pale and unnerved, clearly sharing some difficult news with his distraught wife who is holding his hand. Next to us, in a wheelchair, an Indian man with shoulder and arm amputated, the gap covered by a cloth, asks for the glass of water he can't manage to get for himself. I give him one from the fountain, and his smile is grateful and pathetic.

How easily a victim of cancer is reduced as a person! Everyone has their role in the system, and it is not primarily to embrace you and give you sympathy. There's a hierarchy, with the doctors at the top, and an impersonal power given to the diagnostic machines. The technicians are concerned with clear pictures of your growths, not with you and your feelings. And the system — but that is really the patients themselves, who invest the doctors with almost magical powers, out of their own need for reassurance and certainty, although in reality their power is so limited. Doctors are human, they compete for the prestige and money which come with cures: so many patients die, and quickly, and any prolongation of life, however short, is an easy triumph.

Alone with you in her office, your doctor is gentle, especially when she writes the details of your Auschwitz history into the form on her desk. But she too has her professional objectivity. Cool and kindly, she hands out her diagnosis and her hopes, like a plate of food to

hungry beggars. That weekend she must be at a conference in Istanbul, and we would talk again.

I recall you cringing to her — what other word? — a
fortnight later in the hospital lobby, as she passes through
the mass of waiting patients, as you beg her for news of the
scan. She has become the messenger of life and death for
you. I have never seen you so reduced. I cannot bear it.

Christmas marks the watershed, the beginning of the
end. As the January frost bites the soil, as the bulbs and
branches draw back their life into themselves, so your
life too is sucked back into yourself, and I can reach you
less and less.

You hold back from dying because you don't want to
leave me without your care. On my side, I have the responsibility of helping you to die. For that I have no preparation or training. We wrap death up and leave it out of
sight. But now you are dying in my arms, I am finding
words to say to you, though I'm not sure you hear them:
*It's alright, you can let go now, it's alright, I shall man-
age: you've fought enough . . . Apu and Anyu are waiting for you . . . And Marika is there also . . .* Yes, it's precious that you can die in my arms. No, there's no sense in
your dying. You are too young. It is a cruel interruption.
I am angry and bitter that this is happening. But at least it
is a consummation of our life together that the very last
air you breathe out of your lungs, that long slow sigh, is
while I am holding you in my arms.

I hope I will never gloss over the horror of those last
weeks.The groans of your agony, even while you sleep,
fill the apartment night and day. And as I watch your
body wither and your eyes grow huge in their sockets, I
can't help thinking, isn't this the Dita of Auschwitz again,
this phantom skeleton so remote from the warm flesh,
the busyness, the verve I knew for twenty years. Are they
right, then, those who say that Auschwitz never surrenders its victims, that it strikes them even thirty-five years
later, with cancer as its ally and assassin, only waiting in
the wings for the moment to strike?

Yes, your dying at home is precious, but there's a price.

It's after you've gone that I feel my own anguish and physical exhaustion. When I look into the mirror, I see that the pain of those last days together have swollen the bags under my eyes like skin water bottles. I cry now, uncontrollably when your eyes laugh at me from your photo on my desk, your head tilted to one side. Your clothes droop in our closet like abandoned specters, as if tormented themselves — as I am tormented — by the smells of your body they still carry, and by the sheen of your flesh they imitate. And, without you to wear them, your jewelry seems a sunken treasure fathoms deep.

But the deepest pain is not immediate. For a time, numbness spreads a protective covering, like a snowdrift, so that even my senses seem to lose their sharpness. Things lose their proper shape, as if shrouded in some loose plastic bag, like that black one in which two men from the crematorium carry your dead body out of the apartment, the evening of the day you die. A Friday evening, Sabbath eve, *erev shabat*. And, as if anaesthetized, I see the contorted plastic mass which had been you, shapeless and shiny, carried from the bedroom where you died and out through the front door. While in the living room, packed with hot, swaying bodies of my family and friends, we are praying the mourners' *Kaddish*. *Yisgadal veyiskadash shmei raba. Magnified and sanctified be His Name* — the Name we do not know and is always unpronounceable. Again and again, for every life, for every birth, a death and a Kaddish. One for one, it is supposed to be a fair exchange. The Kaddish, the great paean to Him who gives and therefore has the right to take away. To take whenever He likes. However He likes. In the ripeness of years or in the agony of years aborted, ripped apart and rotting.

I can't bear this ritual and these meaningless words. I can't identify you with that stuffed plastic bag. Anymore than I can believe that you are in the coffin I see disappear behind the curtain which conceals the fire, at the cremation ceremony. Nor are you in the vase of ashes. (You know that Rabbi Albert Friedlander took them to

Israel, as you wanted, and scattered them in the Park of Independence in Jerusalem?) Why did you choose to be cremated? Was it to be mingled with the smoke from the camp chimneys, the smoke of your burned family, the smoke of your childhood ? Why did you choose a grave-yard in the sky, disappearing into the surround of blue like a jet-trail, or like sky-writing made of smoke . . . The smoke from the chimneys also wrote a sign on the sky, one that no-one wanted to read.

A week later, your death is still unreal to me. Coming back from an extraordinary evening, I rush up the stairs to share it with you, as if you are still here. Malcolm Williamson, the Master of the Queen's Music (did you see him at your cremation?), was honored on his fiftieth birthday at Australia House. He wore a *yamulka*, like a Jew. There was a circle of dignitaries standing round him — Lord Goodman, Royal family . . . 'What is that you're wearing, Malcolm?' 'It's a Jewish skull-cap.' 'But why are you wearing it tonight?' 'I am in *shiva* for the death of Dita.' 'Who was Dita, and what is a *shiva*?' He explained: 'A *shiva* is a period of mourning for Jews. Dita was my friend, who survived Auschwitz.' And I drive home furi-ously to share all that with you . . .

I can't help it, the ghosts of Auschwitz haunt your can-cer and death. Auschwitz has claimed you again, thirty-five years after your liberation. I feel that strange, cruel echo: again you lose your hair. A coincidence? Chemical treatments make the hair fall out. The hospital hairdresser comes to fit you with a wig, for him a matter of routine. Yet how the past resonates! That trauma, that threshold which life crossed into death, that moment of shock in Auschwitz when reality burst in on you, as you have so often said to me, when the sheers savagely snipped off all your girlhood hair, and with it your girlhood itself . . .

LETTER FOUR
Dita to Ronald

Entry into Auschwitz

You wrote me, my dear, when the *Requiem* you composed in my memory was performed at Canterbury Cathedral. It was like the end of a chapter, and the music illustrated it. You used to say, didn't you, that your music could punctuate life, as well as reflect it somehow. That's true. Like Capitals at the beginning of paragraphs in illuminated manuscripts, full of promise; or commas, you said, cornucopias half-empty and half-full; or fullstops, black buffers or tiny mandalas. When my lump (I said I'd got pregnant at last! Remember?) became painful, the very day, yes, before the fateful visit to the surgeon, there was the performance of your children's opera, *Francis and the Wolf* in the new Covent Garden Piazza, the day after it was opened by the Queen. I sat up in the southeast balcony, above the crêpe restaurant, with a full view over the audience below to the Inigo Jones portico of St. Paul's Church, in front of which the action began. For all the world like some Renaissance Lady viewing the piazza of her native Italian town!

I loved it. The strutting bourgeois of Gubbio — Gonfalonier, Fine Lady, Furrier; the comic and pathetic (but very sophisticated) wolf driven out of his natural

wits by those greedy capitalists; and Francis himself, mixture of lamb and lion, with music to express these opposites. And I cared deeply about the serious message in all
the fun: the one world, and our broken harmony with
nature. You planned that opera with Peter Porter over
lunch at *Quo Vadis* in Soho (you were conspirators, you
joked, under the very attic where that father of conspirators had lived, Karl Marx!). I remember, too, the macabre
coincidence: that you planned the opera the very hour
his wife was committing suicide. I imagine an invisible
audience of the ghosts of writers and actors and composers hovering round the famous portico. Samuel Pepys
who watched a puppet show there three centuries earlier. And the galaxy of theater giants buried there, Noel
Coward and Terence Rattigan, Arne and Constant Lambert, Marie Lloyd and Marie Rambert, Vivien Leigh and
Sybil Thorndike, Boris Karloff and Donald Wolfit . . .

The weather reflected my own moods. First the heavy
clouds threatened a storm; like my own foreboding of
what that lump was. Then sunshine stole across the stones
of the piazza and the extravagant costumes, cautiously,
as if not daring to believe in life. And no sooner had the
last chorus and audience song ended, the black clouds
returned, as if impatient of all this distraction. As did the
heaviness inside myself.

Yes, you are right about my hair, and that terrible echo
— losing my hair in the cancer as I did in the camp. Her
hair is a woman's glory. Oh yes, *how I hated, hated, hated
to lose my hair!* But there can't really be a comparison. It
was infinitely more violent at Auschwitz, and it was done
by evil men. You see, the shaving of hair was part of the
entry-shock into Auschwitz, into the place of death. Since
the first manned space capsules, astronauts have suffered
from entry-shock into the earth's atmosphere. And really,
that was like entry-shock into the evil atmosphere of another planet. But a man-made atmosphere. That shock
was planned, brutally, in order to destroy your character,
your person. To break up all those layers of trust, all that
you took for granted in morality and decency and author-

ity, all that you'd learned from parents and teachers and friends. To strip you bare, like a city plundered by pirates and razed to the ground. To reduce human beings to mere beasts in the ruins. We were stripped of the flesh of our humanity, as we would very soon be stripped of our physical flesh.

After the ramp and the selections, we were made to strip naked before the eyes of the SS as we were pressed into the showers. Then we stood in the cold glare of bare light bulbs, for hours it seemed, while the strange prisoners in their coarse striped cloth and their inhuman, skeletal eyes mocked us with leering Polish swearwords (but why weren't they on our side?). And we were shaved, no, we were *sheared* as if we were so many dumb sheep, violently, coarsely, non-stop, one after the other. They wielded huge crude shears, blunt from brutal use round the clock, so that large lumps of my hair were savagely torn away. And torn from my pubis, and from my armpits, as well as from my head. There were mounds of hair on the dirty floor, and I saw striped Polish skeletons sweep them up into sacks. We had now become human raw material in a special factory, anything that could be, would be recycled. My hair might have ended up in a German mattress, or in the pipe-joints of German U-boats.

It was then, I remember, for the first time since I'd stumbled from the cattle-truck of the train onto the Auschwitz ramp, it was then, among shivering, half-sobbing strangers and the inhuman, mocking guards, that I knew my real feelings. Cutting my hair also cut through the fog of numbness which had been enveloping me. I felt helpless, I felt alone, I felt despairing. Above all, I felt I was being *defiled. Abased. Humiliated.* And I fell apart, and I know I began to sob, convulsively. But I swallowed my sobs, I choked on my sobs, because I had to. When one of us cried out loud she was beaten harshly by a guard with a whip. Beaten savagely, for no reason except to make her cower and feel subjugated and punished. You still find this hard to believe, don't you, *drágaságam*? Even though you've read about it all, and by now many times over . . .

But we had nothing to prepare us for this ordeal of stripping, for this rape of our human self-respect, of our pride, of our very lives, as well as of our hair. Even the glare of the lamps seemed unreal as we just stood there in a half-trance, not believing what we saw, not believing what was being done to us.

That is what I remember of losing my hair in Auschwitz.

No one, who was not there, can imagine how stunned and confused we were. We had suffocated, crammed in the dark cattle-truck, with only the merest crack onto the outside world, high over our heads, a slit of starlight which turned into a dim daylight and then, aeons later, into dusk again. The air was foul and sweaty and stinking. Sometimes I, sometimes Apu or Anyu, held Marika up towards the crack, as others were doing with their children. We had no food, and we had nothing to drink. We couldn't urinate or defecate except on the floor, on the walls, and on each other. There was a basin someone had carried with them, that had been an improvised toilet, if you could get to it, but it had soon spilled its muck over the floor. The stench was fearful. There were pious Jews who recited prayers at intervals, chanting and swaying. *Baruch atah Adonai: Blessed art Thou Lord. The heavens are the heavens of the Lord; but the earth hath he given to the children of men.* Yes, it seems he certainly has. There were some who strapped their *tefillim* around their arms and foreheads — the little leather black boxes containing the scroll of the *Sh'ma Yisrael* which their ancestors had heard first in the deserts of Sinai. All that Jewish piety was really a completely alien world to me. Yet choking there in that cattle-truck, rattling and creaking along so slowly, only God knew for how long and to where, snatched away from all the life we'd known, I did clutch at the alien mumbo-jumbo of those ancient ritual Hebrew prayers as if they did, after all, contain locked-up secrets, centuries of reassuring Jewish wisdom which had seen many

powerful empires crumble, a long history in which I
myself was now brutally forced to play a part.

Nothing has prepared us for this stifling hell-train.
Many times it jerks and jolts to a stop. We hear clanging.
Trucks are being shuttled and joined. We hear a melée of
indistinct voices shouting outside in German and Polish.
At every stop men and women, Apu among them, batter
frantically on the heavy wooden door. *Water! We need
water! Air! There are children suffocating to death!* Does
anyone hear us, does anyone care, outside this railway
truck, beyond these railway lines, beyond all these villages and towns we pass through, beyond this country?

But the final stop is altogether different. Bellowing,
screaming in German, *'Raus! Raus! Raus!'*. Dogs barking
and howling. Fierce thudding on the doors, then the
clanging of bolts. Groggy people, mothers with crying
babies, dazed children, all fall in confused heaps onto a
platform ramp lighted by long rows of torches, blinding
our eyes. And there is another grimy kind of light, coming from fires in the distance. In those bewildered
moments of arriving we know nothing as yet of the crematoria fires, or of the ditches of flames where human
corpses are burned continuously, sometimes even living
beings, because the ovens cannot cope with the carnage.
But we do see the strange red glows, the colors painters
used to depict Hell. Men and women are shouting to each
other through the confusion. Children are crying, wail-
ing. Marika is clinging to Anyu's hand. I am helping my
grandmother. She is weak and fumbling. We are herded,
viciously, with clubs and riding whips, towards the end
of the ramp, by black uniforms and green uniforms.
Among them we are shocked to see, for the first time,
unearthly skeletal men in striped uniforms like pajamas
with their heads close-shaven.

We have come to another universe. Loudspeakers are
blaring commands in German. 'Leave your baggage behind': and with it our lives, our homes, our memories.
The women are herded to one side, the men to the other.
We are swept along as if by the waves of a heavy sea, yet

we are managing to keep abreast of each other. I go through the motions of walking, like an automaton. At the far end of the ramp there are two officers. This is my first sight of the notorious Mengele himself, the handsome, elegant, devilish doctor of Auschwitz. The other officer, on the right, is some kind of *Arbeitsführer*, or work supervisor. It is he who is asking Apu questions — how old is he, what kind of work he does. Gyuszi, Apu's secretary who has stuck close to us since the brickyard in Kosice where we were first assembled, now shouts across that he is a carpenter in his thirties (in fact, Apu runs a large timber business from his office, and is past forty). It is Mengele who directs him this way with a slight wave of his hand. Other people are routed the other way, including my mother Anyu, together with a terrified Marika still clutching her hand on one side and my grandmother holding her arm on the other. *I am never to see them again.* There is never to be any kind of humane farewell, a word of comfort, a kiss or an embrace. The merest movement of a hand has a divine omnipotence, to spare or to destroy our lives, for it is the hand of Mengele. But we are paralyzed by these few, eternal minutes, and the horror of the truth is hidden from us. We see that there are large motor trucks parked in rows, waiting for them, for these older men and women, for these mothers and their children. And on many trucks are painted large red crosses glowing in the torchlight. We want to be reassured. Those about to die . . . We want to be reassured. The whole world wants to be reassured. And the Nazis, like lizards and serpents, are masters of reassurance and camouflage.

I am not to be murdered immediately. I am to be tortured slowly and painfully. I am well-built, I am among the fourteens to thirty-fives, I am reserved for a slave's death through starvation and exhaustion. I am one of the great herd of cattle branded for slave labor in the war factories built within the huge triple-city of barracks, maybe in Krups, in Siemens-Schukert, or in I.G. Farbern. My own brand-mark is, in fact, for the Farben camp-within-the-camp at Monowitz. This will be my new prison and my condemned cell, with its own army of police brandishing whips, its own daily floggings, its own daily diet of watery potato-turnip soup at noon and a piece of bread at night. I can expect to be dead within three months. The night will vanish in a few hours of sleep. I will be woken at 3 a.m. for the *Appel,* the parade and roll-call of specters that lasts for hours, then I will set off to work at the 'SS trot', sometimes carrying heavy packages of chemicals, with no break for rest. That is if I survive the *Appel,* if the Arbeitsführer or SS officer has not selected me as one of the sick to be sent to Birkenau.

But now I am being initiated. I am being brutally stripped of myself, my own will, my own past, my own face, my own name. To this end, I am also stripped of all my clothes and belongings, as well as of my hair. For this new anonymous non-person, there are massive piles of crumpled clothes and ragged heaps of shoes, captured prisoner-of-war uniforms, coarse peasant coats and smocks, slips, shirts, dresses, lace-up boots without laces, numberless clogs, and there is no time at all to pick something that might fit. And then the rite of tattoo. My name is replaced by a number. An imprint, as if on merchandise, signifying that I do not exist any more. My number is branded into me, forced into the very flesh itself, jab by jab, with a needle. A dirty needle, and certainly infected, because my arm will rebel and swell up afterwards for weeks. Nothing can heal easily in wasted bodies condemned to primitive latrines and polluted water. Ah, that terrible tattooing of a number onto what was once a person! It was a special invention of Auschwitz, a special degradation from which even babies were not exempt. Did the Nazis know that Jewish law prohibited tattooing, because it was the mark of barbarians?

Now in the packed barrack hut, with its rows of coarse wooden bunks, I am standing frigid and stupefied. I am *anaesthetized.*

Is it two days later? Time is as cracked as I am. The most

devastating shock of all. The daytime sun is always half-darkened, like an eclipse, and the sky glows red. The air carries a stench which fills your head and your lungs. It even intrudes into your sleep. I am still naive. But all the world is naive. I ask the coarse Polish *kapo* of my hut: *What is that smell?* and she sneers at me, maliciously. *That's your family going up the chimneys!*

Try to put this in some 'normal' context, if you can. Some comfortable home, a meal after a day at the office, perhaps plans for a holiday . . . And you hear: *That's your family going up the chimneys!* Of course, it doesn't belong, it's just not credible, it's even rather funny, a bad joke, you want to laugh. But in Auschwitz, it is completely believable. It becomes something perfectly normal. And I am ready now to believe it. I am sick inside, but I believe it.

And it is the more shocking because of its disguise. Later, I would see the crematoria from the outside. The front of neat white fences, and behind them trim brick houses with curtains in the windows, like a suburban dream. Yes, I would see the smoking chimneys. Yes, I say I could believe it. But do you think that it is easy to believe that smoke and stench is all that remains of Marika and Anyu and all my family, of so many people I knew, and of *millions* of living human beings who each loved and strove and resented and hoped; now all of them transformed by the chimneys into dizzying rows of zeros, numbers beyond comprehension like the numbers tattooed onto millions of forearms . . .

LETTER FIVE
Ronald to Dita
Oxford

It was always our joke, wasn't it, darling, that you went to a real life University — a University of Life — or rather, of Death, at the same time that I went to Oxford . . .

And I first learned about your concentration camp 'University' while I was at my own, at the end of the War. In fact, I took up my scholarship to Oxford just four months after you entered Auschwitz. That was also three months after the massive D-Day invasion of Europe, too late to rescue your family or all the other thousands, upon thousands, upon thousands . . . During the following year, Hitler committed suicide in his bunker on April 30th 1945; Germany capitulated on May 7th; and the atomic bomb devastated Hiroshima on August 6th. It seemed that 1945 was the end of a Thirty Years War which had begun in 1914, during which dictatorships had all but defeated liberal traditions everywhere. Some years more than others shake with the explosions which drive the pistons of history. Some years more than others are scarred with the crossroads and traumata of our personal lives.

There'd been rumors of the Holocaust, like a distant earthquake's rumble, in 1943, when I was at Marlborough busy with my entrance examinations to Oxford, those initiations to my own university on the light side of the planet. Like a hidden land-mine in my own sheltered landscape, I was horrified to read that one Shmuel Ziegelboim committed suicide in London. He was the representative of the Jewish Labour Bund in the Polish government-in-exile. You remember, *Ditukam,* that my own father had emigrated from Poland before I was born; and I was to discover later that all his family had perished, in Auschwitz, Maidenek or Treblinka, or in the ghettos themselves of Lodz and Warsaw (where my father's three cousins had established an elite tailoring House for the aristocracy, all marble and glass: their connections and their millions of zloty did not help them). Ziegelboim gave everything he had, his own life, as a neon-light advertisement to a so-called civilized but blacked out world which seemed indifferent to the massacre of an entire people in its own heartland, now its theater of war. His suicide was the only way he knew to electrify its conscience; and it was in vain. He wrote in his letter:

> I cannot be silent — I cannot live — while remnants of the Jewish people of Poland, of whom I am a representative, are perishing. My comrades in the Warsaw ghetto took weapons in their hands on that last heroic impulse. It was not my destiny to die there together with them, but I belong to them, and in their mass graves. By my death I wish to express my strongest protest against the inactivity with which the world is looking on and permitting the extermination of my people.

But myself — I came up to Oxford with a young fire and enthusiasm for the new age of humanitarianism which everyone wanted to believe would follow the War. I was convinced I was brilliant, that I had a creative gift which could apply itself in any direction, where others labored. It had blazed a trail of scholarships and distinctions for me out of the deprived rough and tumble of the East End of London, through a privileged private school, and now to Oxford. At the interview for my scholarship, a benign white haired Sir William Beveridge sat at the head of the table and asked me what I knew of economics. His Report had sold half a million copies. He was the draughtsman of the Welfare plan for a new Britain — cradle to grave security, free medicine, free education, — which the prosaic Clement Atlee, who was elected over Winston Churchill, would realize dully and bloodlessly, without any fanfare of revolutionary trumpets.

In the new spring which ended the European war, the cruel spring which bred corpses out of the dead ground of the concentration camps, the spring of Hitler's suicide, the spring when that handsome Russian captain, a red white knight, had rescued you from the death march out of Auschwitz — that was a gleaming sunlit spring for me as remote as Olympus from the Hells you had experienced on the Nazi continent. I moved out of my rooms at the foot of the baroque Bridge of Sighs in Hertford College, the replica of the Venetian original, and into the bustle of 16 The Turl, just off Broad Street, a crowded, curry-stained (it was next to Bahadur's restaurant) and buzzing hive of Bohemian outsiders, of scholars, writers and artists. I had my own springtime energy. I threw myself into composition lessons with Egon Wellesz, Schoenberg's pupil; I went to live with my first mistress Margaret Lane — older than me, following Benjamin Franklin's advice — a writer, wife of the actor and later screen director David Greene (who had just been in Wormwood Scrubs, as a conscientious objector, in the cell next to Michael Tippett); and I launched a publishing company which took its name from my art and literary revue *Counterpoint.*

The Blitz had fermented a crop of little revues in London, wherever a printer's cache of precious paper could be found in those days of shortage. John Lehmann, the editor of *Penguin New Writing,* had compared London to Athens in the Peloponnesian war, or Renaissance

Florence, beleaguered into giving its best. He said he would rather have been in London under siege, between 1940 and 1945, than anywhere else. With their social life centered in the pubs and clubs of Fitzrovia and Soho, young talents flourished in spite of the bombs and black-outs. Their writings and paintings struck a new note of realism and simplicity: like Henry Moore's drawings of sleeping bodies in the Tube shelters, or John Piper's and Graham Sutherland's of bomb devastation. But there was also an art of compensation, a neo-Romantic escape from the scarcities and boredom of the war. *Counterpoint* inherited this legacy. Among other revues of its time — Miron Grindea's *Adam;* Arthur Boyars' *Mandrake;* Tambimuttu's *Poetry London;* Wrey Gardiner's *Poetry Quarterly* with his pacifist editor Alex Comfort; Denis Frankel's *Arabesque*, to name a few of so many — it was a *primus inter pares:* glossy and laden with color reproductions, a paradise for the eyes in those parched years.

In both the revue and in books, I published the painters Paul Nash, Michael Ayrton, Mervyn Peake, Cecil Collins, Gerald Wilde, Lucien Freud, Bryan Wynter, John Minton, Keith Vaughan, Robert Colquehoun, as well as the then unknown art critics Bernard Denvir and Anthony (David) Sylvester; the writers Kafka, Lawrence Durrell, George Barker, Roy Campbell, Walter de la Mare, John Heath-Stubbs, R. S. Thomas . . .

Paul Nash, with whom I lived for a time, was painting his 'aerial flowers' — mystical visions of an earthbound spirit longing to fly. He was prevented from flying by the bronchial asthma he had contracted in the First World War trenches. He was an official war artist in this war as in the first. His *Battle of Britain,* which I published, was a vast abstract epic, a colored patchwork of fields seen from the air, spotted with the exploding white of ack-ack shells, and disrupted by mushrooming billows of red-black fire and smoke. His paintings were obsessed with the skies, and their skyscapes of clouds were spiritual symbols, the mansions of the dead. In the book *Aerial Flowers,* which I published in a limited edition, he wrote: 'Death, I believe, is the only solution to this problem of how to be able to fly. Personally, I feel that if death can give us that, death will be good.' He died not long afterwards. Like the late Paul Nash, the younger painters looked back to Blake and Palmer and to the Romantic and visionary tradition in British painting, but also to surrealism, to Ernst and to Klee. Cecil Collins' landscapes had a supernatural glow and his 'fools' were the holy jokers, the clowns of eternity, freed from the chains of convention.

But Gerald Wilde exploded into fistfuls of paint: he was a pioneer in what the Americans would call Abstract Expressionism. Alternately desperate and wild-eyed, or else soft as silk, he would sometimes spend whole nights in my rooms in labor pains with elastic shapes of pigment and writhing colors. He was a Gulley Jimson out of *The Horse's Mouth* of Joyce Carey (in whose gardenhouse Gerald Wilde would actually live later) but more tragic than comical. He had been conscripted into a unit which removed the fuses from unexploded grenades, and the experience had left him close to madness. How unromantic was the shattered person which lay under this 'true Bohemian'! Sometimes, in a kind of mania, he would burn five-pound notes — a fortune in those days. When Jung heard how Wilde lived, he commented that money was a kind of poison for him.

Many of the poets, too, looked for a powerful new imagery. The most explosive and numinous was Dylan Thomas. Dylan and his wife Caitlin lived in a converted boathouse by the Cherwell in moist gardens near Magdalene College. I got to know him in the pubs — his eyes rolling as beer bubbled into, and speech bubbled out of, his plush lips. I knew the Thomas's boathouse from its previous tenant, Vera Leslie, a dark-voiced refugee from Germany, who translated and illustrated for *Counterpoint* Kafka's *The Country Doctor* — a book never published in England. What a rich time that was, *Ditukam!* So many of my contributors also became my friends, among them Cecil and Elizabeth Collins in Cambridge; Wilfred Mellers who, like myself, studied with Egon

Wellesz, and wrote about him in the first issue of *Counterpoint;* the critic David Sylvester; Thomas Good, the Irish poet whose book *Overtures* we published; Mervyn Peake, who was working on a book for *Counterpoint* called *London Faces*; Michael Ayrton, already a well known spokesman for the neo-Romantic artists, stage designer, illustrator and critic, living then with Constant Lambert at Langham Place by the BBC, who was working on a book entitled *Entrance to a Wood* for *Counterpoint.* The painter Bryan Winter and the art historian Bernard Denvir; John Veale the composer; the half-blind poet John Heath-Stubbs, always with a stick, peering through thick glasses. Hans Keller, who would later play a key role in the BBC's new Third Programme of music. Kenneth Tynan, Gavin Lambert, and Peter Brook (in whose first film, *Sentimental Journey*, I played a minor role. At the première in the Oxford Union, I was pinioned into a grimace on the screen for many humiliating minutes when the projector froze).

And into this cloistered kaleidoscope of my Oxford, the two H's penetrated. The two great cataclysms of our times, watersheds of history, depth-charges into our conscience. One was the Holocaust. The other Hiroshima. The two H's. The two *catastrophes ('subverting the system of things'*, in the definition of the Oxford Dictionary). I found a diary from those days in which I'd written: *Perhaps we should talk now of time BH, like time BC, and time AH. Time before, and time after, H . . . Like the birth and death of Jesus, both H's signify historical moments of truth, of confrontation with what humanity is all about, and similarly they demand a new calendar. In the new Alphabet Primer for our children, H will stand for Holocaust, and H will stand also for Hiroshima . . . What both have in common is a technological planning of mass slaughter, on a scale only before imaginable in myth, in visions like that of Armageddon or of Shiva the Destroyer of Worlds. A slaughter as of herds of cattle, where the humane person no longer exists. The Nazi slaughterhouses and their cold-blooded brutality betray our entire humanist and*

*Christian civilization. But did not those seeds of Europe,
now flowering over the whole earth, always contain its
destruction? . . . . And now the nuclear bomb has raised
the stakes to a degree where the savage game of war, as
we have known it, must become henceforth unplayable.
It's not just the end of a chapter or a book of history, like
the harnessing of fire, or the coming of the Ice Age. It's
like the end of all possible books, of all possible
libraries.The towering mushroom clouds we see in the
newspapers and on the cinema screen mean that all of*
civilization *can now be consumed, not just one of its lo-
calities or strands as before; now all of life on earth, in its
seas as in its skies, can be destroyed irrevocably.*

I first read about your own 'University of Life' (to come
back to our joke, which now seems more and more sick
to me), in the newspaper reports. Auschwitz stood out
from all the other concentration camps. It was the 'crème
de la crème' of evil. Its crematoria, I read, could cope with
half a million corpses. All that remained of the murdered
were stacks of clothes — of 100,000 children in one storeroom alone (*were your sister Marika's clothes there?*); of
human teeth, but without their gold fillings (*were your
mother's, or grandmother's there?*); there were seven tons
of women's hair, ready to send to the German factories
for carpets, brushes, mattresses (*was your own brown hair
I once stroked also somewhere in that pile?*)

   It was Belsen which cast the first nightmare shadows.
A British medical detachment stumbled on it and couldn't
believe what they saw. And neither could I. From my
Oxford diary: *Last night we went to the cinema next to
The Randolph, and we saw something we could never
have anticipated. A newsreel showed shocking scenes of
a newly discovered Nazi concentration camp called
Belsen. I slept badly last night, and I feel sick as I write
this. I could not believe what I saw. And neither could
that cinema audience. Some people giggled and lit cigarettes. Even after the years of war horrors, this was unreal. We saw heaps of torn and ragged dolls, piled up*

*promiscuously, with weird protuberances of stick-arms,
stick-legs, and shriveled heads, and we could not con-
nect any of this with real men and real women. Over the
barbed wire peered vacant eyes that had once been human
eyes. They belonged to black-striped, shuffling bare bones.
They peered at us in our comfortable darkness. The mo-
tionless mounds were corpses. But so were the moving
things, the striped skeletons. And their eyes just went on
looking at us, not really accusing, just vacant, just destroyed, looking and looking at us, their brother Europeans, some of us their brother Jews; and they were looking
at me.*

The war writers were writing, and the painters painting,
before Auschwitz and Hiroshima. But now? William
Golding would write that these experiences were like
black holes in space. Nothing could get out to let us know
what it was like inside. How could you write about it,
paint it? There was a limit to literature. There was now a
gap in history.

The camps did enter into the art world of *Counterpoint*.
A number of artists and performers went to the camps.
Benjamin Britten played at Belsen. Mervyn Peake also
went there in 1945 (the time you were threading your way
back to Kosice on a train bursting at the seams with the
remains of army regiments, victors and losers, and with
the shapeless army of the refugees and survivors, all of
them losers). I published his drawings of a dying Jewish
girl, together with the poem he wrote to go with it:

> If seeing her an hour before her last
> Weak cough into all blackness I could yet
> Be held by chalk-white walls, and by the great
> Ash colored bed,
> And the pillows hardly creased
> By the lightness of her little jerking head —
> If such can be a painter's ectasy,
> Her limbs like pipes, her head a porcelain skull,
> Then where is mercy?

And what irony?
Is this my calling, for my schooled eyes see
The ghost of a great painting, line and hue
In this doomed girl of tallow?

This poem shocked me deeply. Wasn't I a prisoner of my
own kind of insulation, of the abstract power of my own
art, music, of my own mandarin kind of *schooled eyes* ?
Wasn't I too that kind of alchemist, transforming cruel
reality into art. This was the point of one of the prose-
poems which Lawrence Durrell wired to me for inclu-
sion in *Counterpoint* (throughout the war, it was crucial
for writers abroad to hang on to editors at home, even by
the frail thread of an airgraph).

> *On Alexander of Athens.* Alexander was in love with
> Athens. He was a glutton, and exhausted both him-
> self and his subject in his art. Thus when he had smelt
> a flower it was quite used up, and when he had
> painted a mountain, it felt that living on could only
> be a useless competition against Alexander's paint-
> ing of it. Thus, with him, Athens ceased to exist, and
> we have been walking about inside his canvases ever
> since, looking for a way back from art into life.
> *From Conon the Critic on the Six Landscape Paint-
> ers of Greece.*

A parable for all time, but particularly for the antenna-
tangled half-century to follow, the coming era of the global Empire of the Media: which would not merely consume life, but replace it with its own images.

You write, *Ditukam,* how in the terrible transport to
Auschwitz you felt forced to play a role in a long Jewish
history that was really alien to you. It was alien to me too
at that time. Any conflict of my childhood Jewish background and the present Gentile world of Oxford was
hardly in my mind. It was eight years since I'd left the
East End of London, and I had a sense of having fought

my way successfully into the upper-class Gentile world at Marlborough. I was as English as the more renowned English Jews, from Disraeli to the modern Cabinet Ministers like Nigel Lawson and Lord Young. And the situation was different in England to the Central Europe of which you were a part. I never had to say, as Schoenberg did in a letter to Kandinsky, at the time of his remarkable turning back *(teshuvah)* to the origins of Judaism and his Jewish identity: *I am no German, no European, maybe not even a human being (ein Mensch) — at any rate the Europeans prefer the worst of their own race to me — but . . . I am a Jew.* Or as Freud said: *My language is German. My culture, my attainments are German. I considered myself German until I noticed the growth of antisemitic prejudices in Germany and German Austria. Since that time, I prefer to call myself a Jew.* I knew nothing of the alienation and self-disgust of a Kafka, who spoke of Jewish writers in Central Europe having their *hind legs bogged down in their father's Judaism,* while their front legs could find no secure new ground. For Kafka, all German-Jewish writing was *gypsy literature that had stolen the German child from its cradle and trained it, in a great hurry, to perform any way because someone had to dance on the tightrope. Worse, it was merely for someone writing his last will and testament just before he hangs himself.*

Nevertheless, the Oxford I entered, at the end of the war, was cosmopolitan mainly because of the influx of refugees from Nazi Europe, and most of these were Jews. It was precisely their cosmopolitan background, as well as their finely-tuned sensitivity, which attracted me. These refugees were loosely integrated into, but also formed an alternative society to, the English middle-class academia and its Oxford entourage. For me, they seemed to open secret doors not only into the larger world of Europe, but into my own self, into that chequered living-legend history of the Jews which was the soil of my deepest and most unconscious roots. I was welcomed into many immigrant families: the family of Bela Horovitz who founded the Phaidon Press, one of the successful new *émigré* publishers (along with André Deutsch, Walter Neurath of Thames and Hudson, Paul Hamlyn, George Weidenfeld and the infamous Robert Maxwell) whose son Joseph, my peer at New College, was a brilliant painter (his self-portrait in the style of Raphael hung in his rooms) as well as pianist and composer; the family of beautiful Constance Isepp whom I adored, and young Martin who would play an important role at Glyndebourne and the English Opera; the family of Albi Rosenthal who dealt in rare books and manuscripts from his office in the Turl, with whom I spent hours playing the violin sonatas of Mozart and Schubert. There was Oscar Némon, the cynical soft-spoken Hungarian sculptor, busy with his busts of Freud, of Churchill, of Spaak . . .; Hans Cohn — yes, darling, the same Hans dear to us, therapist, poet, whom we knew many years later in our community, but at that time reduced to being a porter at the Radcliffe Infirmary, his medical studies at Prague disrupted by his flight from the Nazis, humiliated by internment (it was said that some of the best talent in Europe was locked up in internment camps like the one on the Isle of Man); or Hans Keller, who would become the BBC's musical gadfly and a hundred others. My own teacher of composition, Egon Wellesz, was an immigrant from Vienna in whom rich veins of musical creativity, as well as of rare scholarship, lay beneath a surface of old-world charm and courtesy. I published his book on Schoenberg, his teacher. He pioneered the deciphering of Byzantine music; and I would also learn from his scholarly work on the origins of Western Chant in Judaism and the East.

My surname, Senator, is one of a family of names which are corruptions of the Greek Alexander. In the Hellenic period, some Jews named their sons after the great general and disciple of Aristotle, whose empire embraced the ancient world and subjugated Israel's enemies: Babylon,Syria, and Egypt. There was a bitter conflict then between the Jewish 'Hellenizers' — those who assimilated themselves to Greek culture, and even distinguished themselves within it — and pious Jews who feared that their religion and mores were threatened by it. That conflict became bloody at the time of the Maccabee revolt against the Seleucids. A century and a half later, it was the same conflict which simmered under the Romans at the time of Jesus. Herod (Antipas) was an example of the assimilated Jew: he was tutored by the same philosophers as the prince Claudius who was his close friend. This age-old conflict, between the traditionally pious and the assimilated Jew, played a key role in the Crucifixition. Jesus was hastily executed by the Romans, with the collaboration of the Jewish Council, because both feared a religious and nationalistic eruption against Roman power and the threat of its culture. When that revolt did come, thirty-odd years after the Crucifixion, the Roman legions under Titus utterly destroyed Jerusalem and its temple.

As my ancestors had gone to a Greek gymnasium, I had gone to an elite private school at Marlborough, one founded for the sons of Christian clergymen. Two thousand years later, I was also a scholar of the Greek and Roman classical civilization, and rich in a modern enlightenment (the tail-end, actually, of an Enlightenment: the philosophies of Russell and of A.J.Ayer, my professor at Oxford, bypassed tradition with linguistic hair-splitting). How much was that ancient conflict between Jewish piety and the great culture beyond it also my own personal conflict? I too was trapped in a double-bind. From my cradle, my parents had ardently and equally wanted me to be both a Jew and an English gentleman. These were two opposite poles, and that polarization was capable of splitting my psyche apart. I sought to grow big enough to transcend that split. To look at Jewish tradition from a vantage point which included the non-Jewish, and to transcend my Englishness without denying it.

I belonged to a modern ferment of culture, an elitist spearhead of culture, European as well as English. I was yeast in that ferment as well as nourished by it: a ferment of diverse and seemingly incompatible elements, difficult to knead into a single dough for the bread of my life.

And as in my life, so in my music. I wrestled with the conflicts a composer of my time had to resolve: the atonal-serial revolution of Schoenberg versus traditional tonality — or versus the tonality of old modes in new guises, as in Debussy, or novel modes like Messiaen's; the single tonal center of tradition versus the multi-layered polytonality that was explored by composers as diverse as Milhaud, Stravinsky or Bartok; in rhythm, the regular two, three, four-beats-in-the-bar, the basis of all Western music since the Renaissance, versus the additive groupings common in India or Africa, once normal in Western plainsong, and now re-emerging in Europe like some recessive gene . . .

The pressure within me to integrate, to make my own sense of such diversity, was fierce. The time came when I left Oxford and rented a cottage near Marlow, set in its own acre of forest and meadow, to cut away from the over-rich diet of Oxford, to be alone with myself. *Reculer pour mieux sauter.* For a time Margaret would visit me. I remember with the pain of nostalgia that old gnarled railway carriage at the back of the cottage, a surreal summerhouse, where we would sometimes sleep together in a sweet sensuality under the whisper of the late summer leaves. But soon I felt I had to part from her — in order wholly to give myself . . . but *to what?*

Wholly to give myself . . . To the struggle to realize those musical ideas of such commanding, exquisite beauty which haunted me. *Wholly* to give myself . . . To an awesome, pulsating sense of wonder at being alive. *Wholly* to give myself . . . To a vibrant feeling of oneness with the nature I walked through, which seemed to breathe in and out with secret alleluias, softly, but sometimes screaming. I was learning to focus a new eye, an invisible eye. I read widely, for the first time, such books as the *Bible of the World*, or Aldous Huxley's recently published *Perennial Philosophy*, which revealed for me the parallel texts in all traditions, and the common spiritual experience beyond the confines of each.

But my isolation was also courting my own personal

catastrophe. Against the backcloth of the catastrophic H's
of history.

Wholly to give myself. To become whole. But it wasn't
that easy, *édesem,* not as easy as a young man in his twenties believed . . . It's turned out to be a very long, unfin-
ished, unfinishable story. That's for my epitaph: *It wasn't
that easy.*

Archangel's Central Office
Report on Russian and German Camps

100111010001101110110110111001100111101010011011001100100111001011010011100101001100101001100111000101

You needn't be so surprised that your Mac is picking this up and showing it on your screen, even if your modem isn't plugged in. Your computer, after all, is a metaphysical machine, in its very conception and structure. It partakes of the essential mystery of Creation — the choice of 1 or 0, which is of being or non-being, of yin or yang.

There's no need to make a fuss about my exact name. You have given me many. Ahasuerus, St. Michael the Archangel, the Reaper, and many others. When you had need of my female side, you called me the White Moon-Goddess, Tara, Isis, Sophia or Wisdom . . . With your new computer screens for me to appear on, it's a conceit of your age that you're the first magicians to see this conjuring-up trick. It's been going on for many ages, from the Babylonians to the magic circles of the Kabbalists, who were the inspiration for my own favorite, Dr. Faustus.

I'm eternally grateful to the Greeks, you know. They understood how much the gods need men. Without your referrals and sacrifices, we couldn't properly exist the way you want us to. Then again, I think that the Greek dramatists understood very well my own cosmic role; in fact they aped it with their Choruses. Consider now this paradox: their Chorus was masked; yet its speech originated in those depths where masks have no existence, where all of life's streams have their sources. Their Chorus was Commentator and Illuminator in at least four dimensions, and its elastic horizons stretched beyond the actors and their every action, beyond their knowledge of themselves, beyond all the motives and reasons they thought they had for their actions. You might say that the Chorus exposed the raw nerves and the hidden hearts of all history, tragic or comic, tragi-comic or comi-tragic.

Then again, the highly inventive Chinese had some sensible notions of what my life and work is really like. They called me, picturesquely, *The Great Emperor of the Eastern Peak, T'ai-yueh-ta-ti*. I started off being the god of the mountain in Shantung, T'ai-shan. But they soon realized that I was delegated (by the great August Personage of Jade) to look after all the affairs of mankind, and even of the rest of creation: and to this end I needed a huge staff of registrars and researchers filing regular reports, a complex hierarchy of departments, with personnel chosen from among the souls of the dead. The Christians called these their saints: there was one for being born, one for journeys, one for dying, different ones for different illnesses, different ones for different pet animals, and so on. And, of course, they all have an intercessionary role. Not only my temple in Peking, *Tung-yueh-miao*, but all my sanctuaries everywhere are brim full with importunate beseechers, just like the shrines of Catholic saints, heated, holy, and greasy from the forests of burning candlewicks.

On earth, nowadays, you are discovering the intricate communication centers of your human brain, a miracle far more complex than many thousands of air traffic controllers running all your busiest and largest airports put together. You know your brain has at least 100 billion neurons carrying and coordinating billions of messages every second along a vast interlocking mesh of electrochemical routes; and it organizes a truly vast hierarchy of hormonal messenger services continually scurrying and flashing back and forth, from neuropeptides to endorphins, from interleukins to enkephalins. That is to say, if you work out the permutations, all the infinite arithmetic, your human brain proves to be pretty limitless. You are endowed with a mind which is a latticed window into all eternity. But I say this, not to gloat in any way — which can have serious consequences for an angel, as it did, for example, for my cousin Beelzebub — but to remind you of your image that I am made in, only more so, and of the great workload we all carry up here in this knotty network of heavenly offices. After all, you see, we are His Brain itself. The Brahma's Brain. That's the raison d'être of my Office.

However, you have thought me up — courtroom Advocate before the Judge, Secretary of State employing a vast Civil Service, the King's bride even, or favored mistress with access to the secret passions of her Lord — whichever way, you should realize that it is a cumbersome burden to be besieged through endless particles of time by tormented souls, asking for interventions into history. My heart is not of stone, it is of liquid fire, luminous fire like lightning, blazing fire like the sunlight you once worshiped, the fallen fire of the demonesses of volcanoes, the same fire which Prometheus stole, the same fire which burned the bush before Moses, the fire which formed a pillar to guide him through the desert night, the very fire Elijah of Mount Carmel called down from heaven ... I know that unquenchable stuff which Prometheus stole has made some of you quite heady — no longer accepting anything that's given, lifting the skin off the world, twisting and warping time, having to know the end before the beginning, the beginning before the beginning, and the end after the end . . . Walking on the moon, now the earth itself rises and sets in the heavens instead of the sun and the moon and the stars . . . The immoveable heavens (into which Elijah and Jesus ascended) now race away in every direction at colossal speeds. And the planets and gods — among them Tammuz, Isis and Dionysus — are dizzy and exhausted from seeking new niches in which to fulfill their role of dying and being reborn.

Well, they used to locate my offices in the supernovae like the Star of Bethlehem, or else in awesome recesses, in fastnessnes of mountains where metals whistle and lightning is born to flash across the valleys, in wildernesses whose rocks may melt into water or whose branches bubble into manna, or in giant Etnas disgorging holy black steaming rivers to consume and fertilize the earth. Nowadays things are much more sophisticated. Our offices are dissolved into the particles of waves and the waves of particles, beyond the elastic humps of time. They are located everywhere and nowhere, inside of the outsides and outside of the insides, pretemporally, coevally and preternaturally . . .

To you I am no longer the terrifying vision, four-headed and multiwinged, of whom Rilke wrote: 'If the archangel now, perilous, from behind the stars took even one step down toward us, our own heart, beating higher and higher, would beat us to death.' On the contrary, I have been reduced to a Christmas cake decoration, bite-sized, so that the awesome challenge I was once is now swallowed up in meringue and icing sugar.

Nevertheless, I continue to be the custodian of that supreme Book of Life from whose pages letters of fire configurate to form the new word of a newly-born child, and to whose pages those letters must always return, enriched by his or her life . . . That overflowing Book of Books, Library of Books, Bibliocosmos of all possible universes, yes, as you have insisted for millenia, my Office is

charged with Its supervision and revision, with the care
of all Recordings on the Cosmic Macro-Micro-Chip which
is coextensive both with the boundaries of the entire Universe and with the still Point of all points which preceded
all motion.

Report to Central Office.
Safer Chayim (Book of Life), Research Department,
Twentieth Century Desk.
Source: Mercury Intergalacticinstantfax.

It is hard to quantify or to compare the suffering of human beings on earth, but our statistics show that no
tyrannies of past times have tortured and executed and
enslaved so many people as have the regimes of the
twentieth century. Sir, we must report our concern that
such extreme cruelty still coexists with notions of human progress, mainly derived, strangely enough, from
the proliferation of human technological inventions,
from telephone and television to big-bellied airplanes
and computers. Inventions which are extensions of human bodies and senses and brains. In all our records,
there has never been that kind of confusion and idoli-
zation of the earlier technologies of other species —
skins, fins and wings, snail shells, spiders' webs and
birds' nests, and so forth. And unlike those dumb flo-
ral or faunal kingdoms, we have now to report certain
all-consuming human ideals revived in modern dress
which, like their predecessors, propose New Edens:
that is to say, virgin worlds pretended to be purified by
fire from the dross both of the aeons of human history,
and the myriads of present doubters. It is a time of
eclipse, when counterfeit suns shine; a cruel era of
ruthless clean sweeps, deck-clearing, and apocryphal

blood-letting; a darkened age of holocaust, of uprooted and murdered peoples.

Under Stalin, hotels and churches, even public baths and mews, as well as the old disused Tsarist gaols like the Lefortovskaia, are converted into the new Soviet prisons, complete with torture chambers in which mediaeval instruments, like the iron maidens, the boxes of nails and the eye-gougers, have a renaissance which far surpasses the dreams of their original inventors. These prisons are part of a network which embraces vast camps in the Gulag Archipelago, like chains of terrible islands quite separate from everyday life and enclosing many thousands of square miles, through which as many as ten percent of all Soviet citizens have passed in as many years. This is a self-contained universe with its own hierarchy of status, and its own special purpose camps, like those for the orphaned children of the executed, or those for the widows and other surviving relatives of the liquidated army officers.

They are both labor camps and death camps, and they are the inspiration for Himmler's network of concentration camps in Nazi Germany and then in occupied Europe. Himmler writes *Arbeit Macht Frei* over the gateway into Auschwitz, in the same way as the horrendous Soviet Kolyma camps greets its prisoners with the sign: *Labor is a matter of honor, valor and heroism.* In those Soviet camps mass executions are common — 40,000 people, including children, are killed with machine-guns in 1938 alone. About half a million people are executed in what the regime calls purges of the *enemies of the people,* mostly summarily and in secret. Yet a million a year die in the camps just from brutally harsh conditions, from starvation, from beatings. Professional criminals are put in charge of the Camps, as they are later by the Nazis. In the *special punishment* camps, like those which serve the gold-mines, men work seven days a week for sixteen hours a day, in the freezing cold sometimes as low as sixty degrees below zero, against which their tattered rags, either of clothes or of tents, offer little protection.

From our historical records, Sir, we find that the sense of mission which both Stalin and Hitler have, their frenzy to exterminate the enemies of their vision, one based on class, the other on race, is not unlike that of other figures in the past, like the Christian Inquisitors of the fifteenth century, or the Moslem *jihad* warriors who have reappeared in the twentieth. But the sheer scope of their power is without precedent, not merely in the extent of their political control, but in the modern technologies available to them for rounding up and destroying their enemies. Stalin can transport and annihilate millions of Soviet peasants who oppose collectivization. Hitler learns from this model when he decides on his *Final Solution* for the Jews.

But this goes hand in hand with his *Operation Barbarossa*, in which all inferior races are to be destroyed, and the Germans will follow the centuries-old route of the Teutonic knights into the fertile plains of the Russian empire, where more than 100 million will settle west of the Urals, and transform the Crimea into a vast German spa. Auschwitz is planned not only as an extermination center, but also as the industrial complex which will supply these huge Eastern settlements when the war is won. Fifteen million slave laborers, over twenty years, would be necessary to this end — that is Himmler's projection. So Auschwitz, Sir, is a compromise between an industrial centre and a death camp. Those who are not gassed immediately burn up their starving bodies in two or three months of labor, and the living dross is shipped to the gas chambers at Birkenau. The human is destroyed as if a used-up economic commodity, except for those parts which can be recycled: for example, gold teeth for the *Reichsbank*, and even fat for soap. This latter consumption is, of course, Sir, a cannibalism once considered extinct by the self-styled civilized world of the twentieth century.

We are appalled, Sir, to discover how Auschwitz processes the human being like an inanimate industrial commodity. The vermin-control company Degesch, which
supplies Zyklon-B poison gas for the extermination chambers, is worried only about their patent when the SS orders the gas without its warning smell indicator. This is
their sole source of uneasiness. The SS are concerned only
with the cost of this expensive gas. Healthy victims are
often stunned by inadequate quantities, and then burned
alive. The language is the impersonal idiom of industry.
German companies compete for the design of the process-
ing unit, which must have the capacity to dispose of 2000
bodies every 12 hours. Five furnaces are supplied and
invoiced by Topt & Company, among their orders for vari-
ous factories. The prize design for the gas chambers, described as *corpse cellars*, is by German Armaments Inc.
But even five furnaces prove inadequate for the scale of
this top priority operation, which must dispose of some
24,000 bodies per day by the time of the Hungarian
deportations in May 1944.

Since, these prisoners are considered sub-human, they
are the material for any kind of medical experiment by
the 350-odd SS doctors. The Polish girls are called *rabbits,* and are regularly infected with gas-gangrenous
wounds to test sulphamonide drugs. The Russian prisoners are sterilized with X-rays. Selected Jews, who represent 'a repulsive yet characteristic sub-humanity', are
gassed so that their skeletons may become part of
Himmler's collection of 'Jewish-Bolshevik commissars'.
And Auschwitz is the dream of other camp doctors. Thus
Dr. Sigmund Rascher, who murders many prisoners in
low-temperature tests at Dachau, asks to be transferred
to Auschwitz: 'The camp itself is so vast that the work
will attract less attention. For the subjects howl so much
when they freeze!'

It is, of course, my duty to bring these matters to your
attention, Sir, and I trust you will give them the promi-

nence they deserve in your filing system, where they will receive their proper perspective, both morally, and in the time-charts of human history.

LETTER SIX
Ronald to Dita

Your photo in Auschwitz. Burial of soap

The truth is, my dear, that truth is up for grabs, and those who control the media can manufacture whitewash to their heart's content. How come the western world did not believe the camps existed, nor the torture, nor the mass murder? Those who approved of fascism were among the most distinguished minds, like Yeats or Eliot, Cocteau or Croce, Maurras or Heidegger. On the other hand, most of the intelligentsia looked to the Soviet Union as to a White Knight, the only power able to combat an almost universal fascism, from the German or Italian to the Spanish or Portugese, from the Polish or Hungarian to the Japanese. They did not want to know that Stalin burned many millions of books, if not as publicly as Hitler did. When they heard rumors of persecution they justified it: 'Just as the Inquistion did not affect the fundamental dignity of Christianity,' wrote Andre Malraux, 'so the Moscow trials have not affected the fundamental dignity of Communism.' 'It would suppose the creative genius of Shakespeare,' wrote United States Ambassador Davies in his book *Mission to Moscow,* to contrive the evidence for the 1937 show-trials in Moscow . . .

Now I want to speak to you about two pictures, both of them dear to us, the one so macabre, the other, for you, laden with nostalgia and pain.

I still have the book in which, by the most unimaginable coincidence (both of our lives are far stranger than any fiction), we found a picture of *you, in Auschwitz!* Do you remember? I saw it first, then showed it to you; and you agreed, amazed.

The picture is called *Auschwitz. Able-bodied women, 1944.* It is No. 19 in a book called *A Story of the Jewish Museum in Prague,* published by Artia in 1968. And there *you* are in the third row. Your right cheek is hidden by the headscarf of the woman in front. Your expression is dark, depressed, confused. All the faces are sullen and bitter. But they still have their flesh on them. This must have still been early days. We thought it was one of the photographs taken by the Nazis for their propaganda purposes, didn't we? *A band of women, alive and healthy, going off to work in a 'resettlement' center.* You see, *Arbeit macht frei!* Serendipity of the Gods, to find *you* in a photo of Auschwitz! I am looking at it, even as I write this letter to you. I am looking at you, then, in that place! A documentary. The past in the present. A black photo for your album alongside all the other more sunlit photos which celebrate your life. You might say, sun and shadow of life side by side. But not really. It's not like the normal chiaroscuro of life. Rather, it's the jostling of completely incompatible planets somehow trapped together under the covers of the same life-album.

And the other picture . . . For some time after you died I was not sure what to do with your grandmother's oil painting. You know, the large Szontag, the country scene, with the red-skirted girl seated in front of the pathway through the shrubs, a pathway which narrows abruptly behind her, unseen by her. It narrows as your own life-path narrowed and disappeared abruptly into Auschwitz, along with all the life-paths of your family and friends. That painting could never be simply a souvenir of your grandmother. It was a symbol for you of the destroyed past of Kosice, maybe even that of all European Jewry — and especially of your own. That is why you transported that bulky painting everywhere with you, bulky with a relentless past: to Israel, to Vineland in New Jersey, to New York, finally to England. You always wanted it to hang in the pride of place in our living room, over the fireplace, and it always did. It overlooked our life, your new life with me, ghosts hidden away in a seemingly innocent pastoral scene.

The painting has found a home now in Kent House, the Jewish Temple where you went to rescue some morsels of meaning from your crumbled life. It hangs there now in the vestry, a suitable place don't you think? The symbolic place of robing and disrobing, where the minister discards the bustle of life in order to probe behind its senselessness and its cruelty for the face of a buried God.

But there was something else which you carried with you, your ghastly secret in a little black box. Not visible like the grand oil painting hanging on the wall, but hidden away at the bottom of your bedroom drawer, just as it was always hidden away in your mind. It was a piece of soap. It was marked with the initials *R.J.F.*, which stood for *Reines Jüdisches Fett (Pure Jewish Fat)*, and it was supposed to have been made from the bodies of the Nazis' victims. I say supposed to have been. I remained rather skeptical, as did others — though not because I doubted the cold and inhuman efficiency of the Nazis, who certainly made ropes and brushes from the hair of the murdered, or lampshades from their human skin.

But the authenticity of that soap was not so important as its value, its power, for you. Like the painting, it was your past, the lump stuck in your soul which could never be digested. The painting came from time before Auschwitz, time B. H. The soap came out of the hell itself, it was closer to the actual murders. Like the living bodies of your family and friends, like even their dead bodies when you imagined the unimaginable, the soap was tangible and visible, it tasted and it smelled. Therefore you needed it. It made present for you the gassed and burned and once living bodies, a reality you couldn't believe, which no-one could believe. As long as the soap existed, as long as you could handle it and smell it, you could believe the unbelievable.

It was also perhaps necessary to lay it in earth, one day, when you felt you could. That day comes, and you do bury the soap with your own hands. And we plant a flowering shrub over it. A symbol of transformation. It is a ritual of mourning for laceration and for death. And it is at the same time a ritual to release from death in order to embrace life. Louis and Daniel and myself recite the Jewish *Kaddish*. Again, the *Kaddish*. Prayer for the dead and affirmation of life fused into a single text. Prayer for life in death.

We all stand around this strangest of graves, this alchemic crucible in earth. It is early springtime, and we are all priests and actors in a unique Rite of Spring. The victims are already slain, by poison gas and fire, in a previous ritual, a savage high-tech black-mass ritual. One ritual to expurgate the other. A novel ritual. An improvised light to expel darkness.

The children stand around, seriously, sensing the atmosphere without understanding. Then Kay explains to them what that soap really is, and what is the horrible cruelty it represents. Amy and Nelly are just ten. But they understand, and they cry pitifully.

Hu ya-asseh shalom alenu, the prayer says, *He will give us peace.* How can he give us peace from such a mangling of souls? How can he ever give you peace?

LETTER SEVEN
Dita to Ronald

What the soap meant to me

Yes, Kent House is the right kind of home for *Nagymama*'s painting, and I thank you for thinking of that. I adored her, my grandmother. She used to gather me up in her short arms, even when I grew quite big, and she would call me her little *dilinos,* or scatterbrain. (You knew that, *édesem . . .* You once surprised me for my birthday with a beautiful leather case for my letters, inscribed *Dilinos* !) But you are right . . . that painting, with its stony lane winding away into nowhere, reminded me of those vistas of my childhood and adolescence, in Kosice, in the Tatras, in Kesmarok. Vistas which were darkened with long shadows, and finally swallowed up completely. Yes, it's true, it was as if the oil painting itself contained lost secrets, a kind of hidden message, and I had to carry it everywhere with me, from country to country, until, one day, I would be able to unearth the secrets and decipher the message.

It was the same with the soap. It was something *portable* for me, and personal, not like those grand public monuments at Yad Vashem and elsewhere. It reminded me of *everything* in Auschwitz: the horror, the shock, not only the gassing and burning of my family and friends; and then that callous 'recycling' — human fat for soap, along with human skin for leather, human hair for carpets or brushes, human bones for fertilizers. *My own family's fat, skin, hair, bones.* Shouldn't the whole world stop rotating and try to grasp that? My own family's fat, skin, hair, bones. Someone was sitting on their skin, someone was walking on their hair, someone was washing with their fat, someone was fertilizing corn with their bones. But the world does not stop rotating.

It *was* hard for me to part with the soap. I cannot say I was *ready* to do that. I can't imagine how I, or any of us who went through Auschwitz, could *ever* be ready to bury it. *How* do you 'come to terms' with a nightmare which was too monstrous to have been real? People who do not listen to our horror stories, people who say Auschwitz never really existed, are after all justified. How *could* it have been? Like the number tattooed on my forearm, that soap kept reminding me that something horrific beyond belief really did happen. I would sometimes take it out and stare at it. *Pure Jewish Fat.* Oh, God, how can it be? Oh, Marika! Oh, Anyukam, Oh, Nagymamam! There were human beings who could cut you up like pig fat.

Do you remember the story we read together once, I think by Ronald Dahl, about a pig slaughter house? The pigs squealed and wriggled as they moved slowly, on a conveyor belt, all trussed up, hanging upside down, towards a battery of sharp glistening knives which were there to *cut them into pieces.* Then came the horror: the human storyteller became one of the pigs, himself trussed up, himself helplessly approaching the knives.

That was, of course, a fantasy, a great spine tickler for readers who were sure that such a thing was quite impossible in reality. *Quite impossible.* And, after all, weren't they right? Wasn't my soap the greatest *practical* joke of all time? And my mother, my sister, my grandmother, were they not the dupes of that practical joke? And all the other victims, the dozens I had known, the millions I had not, were they not all dupes too?

And maybe all of our culture, all of our time in history, *everybody* was duped by the same sick joke? Because, after all, when all's said and done, when we look reality squarely in the face, when the cards are laid on the table, when we call a spade a spade, and so forth, such things are simply *impossible.* The sun does not rise in the West, and a flower does not grow its roots in the air and its petals in the earth. There is a natural order of things, and there is, after all, a moral order also.

You see, don't you, *dragosagam,* why I had to keep that soap? It was the only concrete evidence of an *impossible* reality. Do you see why I had to cling to it, as if for life? Because it *did* contain my life. My past. An impossible past. The whole universe of Kosice, of my childhood, all those teen years, all those human figures, they hadn't really vanished into nothing. *They'd been magically transformed into a bar of soap.* Just as Christian believers say that the body of their Christ, which is also the whole universe to them, has been transformed into a piece of unleavened bread, or *matzah.* This is, for them, their most powerful sacrament — the visible sign of the greatest of invisible miracles. And *my* soap was also *my* special sacrament, of the *Devil's* invisible miracle, his most astounding miracle in all of human history, on the most colossal scale. He had transubstantiated *a whole piece of civilization, an entire culture,* into a bar of soap! And there it was, I could hold it in my hands, *his* special visible sign with his own writing on it — RJF.

I'd always hoarded my 'sacrament' secretly, for years. Hardly anyone knew about it — you did, *édesem,* and Kay my therapist. I was frightened to have it laughed at, to have it taken away. Now my little black box could be taken out of the bottom of my bedroom drawer, and its terrible secret revealed publicly. It lay in my hand exposed to this sunny day which brightened the garden of our community. And I was burying it openly myself and planting over it a young flowering shrub, a very special kind of rite, a custom-made rite, one we'd thought up ourselves. Our own rite of spring, like the ancient ones, to make a miracle of new life. But was there ever laid in earth something so gruesome, in all the history of death, in all the history of cruelty and callousness? The soap that was *me* in a sense, *my* history, *my* family's history. And, like a child, I wanted to believe that this rite had a power to heal, spiritually, magically.

I remember the sadness I felt as I laid that soap in its little grave. A gnawing, an aching that seemed to grow until it filled all the garden, and even beyond it, the whole of nature. As you recited the *Kaddish* with Louis and Daniel, as Amy and the other children were sobbing, and I too, at last, was able to cry, I felt that every bush around me and every blade of grass was also crying with me. I felt that Nature too had been violated by Auschwitz and that, within its own womb it was performing its own act of cleansing and renewal by transforming that vile soap into the living sap of a flowering bush.

I wanted to believe in the magic of that rite. That it was truly purifying all the dumb minerals which made the camp's evil tools, which were infected with that evil: *metal,* the metal of the pumps which pumped out the last of the poison gas from the death chambers; the metal of the hooks to drag apart the bodies, some still alive, clawing over each other towards the ceiling or onto that metal door with its little window leading out to life again; *water,* water once pure and now polluted with hosing the faeces and urine and the splatters of blood from the dead and the still dying; *wood,* the wood of elevators and wagons to carry corpses to the furnaces; *stone,* the stone of mills to grind them to ash; more *timber* and *rubber* of trucks to scatter their ashes . . . I wanted to believe that there were incantations powerful enough to exorcize the curses on all the new wedding rings made from the gold stolen from the teeth of the dead; the curses on all the new clothes, all the curtains, all the new rope hawsers and ladders, made from the shorn hair of the millions of human slaves who entered the camps; the curses on the skirts made from Jewish prayer shawls, and the drums made from the parchment scrolls of the Torah, at the mercy of the drumsticks; the curses on all the spectacles, the crutches and the artifical limbs which were stolen from the bodies of the gassed and the burned.

I wanted so much to believe all that, *édesem.* I wanted to be free again, free of my past.

As if it were that easy. If only it were that easy.

LETTER EIGHT
Ronald to Dita

In a dark time. Monasteries

In a dark time, the eye begins to see . . .

What's madness but nobility of soul
At odds with circumstance? The day's on fire!
I know the purity of pure despair,
My shadow pinned against a sweating wall.
That place among the rocks — is it a cave,
Or winding path? The edge is what I have.

Dark, dark my light, and darker my desire.
My soul, like some heat-maddened summer fly,
Keeps buzzing at the sill. Which I is I ?
A fallen man, I climb out of my fear.
The mind enters itself, and God the mind,
And one is One, free in the tearing wind.

Theodore Roethke

In my own brilliantly dark lightyears, along that winding path, I fell over that edge, and, like Roethke, I also
spent some time in a mental hospital. Why should that

have happened? Of course, *Ditukam,* I told you about that time, but never in such detail as I'm going to now.

I was twenty-five when I was absorbed into what you might call the shaman or seer experience. I was alone, lost, isolated from the culture I'd grown up in. You know, every prescientific society in the past had its core of mystical tradition, its oracles and contemplatives and yogis and medicine men. These men and women were specialists, but in a reality which was widely shared in belief and ritual by the societies around them. A reality which was a 'fact of life', and not something perverse and cranky. Super-real, but not unreal because it could not be classified by the sense-evidence of a scientific age. Societies condoned, understood, and encouraged a young man to spend time alone in the wilderness, a time of his 'vision quest', as American Indians call it. He would usually have had a spiritual guide or teacher. That was important, the line between spiritual ecstacy and madness was a razor's edge. I had none. At least, not at the crucial time. Later, I looked for that authority in monasteries, like a moth seeking the skeleton structure of its own wings. But I was blinded and burned by the fire . . .

That experience is a like an earthquake, whose psychic cracks open up volcanic depths. It threatens to swallow you up, as Jonah was swallowed by the whale. That's a universal myth, isn't it? But then, if you're lucky, you come back to the conscious world, spewed onto dry land from the sea, returning from the desert to the town, from the mountain to the valley. The myths tell of a symbolic period in the whale's belly or the wilderness — three days, or forty days, during which the hero, again if he's lucky, is enhanced by the spiritual visions he experiences. He may be able to share those riches with others; or else the visions fade, and the gold turns to ashes. Yet he can never be the same person again. He will always carry the memory of that psychic Odyssey, of the god-like powers that menaced or helped him, of the ocean of energies that were revealed behind the veil of his previous everyday consciousness.

Ocean of energies! I experienced them, and they drowned me. I was unlucky. Physicists speak of the Promethean, dormant energies locked up inside the atoms of our bodies. E=mc ^{2}, Energy equals the Mass multiplied by the square of the velocity of light. An awesome velocity. When the mind descends into its deepest layers, where the chemistry of the body is one with the chemistry of the universe, where we are normally asleep and unconscious, energy becomes equal to consciousness for the mystic, and the fullness of energy becomes the fullness of light. There is a *vox tremenda* written into the very molecules of our bodies, whose tremors can transform mundane men into seers and prophets.

I never lived out my full three symbolic days, my descent into Hell, my forty days in the desert. They were interrupted catastrophically. I was a monk in the Cistercian monastery of Caldey in Wales when the seas engulfed me. I was psychotic for several weeks, in a mental hospital, before I came to myself.

My middle-aged eyes probe now into the turbulent soul of that young man who was myself, and I'm amazed by the incredibly short time-span in which he became a totally different person. How his compass turned right around one hundred and eighty degrees. That busy extrovert at Oxford, rarely alone, was now a hermit, a recluse, cultivating a mystic third eye, that inward-looking eye. And an extra sense, also, a sense of the sacred, which possessed and obsessed him.

I told you, didn't I, how I rented a secluded three-room cottage near Marlow, built by an old man in the autumn of his life, who'd died peacefully on the porch. Apart from composing music, I was reading and practising Yoga — you know, in Sanscrit that means yoking, or joining together: joining myself to my Source, joining everything around me to its Source. I practised disciplines to rouse the energies of the female Tantric serpent, the *kundalini,*

coiled at the base of my spine; to induce her head up
through the whole spinal stem, releasing the seven
chakras, or circles of energy. This is like the ladder of Jacob
in Western mysticism, or the progressive mansions of the
soul of Teresa of Avila. I did not heed the warnings I read
not to undertake these exercises without guidance, that
those centers of energy could become psychotic
floodwaters . . . I was too frenzied, too intoxicated by the
ascetic bliss I was tasting.

One warning came in the form of a dream around that
time. I dreamed of walking through many corridors and
rooms. I came to one room which was clearly some kind
of temple, complete with burning incense. There stood a
statuette whose upper half was female, lower half animal. She smiled an enigmatic, Mona Lisa smile. She was
talking. Something very wise, something very simple. I
said, *were you talking to me?* In another room there were
all kinds of people, also smiling. But their smiles seemed
to me false. To one man, who wore a black tie and was
some kind of leader, I said: *this is all false. I demand to
hear the truth.* He said only: *I have warned you.* Then
from a case he took out a circular metal box and opened
it. In a flash a serpent with glittering eyes sprung from
the box and coiled itself around my throat and my body,
and I fell to the ground struggling to pull it off.

I imagined another symbolic warning, the following
May, when I all but put my foot into a nest of vipers in
the Ligurian mountains. There seemed to be dozens of
them: tiny, writhing, fearful green energies — premoni-
tions, it seemed to me, of insidious energies within myself which could appear just as unexpectedly, and could
harm me. As indeed they did.

I had gone to Italy for the first time, to Florence for the
Maggio Musicale. Like the giants before me, Goethe,
Mozart, Liszt, I was another Northener dazzled by the
South. Not only by its lyrical, sun-drenched sensuality,
but also by the opposite, its fervent asceticism. I was im-
prisoned for timeless, mesmerized periods by the Fra
Angelico frescos in the San Marco, in cell after cell; or by

the giant Christ icon dominating the San Miniato. I remember how awed I was, how weak, how rapidly my
heart was beating. I left the city's bustle and went up alone
into the massive green mountains towering over the glint
of the Ligurian sea. For the first time I was reading the
account of the mystic Jesus, the Jewish Yeshuah, in St.
John, and in the Gnostic Gospels. And Meister Eckhardt.
And Carl Jung. And Aldous Huxley's *The Perennial Philosophy.* But also Ronald Knox, on Catholic thinking. And
I was reliving the wellsprings of sacramental vision from
which all religious experience has arisen, seeing the dead
matter of the universe made translucent with spirit, the
profane made sacred. Only, like falling in love, it was
unique, it was for me the first day of Creation. As if it
were a symbolic rite to express this transformation of
matter, I took colored pebbles out of a mountain stream,
where they glowed like precious jewels through the crys-
talline water which trapped the sunlight, to see their lustre disappear instantly — then gently laid them back on
their underwater bed to restore their glory. *A rite of transformation . . .* I was hungry and thirsty for some great
ritual of transformation, one that would embrace and renew not only myself, but the entire universe. I was ready
to succumb to the symbolic power of the Mass.

Nestling high and remote in the mountains I discovered a church, its interior heavily draped with wine-red
curtains. The parish priest was small and agile and rather
comical (his face reminded me of the French comedian
Fernandel). *Le chiese inglese sono fredde, non e vero?* he
said to me. He invited me to stay with him in the tiny
cottage which his mother cared for. *Ma non siamo albergo!*
Dinner was a magnificent Mediterranean assortment of
tiny fish. And as I sat almost alone in that church, the
Mass worked its magic on me.

The same effect was repeated often after I returned to
England. I'd left my rooms in Hampstead (in the house
of Sir Charles Forte, not yet a financial giant) and was
living now in Speen, in Buckinghamshire, close to Piggots,
the community founded by Eric Gill. I rented a garden

shed, opposite the pine woods by the hill leading up to Piggots. It contained enough for my ascetic needs: a camp bed, thick discarded curtains which could help keep me warm, a little oil heater. A woman in the village made me a daily lunch for two shillings, and I had bread and cheese for supper, if anything.

I felt my meager shed was symbolic. Kierkegaard wrote of the cumbersome religious edifice of dogma and theology and codified rite which obscures spiritual experience, though standing humbly beside it is a mere shack. I too was impatient of that edifice. What was overwhelmingly real to me lay in the shack of my own experiences. And I distanced myself from the gaggle of geese — again in Kierkegaard's terms — who met regularly to talk, with fervor, about flying, and then always wobbled back home without ever using their wings.

My father was allowing me three pounds weekly, through a bank. I did not communicate with my parents, but they knew where I was. One day the postman came with a telegram: my father was in the emergency ward after a heart attack.

Was his heartache, at least in part, because of myself? I'd become a stranger to him as a teenager, grafted onto that complex upper-class English system with its web of mores and obscure tests of exclusivity, its discreet anti-semitism and xenophobia. Of course, I came to hate it myself, and to rebel against it. But the eyes of the young boy had resented his father for being foreign and Jewish. How could the son appreciate the tenacious and gentle qualities of the poor immigrant who'd made a fortune in a strange land? And wasn't this boy the favored son, the clever son, the future conqueror of the elite Gentile strongholds, who was now withdrawing from the contest, rejecting all he had worked for? And the worst thing of all: that son who was once fluent in Hebrew and in Talmud, was he not now flirting with Christianity?

On my side, wasn't my own impending schizophrenia also precipitated, in that tangled tapestry of cause and effect, by my own violent separation from him — by killing him, my father, in myself? My father lay helpless in bed, his eyes heavy and pleading. I cut short the visit, and at the same time I cut off part of my own self.

He lived on, as you know, *Ditukam,* and years later we became close because I came to love in myself all that he represented. He was a man of great energy parcelled inside a gentle manner. He remarried at 76, a year after my mother's death, and his second wife accused him of being a sex-maniac.

Back in Speen, in my hermit's hut, I was like a puppet of unseen powers that seemed to discharge themselves into and through me. As if 'my' thoughts and actions were like kites sent up into the atmosphere which channeled its electricity into my soul and made it supersensible. My nervous wiring must have been superconductive and tough — why didn't my fuses blow at once?

And even more than in Italy, it seemed that the Nature around me — the austere ghost green clusters of pine trees, the mammalian curves of the hills, the glossy fields of frost, the vast engulfing gray-white skies — all vibrated and shuddered as if close to bursting. They became *transparent,* surface skins no longer impermeable to the pressures of the radiance within them. An infinite ripeness, which sometimes husks and barks seemed no longer able to contain; they were about to bubbleburst and explode. At other times the world seemed suffused with an exquisite peace, as if covered by a very gentle snowfall of light which whitened and transformed everything however dirty — grass, roofs, roads. At these times I experienced a purity of silence which seemed to sing with the agony of the first moment of all Genesis. In which the entire Act of Creation, unique and infinitely variable, was happening NOW. I knew that only if I entered and drank of that NOW would I find sense and fulfillment. It did not feel as if it were my own choice. I discovered myself to be a witness of that Creation, for the evidence surrounded me everywhere. Music, the arsis and thesis of rhythm, the winter pine trees, the orange sun, the Van Gogh swirling tornados of cloud and sky — all reflected fragments of the great Ground or Brahman or Jahweh, the 'He Who Is' whose name we cannot pronounce without distorting him. And a Light, inside and outside, like Dante's, it was impossible to turn away from.

And there was also fear. Sometimes terrible fear. The Valley of the Shadow . . . Sometimes I stood in panic, trapped in fear. Sometimes I could walk through the valley and through my fear. I did not know then, as I do now, that this was a path every mystic or shaman or yogi had to take, whether or not his experience was facilitated and enhanced by drugs like mescalin or *yage*, the 'vine of the soul'. In almost every tradition, this was called the path to a spiritual coitus, to a marriage, to the vision of a single reality which underlies the chopped-up world of disconnected objects and events. Modern science has reached the concept of this reality, if not the experience, by its own routes.

Again, *Ditukam*, I look back now with amazement on that young man who possessed such fierce determination to grope and stumble along that path. This was 1950. The Beatniks in the sixties, and — since your death in 1981 — the 'New Agers', have popularized a variety of spiritual traditions, from Hindu Yoga to Amerindian vision quests, complete with tepees, dream-catchers and sweet grass. They take trips into the wilderness to commune with themselves and nature. The young man I look back on predated them, and was very alone. That was one reason why he was drawn to seek out for himself the mystical traditions still alive within the Christian monasteries around him.

Creation was ongoing. It was also re-Creation. I was obsessed with *purification.* I felt that the white morning mists wrapped and snaked around the sombre hills and the black branches in order to *cleanse* them from the night. Similarly, I felt the burning-cold bite of the morning frost as a purifying antidote. And finally I found what I thought was a supreme antitoxin or catharsis, in the Mass. A deceptively tiny circle of unleavened bread, matzah, embracing nothing less than everything, and the golden chalice of wine-blood, the drink of the eternal Now, the juice and distillation of a cosmic drama of re-Creation in which corruption was transformed into purity. Sacrifice of the God to renew creation was a ritual ancient and worldwide, as was partaking of his flesh and blood: and for all my rationality, I was experiencing freshly its spiritual force. I was also reliving another branch of my ancestral Jewish experience: that of the first-century Jews who celebrated this ritual — extracting it from the Seder of the Last Supper on the eve of Passover.

In its extermination of pagan idolatry, the Christian Church had exterminated all 'magic' except the transubstantiation of this unleavened bread in the rite of the Mass. For the pagan, all of nature was still transparent, luminous, and sacramental. The sacred called out to him from rock and flower, water and fire. As it still did to Francis of Assisi, to Sri Ramakrishna, to William Blake, to Gerard Manley Hopkins, to Dylan Thomas. As it still did to me. The world and all its parts, not merely the Mass, was a powerful sacrament for me. It was not an opaque collection of scientific objects.

I was also on fire for an ideal human *community* of some kind. A community which would embace the *other,* which would transcend Jew and non-Jew, rich and poor, white and black, whatever . . . At that time Eric Gill's ideas attracted me, though he was now dead. I visited regularly the Piggots survivors on the hill in their cluster of farm buildings and houses, the chapel Gill had designed, Laurie Crib in the stone engraver's workshop, Rene Haig in the printshop, Eddie Nutyens in his stained glass studio and his son, Patrick who would become a distinguished architect, and Mary Gill herself, smiling benignly over her spectacles among her grandchildren and cats, whom Gill had listed among his possessions, along with chairs and table, knives and forks.

Gill's community was the first of many on my journey.

Edmund Rubbra also lived in Speen. Many years my senior, he too had a spirituality which shone through his music; he too married Buddhist and Western mysticism. I spent that Christmas at his house.

The role of music for me was central. Not only because it was especially *transparent*. It seemed to be a *source*. The Australian Aboriginals believe they *sing the world into existence,* as did their ancestors. They enter into the Dreamtime, and follow the songlines of their ancestors who brought things into being by imagining them. The source of all creative power was the original Ancestor at the beginning of all Dreamtime. In Hinduism the OM of the Brahman is the soundless sound, the seed sound of all being, the source of energy. And music for me too was a magical force which arose from and yearned to return to that infinite Silence.

I was rational about it. I worked at a musical theory which uncovered the universals in music, of all times and places, those universals which Plato said were pre-existent and lost at birth. Bastiam called them *elementary ideas* and Jung *archetypes* of a collective unconscious. In India, popular and local art without any marked impact was called *desi* or *nagara* (meaning worldly and fashionable), as distinct from the temple art of deities which was symbolic of the inner pathway called *marga.* That is a word meaning the tracks of an animal which a hunter must follow to find his quarry. The art called *marga* creates the footprints of the *Atman* or Universal Self, which lead us towards *atmananda*, or ecstacy of the Self. Plotinus wrote that when men recognize such art as the outward portrayal of an archetype subsisting in intuition, their hearts are shaken and they recapture the memory of the Original. St. Augustine, in his *De Musica,* applied this philosophy specifically to music. There were archetypal *numeri* in the world of sound, in music, and in our own souls. My own quest was similar: the *universal operations* which accounted for all music, in spite of its surface diversity. This was a matter of precise musical technique, but I derived those universal operations from the laws of sound formation in nature, and I also proposed how these evolved their way into the nervous system and the engrams of our brains. Music, mind, and nature; like Pythagoras or Augustine. As all colors refract their single source of white light, so the sounds of which music is made refract their original fountainhead of sound, the sonic sunlight. Even the single note, which we used to think of as indivisible, itself embraces a microcosmic spectrum of sound, refracts the sum of all sound. There are natural laws of sound which are manifested in what we call the harmonic series, a theoretically infinite web of proportional relationships. The overtones of this series become more opaque to our ears and minds the higher the range we explore — though overtones always remain anchored in, and related to, the lustre of their pure prime fundamental. Thus as we explore these ranges — call them heights or depths — we are encountering and penetrating the opacity of matter itself. Preoccupation with the higher ranges of the natural series is typical of the twentieth century. The concordance of the music of Palestrina or Bach or Mozart reflected a (temporary) balance of earth and spirit in their epochs, a balance upset in this century. Our time has descended into the opacity of the world and seeks to illuminate it, to discover the reason and light within chaos. As the heart of the atom has been opened up, so have the finer intervals — the apparent chaos, or 'noise' — of the higher overtones. However, in doing so modern man is also coming up against — trying to transcend — the limitations of his own inbuilt human hearing which cannot distinguish the relationships of intervals beyond a given threshold. The opacity of sound, of matter.

Thus, unawares, I was also rationalizing Kabbalistic tradition, for which the musical *operations* were occult tools, instruments of creation which reflected the divine tools which created the entire universe. Hence music was special in the myths of the West, as elsewhere: its angels have always played music, only rarely written books or painted pictures.

At that time of isolation, I could not have imagined that

this work on the universal operations of music would later mature into the program I directed at London University, that it would bear fruit in a system for many levels of musical education and study, and gain me a reputation in academia.

For the first time, I also succumbed to the numinous experience of Gregorian Chant, or plainsong. Those soaring melismata, that winging of rhythms which released it from the dance and from earthly bondage — here was the European equivalent to the songlines of the Aboriginals. And I discovered that plainsong was the fountainhead of all European music for many centuries, bequeathing a reservoir of thematic shapes which passed into polyphonic as much as monodic, into instrumental as much as vocal composition. I heard the Chant first at Quarr Abbey on the Isle of Wight, a Benedictine foundation settled from Solemnes, whose monks had first revived the Gregorian tradition which had lain dormant, locked in manuscripts, since the sixteenth century. I studied their rhythmic theory (and it *was* a theory) in a book on plainsong by Dom Suñol of Montserrat Abbey (strange, the threads of life: I would later be a foundation member of an association of composers at Montserrat — we were there together, weren't we?) But the experience infinitely surpassed all understanding of its techniques. *Music which wants to die and go to Heaven,* I wrote in Suñol's book.

In Quarr I experienced the enclosure and concentration of a monastery for the first time, and I entered into the timelessness of the liturgy, that two-way mirror for the varieties of spiritual experiences. But Quarr also seemed too comfortable a place for the intense ascetic drive within me. And I still longed for that solitude with its inexhaustible wells of silence I had learned to drink from.

Parkminster in Sussex was the other extreme. The Carthusian monks live alone, each in a little 'villa' with a plot of land attached, which they work. They meet together, silently, only for the liturgical offices. One of these, the prayers to the Virgin, occurs in the middle of the night. I joined their nocturnal procession to the chapel, their lanterns swinging shadows along the stonework. Long shadows, thrown from the early middle ages which the world outside had long since disowned. The Prior wisely recommended me to go off and to think very hard before committing myself to a life of such rigorous deprivation of the senses, such thorough emptying.

At Christmas time I was camping in a bunker in the harbour of Tenby, in South Wales, waiting through two days and nights for the boat from Caldey Island. A storm whipped up the waves and prevented the monks of Caldey from bringing their turkeys to the Christmas market. The Cistercians were an offshoot of the Benedictines, but, following Bernard of Clairveaux, maintained strict silence although living a communal life. I went to them because I wanted their *silence*. It held the promise for me of cleansing, of transformation.

Jonah in the Dreamtime . . . The whale able to descend to depths where sunlight no longer penetrates, and the blind fish have no use for eyes, where the waters are without location or direction, and time has disappeared. But a whale capable of osmosis, transformed together with its environment, but preserving its own identity. A special skin. One that mystics learn to grow. If that skin fails, the diver drowns.

The skin did burst for me, and I drowned.

It was sometime in those chapels on the island of Caldey, among its windswept fields, under the glare of the winter sun, sometime during those pre-dawn Matins and Masses, sometime during the chant and ritual of that in-and-out-of-time liturgy, that I crossed a fragile line between Dreamtime and the norms of everydaytime I'd been born into. Between one kind of reality, call it super-reality, and another. And the stuff of symbols became confused.

I tried to die and be reborn, but *literally. Yes, literally.* One afternoon a monk found me lying down in the novitiate, holding my breath, my eyes bulging. *In order to die.*

Holding my breath was the mad ghost of the Hindu Yoga exercises I had practised. The monk spent the evening quietly with me. He was ironing some laundry. Another mad ghost appeared: I tried to electrocute myself on the iron. *Death and rebirth.* A ghost of reality, the mysterious energy of electricity, the invisible power which can transform darkness into light, even the darkness of a whole city, of a hundred cities. *Symbol and reality, confused.* Electricity had to be a manifestation of Spirit: ignited by its power, like Frankenstein's creature by lightning, I could die and be reborn.

By now the Abbot had rung my parents for advice, and my mother arrived the next day with my older brother Mac, driven down from another world by her chauffeur in the Daimler.

I found myself in a clinic near Regent's Park under the care of the famous psychiatrist William Sargant, whom my parents had consulted. And I flickered, like a film seen from a faulty projector, between clear perception and distortions, between my surface and oceanic realities, between presence and madness.

LETTER NINE
Dita to Ronald

Inside Auschwitz, my life saved by Livy

It wasn't only Livy who saved my life, there was also Rachael. No one who was not in Auschwitz can imagine what it was like to find friendship there, amid such hatred and brutality. To have someone who cared not just for herself, in the desperate struggle to stay alive for another day, sometimes it seemed another few minutes. It's hard to describe what it was like, *édesem*. You must try to imagine a hunger which gnaws at your insides continually, every hour of the grinding day, and gnaws on through the stunted night also, a hunger which intrudes even into the refuge of our dreams as we lie contorted in the dark, each one squashed against a dozen other sleeping, tossing bodies, all pressed into that one narrow *Pritsche*, that bare wooden plank without pillows or blankets. The crush of bodies and stinking breath every night. In another barrack the top planks have been overburdened and collapse into splinters onto the bodies below. Imagine seeing the faces you thought you knew turn hollow, yellow, ashen. Imagine the bellies swelling. Imagine all your strength sucked away like an egg out of its shell. Imagine sores burned into your feet that never go away. And above everything, clutching everything, penetrating everything, imagine the most vicious, cruel, unceasing cold. Imagine those winter knives of ice, unrelenting, day by day, hour by hour, which pierce through your skin with a hundred cutting edges, under your skin, into your flesh. Against this torture we have only rags to wear, tattered remnants of what had once been proper clothes. We are lucky enough to have that, the Germans seem to be short of clothing. Some Hungarian women in a barracks block near us are almost naked. And you cannot, at least not for long, hoard extra clothes against the cold, even supposing you are lucky enough to find some extra rag of a vest to steal, or barter a precious piece of bread for some frayed scarf, because every so often we are doused in a bath of smelly camphor, against infection, and you've left all your clothes on one side and then you pick up only one dress or skirt — any old size, any old shape — and any two wooden shoes, never a pair, on the other side. In clothing, as in food, the yellow-starred Jews are always at the bottom of the Auschwitz pile. And there is another terrible source of clothing, lice-ridden rags from the bodies of the newly dead, dragged each morning to the front of the Block to be picked up by the special *Totenkommando,* or Death Squad — if you are quick enough to steal them in time.

Imagine being frightened most of the time. Imagine not daring to trust anybody. Imagine being treated like some filthy refuse or scum. Imagine how callous we have become: we trade anything useful — a button, a needle, a piece of cloth, for a piece of the powdery sawdust bread or rotten sausage (our usual 'evening meal') or for an extra spoonful of the midday 'soup' (especially from the bottom of the pot where there might be potato peel or a piece of real turnip).We whisper sometimes about the women who manage to barter their wrecked bodies for food, who give themselves to German and Polish political prisoners, those who are more privileged in the camp hierarchy than mere Jews like ourselves.

Imagine a fatigue so overwhelming that lifting your arms or dragging your feet is a torture. Imagine endless hours of standing for the daily pre-dawn *Appel* or roll-call, in a heavy wet mist that permeates everything and seems itself to be laden with evil, like the bad breath of the monster which was Auschwitz. And then, in columns of already exhausted and starving women, in a make-believe of efficiency which would be comic if it were not horrific, we are forced to 'trot ' to the factory. I am one of a dozen straining, burnt-out prisoners who have to carry heavy boxes of little metal hubs from a storeroom to benches where they are fitted into *Panzer-Fausten,* the mini-rockets for German tanks. Dazed and breathless from the exertion. Lurching under a weight which seems always beyond my capacity. With only a short break for the watery soup.

We glimpse a few German civilians in this factory, managers and executives, who have little contact with the starved and misshapen slaves around them. These overlords from the once real world have real clothes which fit them, and their flesh is pudgy. I want to hate them, if I had strength to hate. To hate their clothes and their flesh and their smugness. To hate the way they ignore us.

Do they know about the gas chambers at the entrance to the camp? And do they ever hear the shrieks of women and children thrown alive into the pit of flames near the gas chambers?

And yet there comes one unbelievable moment, *édesem,* when a manager of some kind passes by me, near the end of an endless day, looks at me with unseeing eyes, pulls a piece of chocolate from his pocket and gives it to me. *Chocolate!* A paradise of nutrition! I gulp it down in two mouthfuls. No question of making it last. What does it mean? Is he sorry for me? Sorry for the scraggy subhuman slave with sores, no hair and a terrible stink? Does he see a human being, not just some kind of trained animal? The chocolate makes me hate him all the more. It is a hatred that helps me feel more human. And he never comes near me again.

We have become like little children, without any sense of yesterday or tomorrow, fighting each other, or promising a friendship that is over before it begins. Childish, especially towards the ones with power, like our Block *kapo*, a burly coarse spotty-faced Ukranian peasant woman who curses us every other minute. Or towards the guards, who themselves take pleasure in treating us like foul, abominable infants. Oh, those desperate, horrible visits to the latrines! We have to crave permission to go there: they really prefer that we soil ourselves. They want to see that happen. They want to relish our filthy humiliation. They want us to hate ourselves. And we do.

And my dreams in Auschwitz? Dreams, the only privacy, the only remaining refuge of my spirit, while my body collapses into that nightly tangle of human arms, legs, and necks distorted on the coarse planks. There must be many more dreams than filter through into the cruelty of daylight, even in a sleep as weighty as lead, and gone before it begins. I do remember the dreams of food. Not huge and incredible banquets of gorging. Rather one or two favorite things, like poppyseed cake, or hopplepopple. Eaten in an atmosphere of love, round the table at home with Apu and Anyu and Marika. Or a picnic in the Tatras near Kezmarok, bicycles, the smells of grass and moist leaves and ripe plums, with Petr whom I once loved and kissed and caressed. The food I dream about is love-food. Do I have orgasms in my sleep, perhaps dreaming of Petr against my thighs, or some other man? I just don't remember. Perhaps my sex is too crippled for dreams. I entered Auschwitz a golden girl of eighteen in the full springtime flush of my sexuality, and my womb and my heart have been cropped and sheared along with my hair. And isn't it truly symbolic, that Auschwitz gives me a disease of the womb in its latrines?

It's in the latrines, I suppose, that I catch the infection which should have cost me my life. You couldn't imagine the filth and sickly stench of these overflowing latrine-pits. Auschwitz has no proper drainage or sanitation — water is foul, and soap is a dream. In spite of that cesspool of a latrine, it feels fine to be able to move our bowels, it is a sign that we are still living beings, even

when our excrement oozes out in a thin stream of diarrhea.
But what to wipe ourselves with? That is part of the dignity of remaining human. Paper would be like gold. Instead, we tear off tatters from our dresses, so that as the
days pass the rags become more ragged. And it is common to see the bare bottoms of prisoners.

My infection is vaginal (in Bartholin's duct and gland,
I will learn years later). The swelling is monstrous, and I
soon have a terrible fever. I cannot stand on my legs for
long, my head is a furnace, my eyes are glazed. If any of
this is noticed, I know that I'd certainly be killed, either
straight 'up the chimney', or else in the 'hospital', or
Revier, block. We've all heard what goes on there. Lethal
injections to the sick, usually. It's said that the sick wards
are run by common criminals, actually sent to Auschwitz
instead of to prisons, because of their heartlessness and
brutality. But even Jewish prisoner-doctors, we hear, have
to take part in the killings. It is their own way to survive. Years later in Israel, I would be dated by just such
a doctor, Ariel, who would survive and have to make
peace with his conscience. 'We knew that we were all
doomed to die in Auschwitz,' he told me. 'The doctors
in the medical block had to choose all the time. Medical
drugs were very few and precious. The more healthy had
a better chance. We thought of it as saving some lives at
the expense of others who would die anyway.' We hear
about the callous roll-calls, even of the very sick. They
are compelled to stand to attention in front of the hospital block in their underwear, even on frozen mud in the
bitter cold of the Polish winter. Sometimes the guards
slosh them with dirty, freezing water. That is one of their
vicious games.

We are warned about the hospital block from the very
first few days in the camp. It is the alternative to suicide
on the electric fences, and much more prolonged. And
we also hear about the horrific Block 10. (I say *horrific*.
But in Auschwitz, on this other planet, *horror* is not what
it is elsewhere — we have lost our normal human feelings, we are numbed automatons.) Block 10 is situated

in the men's part of the camp, where many hundreds of women prisoners are the living guinea pigs for experiments in sterilization. The rumors say that many of these die in terrible pain, after being injected with chemicals intended to close up their wombs. Others are burned up inside by X-rays. We understand that the Nazis want efficient ways to sterilize millions of women prisoners, all considered by the Nazi ideology to belong to the inferior, sub-human races. Block 10 at Auschwitz is their experimental center. We hear of artificial insemination, and of women giving birth to monsters. Rumors speak of other means of sterilization, like tasteless chemical powders in food. I will never be sure afterwards how true this is. You remember, my darling, when you and I wanted a child in the late sixties, we discover that my Fallopian tubes are blocked, so that I cannot become pregnant without an operation. Many of us in Auschwitz, the women prisoners, believe that we are being sterilized in some surreptitious way, because our menstruation has stopped. Most likely, we think, by drugs we can't taste in the daily ration of watery soup.

That is the sinister, notorious Block 10. Incredibly, the rumors go, under the same roof as these horrors, it also houses a brothel for the elite of prisoners, mostly Germans. It is also a kind of clearing-house where the prostitutes are chosen and shipped in and out, like so many material goods. These camp beauties, they say, are sometimes Jewish women, but mostly German, Polish, and Russian prisoners.

We all feed on grisly rumor because we can have no real knowledge. Our talk to each other is always furtive, our words are squeezed out of wasting bodies. And everything, the most monstrous, the most incredible, becomes believable here, because Auschwitz has its own kind of truth. The everyday, commonplace truth has been suspended. Yet with hindsight, viewed years afterwards from planet Earth, even the most bizarre and atrocious of our prisoner rumors prove to be not far from the truth. There *is* a museum of skulls, of preserved embryos, of mummies. There *is* a shelf of glass jars containing human eyes, for experiments to change their color. There *are* special blocks full of human dwarfs, hunchbacks, all kinds of malformed people — and also of twin children. A mother of one pair of twins has been sent back to our section of the camp, and she spreads the word that twins are being used for experiments. Probably so that German mothers can have multiple pregnancies, the rumor says, when injected with the blood, or even the semen of twins. And there *is* a dissecting room where strange and ghastly operations are performed, nearly all of them excruciatingly painful, and usually fatal. There *is* a laboratory for strange experiments with needles in the ears and eyes and spines of victim prisoners, leaving them deaf or blind or paralyzed, but usually dead.

Our own immediate world is one of endless selections. How we live in terror of that word! Selection. These are the occasions for the SS doctors to sit in judgement on our life or death. Their God-like power. The joy of killing. The Last Judgement Day did not end at the ramps, with their trainloads of new arrivals: it continues to make a Last Day of every day since. Not that the SS do the dirty work of beating and killing: that is left to Poles and Ukrainians, who have inherited centuries of hatred for Jews. The Polish *kapo* shouts at us to undress for a Selection, at any time, in any weather. Selections are usually presided over, and most often conducted by Josef Mengele himself, the fearful Auschwitz Angel of Death, in one year already a living legend of evil incarnate among the camp prisoners. He first arrived at Auschwitz in May 1943, exactly a year before I did on that May day of spring blackened with ashes. Mengele is the devil-doctor of the ramps who condemned all my family, excepting only Apu, to be murdered in the gas chambers. Like the myths of Mephistopheles, Mengele is dark and diabolically handsome, he is graceful and dressed most elegantly, he is some kind of unreal radiant vision, a prince of this horrendous city of hell with its suburban miles of streets of barracks.

I see him many times. He wears an Iron Cross, and sometimes other medals. His manner is polished and cold. He whistles to himself, Wagner, while making his selections. He even has a perverse erotic attraction for the women prisoners who form the immense pool of his victims. We hear so many stories of his outbursts of rage, and of his savage cruelty. How he often beats prisoners with his riding crop. It is he, above all, who supervises and performs the lethal injections, the dissections, as well as the lashings and the executions by shooting.

That I survive selections, in spite of my fever and faintness, is a miracle. Above all, it is due to the help and protection of just a few persons in my barrack who have kept their humanity, and risk their own lives for me, perhaps risk tortures worse than death. Strangely enough, I have to be grateful, even to the coarse *Blockälteste,* who does not report me, and even allows me to spend extra time in the hut. But it is Livy and Rachael who really save my life.

They give me their bread and their soup. That is like giving me their blood, their own hope of surviving. They give me their underwear, leaving themselves to shiver. Bread, soup, clothes . . . not a long list, reckoned in material items, though it is all they now have in the world: in value it is *everything,* in that world life itself. I can't refuse, they won't let me refuse, I am weak and reeling.

The real tests are the dawn *Appels* of every day, each of them a Selection. We stand shivering for hours, while the SS pass along the endless rows of prisoners, stripped or grotesque in badly fitting clothes, to count and recount us, the continual inventories of stock, of barely living livestock, counting and recounting like a bureaucracy gone mad. Now I can feel the dawn frost chop off my feet and hands. Now I can scarcely clench away the clatter of my teeth. Now I can stand up no more. No more. Enough. How can I? After months of hunger. I do not have the strength, my body does not have the immunities, it cannot fight disease. But Livy and Rachael are on each side, holding me up. And just as the SS come into sight, there round the corner of the F Barrack, by the barbed wire fence, Livy and Rachael pinch and slap my face to bring some deceptive blush into my cheeks. I tense myself. And I manage to stand up by myself till the SS have passed. And nothing is noticed.

Rumor chases rumor of a *special* Selection. In my hut it is Esther who hears about it first. Eva is sobbing that the chimneys are belching smoke continuously, every day and all through the night. Alena has picked up news from someone with access to the main office: twenty percent of the camp are to be eliminated. It is to be a murderous selection, to make room for hundreds of thousands due to arrive in the transports. There is panic in our hut. But I am by then too sick, too dazed to feel anything. I only want to sleep.

During the next day the bell rings for a second time — the first was for the morning *Appel.* And that means a confinement to the huts, a *Blocksperre.* Our *Blockälteste* orders us to undress, with curses and screaming. She gives us each a card with our number and age and other details on it. It is all so efficient. So insane. So terrifying.

And then we wait, and wait, naked. Some women have pricked their fingers and are smearing the blood on their cheeks to give them color, a substitute for rouge, literally a life-blood. I am lying on my bunk, dozing in half-sleep, haunted by phantom figures from my childhood who whisper to me in Hungarian and Slovak. Dimly, I see Livy who is covering my bare shoulders with a torn jacket. The camp noises have been dampened into a mere background murmur. A murmur suddenly burst open by explosions of shouts and curses. There are guards, and the *Blockälteste* herself, driving us out through the dormitory door into the guard office connected to it. I am shaken to my feet. Livy, unbelievable Livy, is supporting me. Now we are all jam-packed, completely naked, into that small room, only a few yards wide, each of us clutching our card. Terrified, terrified. I am pressed hard against the wooden wall by the bundle of smelly bodies. Only their pressure holds me up, my feet are sagging.

Someone opens the door to the frosty autumn air. One by one, the naked women must run outside. And run fast. As the office empties, I see the SS officer standing, the guard and the *Blockälteste* on each side of him. And it is Mengele himself who is the Judge! It is Mengele himself who passes your card — and oh, so casually — to the one on his left or to the other on his right.

On one side, we don't know which, the card becomes a death warrant. The prisoner has to run out of the office door, back through the freezing mud to the other dormitory door; and in those few moments it is Mengele himself who is deciding life or death. Rather, what kind of death, if we can face the truth, death by gassing or slower death by starvation and exhaustion. And I am to have the Prince himself sentence me . . . As my turn comes, Livy again slaps me, again and again, and very hard. I am holding my head up and my shoulders, maybe for the last time, and I run with the last dribble of energy left inside me.

I am sleeping again on my rough planks, exhausted. We are still confined to our Block. But the Selection officers have moved their cat-and-mouse games of torment and murder to other barracks. Livy wakes me for my bowl of soup. As she supports me, her arm round my shoulders, she is saying, *Ditukam, dragasagam, I am sure your card went to the right. Everyone knows that just couldn't be the side for the chimneys.* I hear other voices, as if under water: *I'm sure I'm for the gas, I'm sure this time, I know it in my bones . . .* and with crazy sobbing: *They've let me go again, they've let me go again . . .* and behind me another hollow voice is reciting as if in a trance: *Anyu, where are you, Anyu, Anyu, where are you, Anyu . . .* It is the litany of a madwoman, it lulls me as I slip again, way down, deep down, into an everlasting oblivion of only a moment, pierced and destroyed by the next morning's bell and the *kapo's* shouting.

How will anyone ever invent a language for the desolate feelings we have? Most of us want to die most of the time.

It's easier. To make no more effort, to give up on conserving the last ghosts of your vigour, just to drift, until you drop. It's as if you are dead anyway: you really are ceasing to exist, hour by hour. You have lost your humanity, you have, in truth, become that grisly blue number tattooed on your arm.

But I have seen how human feelings can flicker again out of that terrible apathy, when they are sparked by human caring. Livy made me feel a human being again, however sickly a human being. It was a person she saved, not just a physical body. I owe her my life in that double sense. So that her heroism and her concern for me was also a double victory against the SS, who planned Auschwitz and all its cruelty not just to kill us physically, but also to reduce us into non-human beings, to crush each heart into one impersonal number among millions. It was even a kind of daily triumph to use our real names to each other — Livy, Rachael, Eva, Esther ... That was to defy the whole system of faceless numbers, to address a person who once had a human face which was now distorted.

I learned much later that Eichman always chose Jewish Holy Days for the major Selections. That great October Selection during my fever was on Yom Kippur, the Day of Atonement, the central Day of Lamentation of the entire Jewish Year. But it is also the day when God is said to renew the universe, when he recreates it.

Every day in Auschwitz was a Day of Lamentation, and every mourner has a meaningful day to remember. On each Yom Kippur since my liberation, as you know *dragasagam,* I lit candles for my family and mourned their first and last Day of Auschwitz, that Day of our arrival on the ramps, that Day of the gas-chambers, that Day of the murder of Marika and Anyu, and so many others. But I also honor that day of the October Selection. It is a special and terrible day in my personal calendar: a day to celebrate as well as to mourn, because I myself was re-created on that Jewish Day of Re-creation, when the flame of my spirit was rekindled by some human care.

LETTER TEN
Ronald to Dita

Montserrat. My imprisonment in Barcelona

How can I possibly grasp your experience? When I try to feel what it was like to be locked up within an impersonal system at the mercy of guards, then I try at least to extrapolate from that week in Barcelona, when I was imprisoned without trial in a Spanish jail. But I'm ashamed, really, to mention the two things in the same breath. It's like extrapolating from a cold in the nose to the plague. It's bathos, almost comic relief. Prison for me was not prolonged (though I feared it would be), nor was I marked out for a terrible death by gassing, starvation and exhaustion. Still, it was for me just a taste of a totalitarian prison.

That story has to begin with Montserrat, and Montserrat makes me lyrical as it has so many others. The Abbey nestles improbably in the lofty crotch of a giant mountain which rises from a wilderness of burning red earth and rock. The name means a 'sawn mountain' in Catalan, *sawn by angels* said the poet Verdaguer. Other poets compared the mountain to immense petrified flames, to a gigantic organ, to a huge ship docked in the landscape in the very center of Catalonia — indeed a divinely appointed flagship of Catalonian aspirations and identity. Since the Civil War, when Franco had crushed Catalonian resistance (Barcelona, thirty kilometers south-west, was the great bastion of anti-Franco troops), there are many stories of the Montserrat monks harboring enemies of the Franco regime, and engineering escape routes through the Pyranees. But Montserrat has been primarily a spiritual and not a political symbol. *Montserrat sucks a man in from the outer to the inner world*, said Schiller. *Nowhere but in his own Montserrat will a man find happiness and peace*, wrote Goethe in his old age. The cult of the monastery's Black Madonna was carried into hundreds of churches in Italy and Austria, and into America by Columbus' companion Bernat Boïl.

You remember how pleased I was in 1968 to receive the invitation from Dom Irene Segarra, the director of the renowned *escolania* of Montserrat. The Abbey wanted to renew its ancient role as a center of sacred music, to embrace all that was numinous in modern music. For me music was inevitably 'sacred' in the Pythagorean sense, a reflection of the silent rhythms of the universe without, and the 'temperament', or tuning, of the human psyche within. And 'sacred' and 'secular' musics have always been uneasy bedfellows, with much give and take between the two. The composers invited, all of whom responded enthusiastically by letter if not in person, included Stravinsky (who wrote the 'secular' *Rite of Spring* as well as the *Symphony of Psalms* and the 'sacred' *Mass),* Krenek, Messiaen, Jolivet, Penderecki, Britten, Petr Eben, Karl Huber, Vic Nees, and many others. Don't you remember how honored I was to become a founding member of that Association of composers and musicians, to take such an active part in the meetings at Louvain and Geneva, and even as an organizer of a daughter-conference — at Liverpool in 1978, two years before your cancer. Liverpool was a feast. Hope Street, with its Philharmonic Hall, joining the Anglican cathedral to the Catholic, towering over the town of docks and pubs which had spawned the Beatles. Together with the BBC, we commissioned Anthony Milner's Second Symphony for per-

formance by the Philharmonic. In the Cathedral down
the street we heard French premières (a Mass by Xavier
Darasse, commissioned for this occasion by the French
Ministère de la Culture), Spanish premières (Tomas
Marco, and the oratorio *The Creation* by the Catalan composer Homs, both commissioned for this occasion), an
original 'liturgy' in word, music and dance, called 'Light'
with music by Peter Wiegold and dance by Irene Dilks
. . .

It was after the second Montserrat Conference-Festi-
val, in 1968, that I ended up in a Barcelona gaol. We were
late getting to the airport for our charter flight home. I
was very anxious. An Iberia booking clerk showed up
only ten minutes before takeoff. He was sleepy and rude.
He checked in other people and left us waiting. I got angry and said he was being stupid. He went red, and called
you stupid. I lost my temper and slapped his face. He
walked over to where the two civil guards with
tricornered hats were standing. They politely asked me
to accompany them to the Security Officer. (My Spanish,
you remember, is poor: I get by because of my fluent Italian.) Now he turned out to be a very charming man, fluent in French and English. Profusely apologetic, he explained that he had to make a report, since this was tech-
nically some kind of assault on a Government official,
and that I would have to present myself for a short while
at the *Jeffetura*, the police headquarters back in Barcelona. But never worry, he assured me, we should be out
on a later plane. I was naively trusting, but you knew
better. At the *Jeffetura* a brute of a police officer took away
my passport, jerked his thumb at you to get out, and jerked
it again downwards for me. Then the reality hit me. I said
to you, go to the British Consul. But it was to be a week
before I saw you again.

Downwards meant the prison cells. My pockets were
emptied, shoelaces removed (in case I wanted to hang
myself, I suppose). I was photographed and fingerprinted
— a messy business. I was led to a cell, perhaps ten yards
square, which was crammed tight with about a hundred

prisoners. Most of those I talked to were youngsters who had been in a suspicious cafe or house when the police raided it.This was the time of Franco's last illness, and the Spanish police were filling the jails. Especially in Barcelona, the traditional center of anti-Castilian and anti-Franco ferment, both left-wing and separatist. I heard stories of those who disappeared forever. There was also one young deserter from the army who had been picked up, and badly beaten too. He sat hunched in a corner. He bunched his fingers to his lips, blew a kiss towards me, and said *¡Ah, Inglaterra, la libertad!* We all slept badly on the stone floor. Next morning the cell door was opened, and I found myself, for the first time in my life, at the wrong end of a machine gun. Names were read out, mine among them. There was a pile of shiny handcuffs, and they were clanked onto the wrists of nearly every prisoner. Only a few were not handcuffed: I was one. We were pushed into sealed armored cars. I, with only two others, into a much smaller van. There was no window. We were driven for about an hour. I dread to think where the others were taken.

When our van stopped, we were led into the basement vestibule of a large building, with one solitary policeman on guard: a barred door on his left led into a short corridor, with two cells off it. I remained a prisoner for seven days. The Consul could not even find out where I was. And I was released only because *you* wired home for money, on the advice of the Consulate's lawyer, and bribed a senior official of the Government. You knew something about all that. Your mother had done the same for your father in 1943 in Czechoslovakia.

But I knew nothing of that then: only a timeless, helpless tedium, locked up in a dark cell, with nothing to do, or read, for endless hours. The windows were mere slits, high in the corridor beyond the cell. There was no communication with the guard. You could call him only to go to the lavatory, which was at the far end of the corridor. There was no word of any trial, and I'd heard of even foreigners disappearing indefinitely. This was my meager taste of a totalitarian bureaucracy. But then I did become a real criminal, I thought, at any rate an accomplice to a crime, through some fantastic events which seem to have spilled into my life from some second-rate film . . .

On the afternoon of the third day, the cell door clanged open and two youngsters were led in to share my cell. We talked, in my bad Spanish. They had stolen a car, had knocked down and injured a woman. One of them, short, wiry, callous, produced a bag hidden in his pants which contained a razorblade and a key. He said it was the key to the cell door. That night, they would unlock it but leave it shut. They would scream with pain. When the guard came into the corridor, leaving open the connecting door from the vestibule, they would overpower him and escape. He said I should help them, otherwise he'd cut off my testicles.

It was an empty threat. I said I was going to sleep in the top bunker at the back of the cell, and they could do what they liked. But I did not report them, and at night fell into a deep sleep. I woke to shouts. The guard was on his knees in the corridor, blood streaming from his right cheek, crying *¡Ayuda me!* I joined in, diplomatically, shouting *Help! Au secours!* and so forth. The kids had escaped. Two policemen appeared, helped the guard to his feet. I remained quiet in the bunk. Later a senior officer came, and talked to the guard, who was now bandaged. He pointed at me. The guard shrugged: *¡Hah, el Inglés!*

I couldn't believe I wasn't to be implicated.

After the bribe, I was taken to a magistrate's office, given back my passport without a word, and summarily released into a world of traffic and sunlight it took me many hours to adapt to. You remember, darling, how we stayed on in Barcelona for several days, waiting for another charter flight: and how all that time I felt pathologically hunted, certain that every policeman I saw had my photo? How I couldn't believe they'd let me through the airport, even though I changed my appearance by shaving off my

beard? How I hugged like a lunatic the first English policeman I saw at Gatwick, though he took it all very placidly?

That's what a totalitarian regime did to me in a week,
only a week. Just a taste, a savor, a *soupçon* . . .

LETTER ELEVEN
Dita to Ronald

The insane march. The Russians arrive

There are new rumors every day. *The Allies have landed in Normandy. The Allies are being driven back into the sea by the massive German counter-attack. The Russians have launched a huge new offensive, and they will be at the gates of Auschwitz within a week. The Allies are being defeated by the new German secret weapons, the rockets, the giant tanks with impenetrable armor, the missiles. Hitler has been assassinated.*

None of it is very real. Our lives remain the same moment-to-moment survival. The only war real to us is against the pangs of our hunger, as continual as the weather outside. The war against that thick sticky ocean of mud which has everywhere replaced the solid earth. An ocean which swallows up our clogs, sometimes together with the staggering feet in them, sometimes even together with the prisoners who wear them. The war against the bite of the merciless cold as we stand, hour after timeless hour, waiting for the dawn which refuses to come, waiting for the *Appel* ritual of roll-call, waiting for the collection of nightly corpses from the huts, waiting finally to form the column, five in a row, which will be whipped into the 'Auschwitz trot' en route for the hard labor which is fatal. The war, above all, against sliding into the zombie death of the *Mussulmen*.

I am lucky. To be working inside the factory means that for many hours each day I am protected from the worst of the wild Polish winter. In these last days (but we do not yet know they are last days), strange to say, the Germans are stepping up the production of their *Panzerfaust* rockets. For insane hours without end, my skeletal hands and shoulders carry the weight of the same hard shiny metal caps, hundreds of caps, thousands of identical caps. I am an automaton someone has switched on into a nightmare of meaningless caps. But the batteries are failing.

An evening has come which breaks the link in the chain of Auschwitz evenings. It is amazing, but I have no heart left to be amazed. The *Blockälteste*, silently, is giving each of us a full half-loaf of bread. Rachael is crying tears from dried-up ducts. 'We are selected for the gas,' she is saying. Esther joins in, shaking her shrivelled head. 'You know that those who go to the gas after a Selection are given extra bread.' So has it come, at last? It must be true. *We are all going to be killed.* I am already too dead to care any more, too dead to be frightened. Zita, who was a teacher of history in a Budapest high school, says in a brave and steady voice: 'The Russians are coming, and they are going to destroy us because we are the evidence. No one will ever know that they are such monsters.' Sarah whispers from a hoarse throat. 'It'll be as if nothing has happened at all. As if we never existed, or the camp.'

You must try to picture this group of scraggly, despairing women, my dear, clutching and biting into our precious pieces of bread. It's true, the *Blockälteste* and the guards have often taunted us: 'Do you think anything will remain for the world to see? And even if you did ever get away, you stinking filthy cunts, would anyone believe you anyhow?' But Livy just comes over to sit on the bunker beside me, without a word, and puts her arm on my shoulder.

In the cramped darkness of the hut, I am forcing my-

self to keep awake, for the first time since I entered
Auschwitz. Outside, before we collapse on our bunks, we
see the eerie moonlight drape over huts and barbed wire
and watchtowers. I can't sit up in the bunk, even if I had
the strength. It's hard even to turn over. There's no room.
It's like the holds of the old slave-ships. And like the negro
slaves, we too are cut off brutally from our families.

The stench is the same, of excrement, of disease, of
wasting flesh, but mixed as always with the stink of the
chimneys' smoke, sometimes stronger, sometimes fainter,
but all-pervading. Even if I survive, I will never, I know,
be free from that smell. It is imprinted into my nostrils
as my Auschwitz number is imprinted onto my arm, a
signature in smell as well as in tattoo. I am listening to
the familiar night noises. Rats scurry. The man-killing
dogs howl like wolves in the distance. Sudden, coarse
shouts in German. Somewhere heavy transport trucks
cough and start up. Distant rumbling: gunfire? And the
continuous backcloth of the wind's whining through the
electric fences, through the dark zombie-town of wooden
barracks. It is, as always, matched by human moaning.
Pains of aching muscles and limbs, of starved organs, of
souls amputated from family and all humane life —
those pains surface each night through the waters of our
sleep. Shallow waters, oh! so cruelly shallow! And shallow too is the whine of our breathing through shrinking
lungs.

I can't keep awake, of course: we all need to dream, as
well as to sleep. We sleep to dream as well as to rest. What
is so special about tonight anyway? Every night in
Auschwitz has been my last night alive.

In the streaky gray-black morning, we wait helplessly
in our stripes and our rows to be counted and recounted,
methodically and endlessly, as always. The counting of
slaves, of heads of cattle. It is snowing now, heavily, onto
our bare heads, into our eyes, and the January cold gnaws
at the tips of our fingers and toes, our noses and ears. SS
officers come and go. More frozen, stalactite waiting. The
orange sun moves imperceptibly through the heavy

hours. Until, at last, stripes and slithering rows, we are ordered to march.

But we are never to return to the huts again. We are marching out of the Camp, out of Auschwitz, out through the iron gateway with its mocking *Arbeit Macht Frei*, that gateway we passed through once upon a time in another life, like a legendary memory. A long, winding, shivering snake, an army of skeletons, its eyes half-blinded by the snow, dragging its sore feet faster than they can move to avoid the blows of the angry guards and their whips. We've heard the rumors and not believed them. *So the Germans are going to preserve their slave labor. We are not to be killed after all.* At any rate, not yet. And not in those gas chambers. We know that many prisoners have been left behind, too sick and too wasted to move. The Russians would find them, along with the unreal mounds of clothes and shoes, the piles of false teeth and tooth-brushes, the mini mountain ranges formed from tons of human hair.

And so begins an insane march of many weeks, a zigzag through countless miles of open country to avoid the thrusts of the Soviet armies. Day after dank, cold day. Re-lentless. The stops for rest are rare and short, and we for-age the winter fields like animals. If we are lucky, there are roots and berries. If we are not, we eat nothing at all for as much as three days at a stretch. We sleep mostly in the open fields, protected from the razor wind only by hedges or trees. But rarely in the incredible haven of a farm's outhouses and cowsheds. Always under the noz-zles of the guns. We have only clumsy wooden clogs to walk in, and our feet are swollen. We limp on running sores. Many of us have dysentry. We have hardly the will left to drag further our sluggish and sick bodies. Even so, there is still some rock-bottom humanity possible. For many miles, I have Rachael's arm round my shoulder, and we stagger together. Later — two days, a week, an aeon? — Paula on my left does the same for me. The Ger-man guards have noticed, but have not said anything.

Livy, who saved my life in the camp, is much further down the column. The price for dropping out is fixed. A bullet in the head. Frances and Eva, who march in the row in front of me, die like that. They have no will left, after a midday break, to lift themselves up again. The rest of us are herded back into our mad, dragging march. The echoes of the shots which kill them follow us through the crisp air to disappear forever, as they have done.

We are on a winding lane somewhere off the main road to Breslau. Always we avoid the towns, but there are sometimes villages. People gape at us; some children laugh at us, striped monkeys on parade. We are prisoners, it is none of their business. It was never their business, under the Third Reich. Our blood was never on their hands, only someone else's.

We march in snow and winter sunshine, dawn to dusk. The guards treat us viciously. They wake us from sleep with blows, kick us to our feet after a break. We have no strength left to talk to each other. I have lost any idea of time. Has it been three weeks, four weeks? I can no longer imagine myself without blistering feet, without dirt, without faeces or urine over my thighs and legs, without cramps and pains in my stomach. So, finally, I too give up. I cannot care any more about anything. So they will shoot me. I have collapsed beyond caring.

There are about twenty of us. Rachael and Livy are not with us. The guards do not shoot us. They push us over to a barn by the road, and leave us. It is evening. We collapse in the hay and we sleep. And sleep. And sleep.

I hear birdsong. I hear distant gunfire. I see sunlight. Then I sleep again. More gunfire. More sleep. Sleep. Sleep.

I wake to the voice of a tall Russian officer. He stands at the barn door, alone. It is really incredible, but he is speaking to us in *Yiddish*! *'Sag nisht die andere ich bin ay Yid'* — don't tell the others I'm a Jew. He means his comrades waiting outside.

These are the first words we hear from our liberator! Our liberator from the Nazi Final Solution for the Jews! Our liberator is so frightened for himself as a Jew among his comrade Russians that he has to ask us, the nearly-dead victims, to protect him . . . And this is our very first taste of the free world beyond the SS, beyond the guards and the dogs of Auschwitz.

What can 'liberation' mean to a sick body and spirit, too sick to cry or to feel elated? For a long time, just terrible confusion. Who am I? Where am I? Where was my home or family?

Out of the barn, down a country road, the Russians take us to a German village. They are compassionate towards these strange hairless and bony women. Many they hardly recognize as women. But that will change soon enough . . . There are trucks and armored cars outside the village hall, which is their headquarters. Some houses have been commandeered by the Russians, but many have simply been deserted by Germans fleeing from the advancing guns. I am to share a cottage with two others, Anna and Natalia. It had belonged to a carpenter, there is a workshop at the rear. The officer (whose name, I will discover, is Igor) takes us personally to the village store and orders a terrified old man to give us anything we want. I sink sleeping into a deep quilted bed as soft as butter. But I am still expecting the *Appel* bell to wake me from another dream . . .

What has become of my family? Are they really dead? What has become of everyone I knew in Kosice? Who is left alive? Where are they all? What has become of the precious friends who saved my life in Auschwitz, Livy or Rachael? Are they still dragging their swollen feet in the column of swollen feet zigzagging through German fields and forests, have they dropped out and been shot, will I ever see them again? What has become of the whole world?

What will become of me?

LETTER TWELVE
Ronald to Dita

I can't bear it anymore

The truth is, I just can't bear it any more, my love.

There is too much pain. Just too much. Too much for any human being.

I can't take it any more. I just can't. Please.

Ditukam, we are forgetting our years of happiness together. Do some sums, and that adds up to thousands of days of happiness, or to millions of moments of happiness. A sort of private bank account of living we have in our joint names. All that credit! We are millionaires, you know! Why can't we cash in some of that wealth? Why only this talk of pain, pain, pain?

LETTER THIRTEEN
Dita to Ronald

All the good things

Of course, bumblebee, of course.

There was so much happiness. So many riches. We even grew fat on all the good things we shared.

Where to start? Ah, I'm going to have to ramble. You always said I rambled, didn't you? That's why you picked up the *dilinos — scatterbrain* label from my grandmother . . . So — some random memories. They don't match, like the beads and stones in that necklace you bought me for my birthday. Some more precious than others. But they hang together all the same, because they're strung on the same thread of our life together.

I remember the beaches we shared. The fringes of so many countries. Some beaches were naked, even awesome, because they seemed unchanged since the ages before men walked on them, like the Queensland beach beyond Townsend, where we ambled for miles while the sunset sea was swallowed up alive by the night. And we were swallowed up with it, remember? — our flesh as hot with loving as with the tropical heat. Unlike those other beaches, the polluted Paradises, the miles of commercial garbage pock-marking the shores. (*Surfers' Paradise* was where Hans Sittner, the director of the Vienna

Academy, conducted a *bus* — out of a parking lot, remember? Hands only, no baton. A bus load of us from the UNESCO music conference at Brisbane). There were beaches where we could escape the world, and beaches where the world flooded in. Like that French Riviera coast we swam from in August 1969, and there on the sands a chance Czech couple on holiday with whom I talked Czech. The next day, the same sea, the same sands, the same couple, but now homeless: Russian tanks had rolled into Prague, into my childhood country in which I too had been betrayed . . . Remember how we'd followed on TV Dubček's headstrong Prague Spring just a few months before?

Do you remember discovering Portovenere in the dusk at Candlemas, the road to the old Temple of Venus on the tip of the promontory shimmering with a fringe of candles? Or the beach by Saul Novak's house in New York? I spilled wine over myself, remember, and his wife loaned me a dress. After your lecture at Queens College the next day, you returned the dress to Saul saying 'Do thank your wife for a lovely evening.' How the students laughed!

And the yellow-white Israeli beach where we swam naked in moonlight and scores of tiny white crabs scuttled from our barbecue fire? And we loved each other, and I remembered how I'd first danced on those beaches after the camp, my feet I'd thought swollen for ever from the death-march again twinkling like a child's; how my flesh was kissed as if it had never been wasted in the camp, caressed by arms that had never known numbers tattooed on them, and thought beautiful by eyes that had never seen my skeleton in Auschwitz.

We shared the tough delicate tracery of many coral beaches: Bali, Hayman's and Green Island in the Barrier Reef, and its eerie fantasy-land of underwater sculpture! The fossils at Chapman's Pool and Kimmeridge in Dorset with millions of years locked up inside them. Marvels! Both despair and stimulus for my own imagination. You know how I collected shells and corals by the dozen, with their mysterious mazes, because I wanted to copy them in my own stoneware and clay ceramics. You put up with the shells and stones crowding our living room as well as my pottery, every shelf or ledge, mantlepiece and radiator, the top of the black bookcase — remember? Next to my big heavy graystone ceramic — the one with the hollowed eye whose form I copied from a simple nut, and enlarged into something massive. Massive and durable, in a way to ensure that the tiny, fragile case of new life would have a sort of monument, a pyramid. It looked huge and gray above the array of miniscule colored glass vases from Jerusalem in the shelf below, didn't it?

It's not just a word, I really felt those natural objects were *miracles*. I didn't just 'use' them for my ceramics, I felt I was sharing in the miracles, the way a painter does in the refractions of light and color and the endless clash and harmony of forms. A commercial potter of mugs and plates may miss out on that kind of feeling . . . I don't know. I myself often felt the kind of fulfillment Bernard Leach discovered for himself in Japan, as even the gentlest touches of my fingers on the spiralling soft clay turned it magically from shape into shape . . . And then that rich universe of glazes, again miracles of minerals, the colors and glitters and textures, and finally, finally, the firing, the hours of secret chemistry in the kiln, and at last the door is opened! The Raku firings (in the backyard of what had once been the old Fire Station of Richmond) were always a kind of celebration, and you used to share in it, didn't you? Everyone brought food and drink. We were sharing in some sort of magic. A ritual, really — of transformation. Out of the kiln, like out of a womb, came the new things which had never existed before. And we ourselves, a bunch of sophisticated women chatting about this and that, had brought them into being, we were co-creators.

But back to our necklace . . . I remember mountains we climbed together. In Israel. Mount Moriah, where Solomon built his temple, where I found shards centuries old. Mount Tabor, and Safed cradled in mountains, with its strange light like an energy coaxed out of its stones. But above all Mount Carmel. That was where I first worked

when I came to my promised land after the camp, in an
insurance office. I used to watch the ships in the harbor,
the hundreds of immigrants straining at the rails, and I
was haunted by their faces, themselves haunted, tearful,
barely hoping. Remember the little villa we lived in, high
on Carmel, the sea like crumpled silk far below, the city
spreading semicircles of streets like a hooped skirt, which
glittered at night with lights like ornamental sequins? It's
little things I remember and cherish most. Like the king-
fishers building their nest in the bank of earth by our
porch. They'd disappear inside with wings of beetles and
butterflies, and even fishbones. Perhaps goldfish bones
from garden ponds, for the sea was far away. Remember
how once we saw a kingfisher feed his wife with a field-
mouse, both of them sitting on our radio antenna? We
thought it would break! Then they flew away chuckling
and snickering.

And other mountains, elsewhere . . . The plateau high
in the Rockies the American Indians called the 'Garden
of the Gods'. Purest air, the nectar of gods, too rarified for
lungs used to the plains. A place for visions. We thought
we saw so far. We'd been married only a year. Life was so
rich, and the Gods were laughing in their Garden. But
maybe crying, too.

The Mesa Verde in the Rockies, where we collapsed into
our own private canyons of loving, with its own private
caverns (one of those special times), in a cabin perched
dizzily on the edge of a towering canyon, opposite the
dark mouth of the cavern hollowed into the canyon's cliff
which was once the home of American Indians. The peaks
and crags of Montserrat, gargantuan in the clouds near
Barcelona. Leaning on my shoulder was a limping
Laurence Bevenot, the gentle English Benedictine monk-
musician who'd sprained his ankle. That's where we became friends. Except for me, everyone scaling the heights
of that world was a composer or musican invited to the
Abbey music Festival. Then again, the smouldering volcanic mountain of Bali. Do you remember the tawny
greedy-eyed girl who was our guide, with dollars bulg-

ing out her breasts in her brassiere? That was in 1969. An omen, we both knew, that tourism would soon reduce to another commercial show that so beautiful, *petite* people whose lives were still woven in and out of their religious dramas and gamelan orchestras, their woodcarvings and batik . . . And again, I remember flying together eastwards over Afghanistan and India, your waking me up to the vast grandeur and the unfathomable silence of the Himalayas to our left, beyond the reassuring purr of the 747: the night was broken into red slabs, and the white summits of the mountains caught fire.

And then, the cities we shared. Sydney, skyscrapers and a maze of intermeshed, ballooning bays. As we approached to land, we told the Englishman sitting next to us we were anxious, we were being met in the airport — in fact by the ex-Mayor — and we didn't know where. He smiled, and then described where we should go *in exact lengths of meters and degrees of angles!* He was the architect who had designed the airport — as well as the University Senate House in London where you were based in those days!

Sydney was both a great pleasure we shared and also a busy round of engagements for you. Adjudication (of choirs, the first evening, at the Town Hall): conducting your own music on TV: two early morning interviews on 'In Sydney Today', competing with a fashion show, the weather report, and a talk on the moonrocks (we'd watched the first men on the moon a few days before in Bangkok): your lecture at the Conservatory near the Governor's House, from which the UNESCO car whisked us away to catch the Ansett to the Conference in Brisbane . . . I loved the great green ferry boats which ploughed through the bays to and from Manly: and I loved the white Millers Hotel overlooking the bay at Manley where our stay was sponsored by that generous ex-Mayor, with its Czech waiter who made my childhood Czech plum dumplings just for me, and that squeezed corner beach where we swam in winter-warm water. Above all, I loved Sister Gabriel who engineered our first visit to Australia:

'Gabe', plump as a pumpkin, rosy-faced, laughing, and, oh! so generous. I was always included in the dinners given in your honor . . . And I went with you to meet dignitaries — like Archbishop Cardinal Gilroy (though the talk, as I remember, was mostly about the song of the Australian birds, the kookaburras and bellbirds and the rest) . . . But Australia was your thing really, much as we shared: until we went to Melbourne.

You had no engagements there in that year. We went to Melbourne because that's where Livy now lived. Livy who had saved my life in those other-world barracks of Auschwitz, and whom I'd not seen for almost twenty-five years. Livy, who'd lighted a fire for me out of some unbelievably precious human material, the stuff of caring, that the camp was designed to stamp out completely. As if it were the most obvious, the most natural thing in the world to risk your own life for the sake of another's. The woman who met us at the airport was now middle-aged and spreading, now the mother of a beautiful black-haired daughter at the University, now living in a luxurious apartment filled with the same stolid Central European furniture and the same food smells as in the buried world of my childhood. And now the airport bustle became a far away blur, and Livy and I just stood there and hugged each other, and we just cried. We stood there hugging and crying as the world went by, passengers and baggage carts and air-hostesses. We couldn't stop hugging each other, and we couldn't stop crying. Then we talked our childhood Hungarian.

But we didn't talk about the camp. The Auschwitz we had once shared remained the silent background, the unspoken heart of every sentence. For the rest, after all, we were now almost complete strangers to each other in our new lives. We had written once or twice, but never met. Twenty-five years is half an adult lifetime. It is a whole generation. Yet there was no question of a doubt, something was written plainly in our eyes, a terrible shared secret. Like the love of lovers, our bond was of a time out of time, of a time which could have no parallel in the rest of our lives, although, unlike the norms of lovers, it was a time of horror and agonizing cruelty. We were bonded by living in death and defying it.

Then back to the present, to Canberra, where you were a guest of honor (along with dear Gerald Hendrie of the Open University), where I mounted the exhibition of your music color-system: only you didn't show up. An air traffic controllers' strike left you stranded in Hobart. Eventually came the phone call 'The Doc's landed at Kooma' — they'd charted you a private Cesna which couldn't land through the mists at Canberra, and I set off the sixty kilometers to fetch you by car. I was very anxious. We laughed that Kooma was where a pioneer flight crashed in the thirties.

Beautiful cities for music festivals. Dubrovnik and our walks round the city walls. Lucerne on its diamond lake. Aldeburgh, where we met Britten, and once Kodaly (I spoke Hungarian), and so many others. Venice, and our own near Death in Venice. We crossed from the Lido for a concert at the Fenice (remember? we chatted with Alvar Liddell, the BBC announcer who was a legend for you from the war, who narrated the Walton *Façade*.) The next morning, the maid came in ashen faced: 'Did you see the swollen bodies on the shore?' A tornado had swept down through Venice from the mountains: the *vaporetto* after the one we'd taken had been sucked up and every passenger drowned. Those were their bodies by the Lido harbor. We crossed the Lagoon again, and it seemed a giant had stalked around at random, in and out of the shoreline, uprooting great trees and smashing the roofs.

Again, animals and plants . . . I think I can hang our travels on images of animals and plants. The friendly chipmunk at Mesa Verde. The ladybirds I love, in France. The midget monkeys in Singapore scrambling round our legs. The giant butterflies of the Barrier Reef. The baby kangaroo, still inside its mother's pouch, I fed in Sydney. Curtains and carpets of red bourgainville like weeds. The screaming of the birds and the mad tangle of branches and tendrils in the early morning rainforest above Brisbane, where we were taken for a barbecue breakfast, remember? The huge brilliant orchids. The aquarium at Manley, fish glossy with rainbows, the feeding of its Port Jackson sharks. At home, the deer in Richmond Park and the ducks on the lake in Kew Gardens: they reminded me of the ducks in the *Hornad* outside my childhood window in Kosice.

All this, for me, meant life renewing itself. Animals and plants have no option but to fulfill the thrusts of life, to surrender themselves to sex and the blind miracles of birth, to obey the secret clocks in their flesh which regulate their times of seeding and breeding, growing and multiplying. I needed to be reassured by this lavishness of life, because within me remained unforgettable images of death: images of Auschwitz, of wasted human limbs, of zombies, of stinking corpses: outside the gates, of the black fields we were forced to march through, that winter of 1945; later images of mutilated trees torn apart by shellfire, of the carcasses of pigs beside a smoldering farmhouse, of burning silos of grain, of dead squirrels and rabbits in the fields the Russian tanks had rolled across.

You know how you loved the feelings for new life which bubbled up in me! In spite of everything. That wonder. And for how nature protects its own . . . The pips in the flesh of a watermelon when I cut it up to eat. Or in apples. The seeds in grapes (I didn't *want* to buy 'seedless'.) The nut cushioned in a peach. Life's secrets in a pip and a nut.

And I myself longed sometimes for the juices and the guts of a sensuality, a freedom, a big yes to living. This I knew would always be beyond my reach. You know that, *dragasagam.* There were too many knots inside me. Sexually, you meant so much for me! (But you had your hang-ups too, having been a monk and all that). From frigidity, from coldness, I thawed. With you, for the first time, I experienced those bottomless orgasms, inside as well as outside. Sometimes, only sometimes . . . But our sex remained a problem, most of the time. I'm sure a lot was due to me. I couldn't really abandon myself. I could never be free from something which overshadowed and burdened my womb. Perhaps that's why the cancer, if it had to break out somewhere, chose my womb. It gave me my pregnancy, we joked, remember? My womb, the carrier of life, or of death. There's a Paul Klee drawing we saw together called *Fertility.* He draws a woman's womb filled with a tangle of new shoots of life, a writhing riot of life, like the tendrils of the Australian rainforest we walked in together. But it's a picture that, for me, flickers between life and death, between new life — and new death. For those shoots of life can also become the tendrils of cancer.

BUT I'M BACK TO THE PAINFUL THIHGS AGAIN!

I'M SORRY, BUMBLBEE! SORRY!

LETTER FOURTEEN
Ronald to Dita

Your ceramics. Kiss of the frogs

Thank you.

But, of course, things are never all beautiful. I'm thinking of the cities you left out — the American cities we toured in the explosive summer of 1964. Riots and looting in Harlem, down in New Orleans with the *Whites Only* on the toilets smeared with excreta, my walk into Kansas City (you stayed in the airport hotel) through the black quarter where they threw cans at me . . . The civil rights laws have changed, but the violence still erupts. Only last week three young blacks entered the subway car where I was sitting, a fellow was lighting matches and throwing them on the floor, the others were laughing. I said, 'That's dangerous.' He set fire to the whole box and threw it at me, the others laughing all the more. I stamped out the flame, got up and said, 'would you laugh if I tried to set fire to you?' And then: 'Is this what they teach you at school? Is this what being a good American means?' Maybe because I looked them in the eye, maybe because of my English accent, anyhow, they didn't pull a knife or attack me. I was lucky. I turned to the rest of the people in the car and said, 'Why don't you tell them? I'm the foreigner.' They hid behind their newspapers. The young blacks got out at the next stop, a bit sheepishly.

You write about your bond with Livy, and yes, I felt it like an invisible circle of fire. Like lovers, you say: yes, and just as fierce and exclusive, perhaps more so, because the shared secret is such a terrible one.

An invisible circle into which only survivors may enter. I have felt it many times, whenever we met survivors. Like Dlugatz the acquaintance of Apu's who was to give us money from your father's account, whom we found in a dingy basement behind Ha-Yarkon in Tel-Aviv. He was a shocking caricature of a man, a rubberized twisted-out-of-shape replica of a man, whose life had been once and for all drained out of his bone-marrow in Auschwitz, so that what passed for life now was just some kind of grotesque and even ridiculous spill over. But with you there was a strange rapport.

Or that hunchbacked, dwarfish woman in Safed, one leg a full foot shorter than the other it dragged behind, a leg mutilated by iron rod beatings in Treblinka. She spoke to you in your native Hungarian — cementing the bond. She wanted nothing to do with *Wiedergutmachung,* restitution money. She was trying only to forget. If she could, she said. As if her mind, like her leg, could simply erase its deformity, its imprints of torture.

And then the woman at the kiosk in Jerusalem (jutting out into Jordanian territory, that was before the Six Day War). A woman so thin, a woman like a tenuous statement withdrawn almost as soon as it is uttered. From the number tattooed on your forearm she recognized roughly the date of the transport which rumbled and screeched you into Auschwitz. One of those wordless stigmata of camp culture, belonging to an almost private language of survivors: icons of terrible feelings from which the rest of us are, mercifully, excluded.

And I'm glad you talked about your ceramics. You had such great gifts. And I have loved them in you as well as loving you in them.

I keep your four little brown ceramic figurines arranged

in a group. They're by me as I write to you now. They are
a family: two are larger and older, a standing father figure with his wife sedately seated beside him, hands in
her lap; and there are two much smaller girls sitting in
front of them. I used to think these two girls were symbols of yourself and your young sister Marika murdered
in Auschwitz. Now, I think of them as twin images of
yourself. One is free and abandoned. She leans far back,
her head cocked coyly to one side, her arms pulled back,
and with no shame she offers me her delicate virgin
breasts and belly while she rests on her bended knees.
The other girl is hunchbacked. Her head droops down
towards her raised knees, and these are hidden in her
skirts, which like shrouds cover the womb which her sister flaunts so openly. Innocence and Experience,
maybe.The one fresh and trusting, poised eagerly for life;
the other beaten down and self-enclosed. Truly they are
your twin images.

There remained a wide-eyed girl-child in you who'd
never died, whose spontaneous delight in the world was
a natural spring, forceful enough to push past blockages.
But then there was that other, that bent-over spirit, a girl
shocked into paralysis by her secret memories.

I knew both of you.

I am surrounded by your ceramics as I write. On my
desk, my bookcases, my tables. And I see them differently on different days.They have taken on a life of their
own, a life you couldn't have foreseen when you made
them; a life which also depends on me and how I see them.
And how everyone else sees them. For better or worse,
this is the afterlife of things we create, which we can't
control or anticipate.

I know this when I hear my own music in a strange
hall, performed by strangers, surrounded by an audience
of strangers. The performer brings his own background
and temperament and makes my music something new
at each performance. And each audience makes it new
for itself in ways I can't fathom. So I sit at concerts of my
music like a parent recognizing and not recognizing his

own children who have become independent. No, it's really a rebirth, brought about by the performer, but in conjunction with the audience, of whom I am only one member. I'd like to share with fellow humans the feelings (wonder, pleasure, sadness — untranslatable feelings) I had in discovering the music originally. But I can never be sure that is happening when I listen to my music among them. And I can never really know what quality of experience is signified by their applause afterwards, however enthusiastic (like the St. Petersburg audience, which broke into rhythmic handclapping).

So I remain a solitary midwife, among many other midwives (for all the audience is included), at the rebirth of my own children.

You know, *békachkam,* of all the intimate words you taught me in Hungarian my tongue (or is it my heart?) keeps getting stuck on this one, *békachkam*, my little frog. And I'm wondering why. And I think I know.

Because of the fairy tale. You know, the Princess kisses the frog, and it turns into a Prince. Or vice versa, the Prince kisses the frog, and it turns into a Princess. Or better, two frogs kiss (but how do frogs kiss, I wonder?), and they turn into a royal couple, Prince and Princess, hand in hand. At this stage, finally, he can put a ring on her finger, a rite which would have been quite impossible when her fingers were lost in webbing.

There's an important question nobody asks: how far did the Prince know from the beginning that a Princess was hidden in the frog, or the Princess know her Prince from the beginning? That beauty was veiled by the beast? That's the heart of the matter, it seems to me. But *we* saw something in each other, beneath the frog skin, didn't we, *békachkam,* my little frog? Yes, that was our fairystory in a nutshell or perhaps, we could say, in a kiss. A kiss lasting twenty years (on and off, of course). I loved my Princess though she was alienated and disfigured. You loved your Prince though he was too. The causes for this disfigurement were very different—the Nazi camp, the leucotomy: nevertheless, each of us had been turned into a frog.

Some people talk so rationally of psychological work. Let us rather undemythologize our belief in spells and wizards, *dragam*. After all, that twenty-year kiss (on and off) worked on us as mysteriously as the potions of legend: so that our fingers lost their yellow-green webbing, we stopped croaking and learned speech, even poetry, and our faces grew human again.

LETTER FIFTEEN
Dita to Ronald

Going home! What is home?

In that German village I sleep on and off for a week, until my fever leaves me at last. Sleep in a limbo of dreams — sometimes healing, sometimes nightmarish, comas to protect me from my wounds and from the reality I will have to face outside.

It will take months for my feet to heal. At any hour of night or day, I eat from the medley of foods we've taken from the store — tins of sardines, dried eggs, *ersatz* sausage. They make me vomit. I wash myself in a real bathroom. I keep running to a real toilet with a real flushing system. But they are not fully real, not yet. I look into the mirror, and try to recognize who I am. My hair is growing again, short and straight, but my cheeks are as hollow as a skull, and my eyeballs huge. I'm still deformed.

Anna and Natalia also sleep. At first I float in a vacuum. In a freedom which means no guards, no rasping orders, no rumors, nothing, except the pains in my feet, nightmares and vomiting. But soon comes the worst pain of all So far as I know, all my family and friends have been murdered, the entire world of my childhood. I have no home. I am lost. I realize that I'm orphaned not only of my parents, but of a whole life.

I'm beginning to wake up to the world around me, still as half-real as the frosty winter light. I'm waking to the distant thunder of artillery and the rumbling of warplanes, to the screech of Russian jeeps in the village. The Post Office-cum-shop has been turned into an office and local headquarters. With Anna and Natalia, we're escorted there by a rough soldier whose oriental eyes undress me and glisten greedily over my boyish body. I am frightened, but also paralyzed. I'm without sex, my juices are still dried up. But the officer Igor is there, his face now heavy and tired, but again with a reassuring smile. I understand some Russian, it is a cousin of the Slovak I once spoke in Kosice. Our names? Where was our home? Have we news of any relatives? Have we enough to eat? Kindly tones, foreign music strange to our ears. We are at the beginning of a long lesson, learning to trust again. We have forgotten how. It's going to be a difficult lesson.

We were marched into Germany through Silesia, where the Nazis built factories out of reach of the Allied bombers. Igor tells us of the fierce battle around Breslau, the nearest big town. We are in the midst of two of the Russians' enormous armies, under the generals Zhukov and Konev, multitudes of men and armor advancing into Germany with a savage fury and a lust for revenge. Hundreds of small towns and villages are burning, thousands of German families are being killed in their own kitchens. Hundreds of thousands, no *millions* of Germans who had settled in the East for centuries are now blocking the roads in carts or on foot, fleeing in terror from what seems to them an Armageddon, a Day of Wrath, making for the German interior or for the ports of Pillau and Danzig. Many are being battered and crushed to death mercilessly and deliberately by the racing columns of Soviet tanks. Families hide in ditches, in the cellars of their houses. There are suicides. Captain Igor tells us that orders come from the Front Commands to stop this brutality, this rape, this devastation, to follow 'norms of conduct' with the German population. But these orders cannot stem the tide of soldiers who have seen their own towns and families ruthlessly destroyed by the German armies and the special SS extermination groups who accompanied them into Russia and the Ukraine. And among those soldiers there are now many Russian ex-prisoners of war who avenge themselves viciously. Beasts are devouring beasts and innocent alike.

There have been some brutal scenes of massacre here too, in this village. I was protected from them in my feverish sleep. Two families were slaughtered by Russian soldiers who saw photographs of Hitler on their walls, and their houses gutted by fire. The women were nailed, yes nailed to a wall and then raped repeatedly by one Russian soldier after another. I see the ruins of these houses in the main street. It seems that Captain Igor has stopped this frenzy with the threat of the severest penalties. Perhaps that is why none of us have been sexually assaulted, we the Auschwitz scarecrows whose breasts and thighs are now beginning to fill out again.

I am filling out also with feelings of horror. With feelings of hatred. With feelings of revenge. What do I do with this hatred? On whom do I take revenge, and how? The Germans I see in this village are very ordinary people. They offer me nervous smiles, they offer me food, their greetings are friendly. I don't see any fiends under their skins intent on torturing me or gassing me. And if I had an Auschwitz guard in my power, would I be torturing him, taking his life, an eye for an eye, one for one, perhaps a hundred guards for every hundred dead prisoners? I don't know. It's usually the victims who have to desist and be merciful, never the original tormentors.

The village is joined to the main road by a mile of snowy lane secluded behind evergreen hedges. The quiet is shattered as the lane winds uphill into the hubbub of the highway. I walk along it often to watch the confused traffic of bundled people on foot, of horses and carts, of tanks, of Russian soldiers in armored cars. It is always a two-way traffic.There is purpose in the chaos. Westwards, straggling groups of German civilians, jumping aside into the ditches to avoid the fast roaring Russian army, frantically pulling their horses and farm-carts into the fields. West-wards, it is a road of panic and of terror of the conquer-ing armies. Eastwards, it is a different trail, a pathetic one, of refugees. Eastwards, it is a road of hoping against hope, of new life from ruins. Refugees freed from the concen-tration camps, from the death marches, hobbling their way towards home. Home! What is home? Clusters of survi-vors, my own people, my own cousins, my brothers and sisters, my uncles and aunts, all of whom I recognize but none I know. For there are trains leaving, they say, from Oppeln, from Czestochowa, from other places. Trains to home.

What is home?

I come not only to watch, but also to hope. Perhaps Anyu and Apu and Marika and Nagymama are all alive. Those men there are Polish, from Lwow. The women yesterday were Czech, from Prague and Brno. But the men today are Hungarian, from Budapest, and from Miskole which is not so far from Kosice. Yes, they were in Auschwitz. No, they did not know Apu. Did I have news of A and B and C, they shout to me, who were taken to Auschwitz, also in the May transports?

And the day comes when I too join this straggling trail eastward. In his office Captain Igor has given us identity cards, and travel permits. Ah, I have my identity now, the card which tells me who I am. I have been recreated out of chaos. I am a survivor of Auschwitz. A liberated prisoner. I remember another card — in the selections, when another officer, Mengele, also decided my identity — slave-laborer or fuel for the chimneys. *Who am I?* Ah, now I know, the card has it in black and white.

I am going home ! I am going home ! Home!

What is home?

I'm on the move again, now in another column, on yet another snowbound road. But this is a shapeless procession, loose groups of people, not driven by whips. Horse-drawn farm-carts heaped with men and women and bundles. But, I am thinking, there are no more children. The children are all murdered. A million murdered futures. Where are the million ghosts? Are they haunting this road back to the homes they were snatched from, as they will haunt the homes themselves? Will the ghost of Marika be waiting for me in Jacob's Palace by the river Hornad in Kosice? How shall we ever lay so many ghosts?

Anna and Natalia are with me. Their home is Radom in Poland. They will take a different train going northeast. We have a big bag each, stuffed with bread, sausage, pickles, and the badly fitting skirts, shirts and underclothes the Russians gave us, taken from German women. After a few miles we are offered a ride in a cart already crammed, driven by a hunched figure in a black coat, his face wild and bearded. His name is Samuel, he too was in Auschwitz, his home was Bialystock. To each of us home means a different place. Each of us was seized out of a different home in different countries and thrown into different death camps. But now, in this cart, on this road, under this dark winter sun, we all belong to the same realm, a kingdom of the dispossessed, of the bereaved. We have eyes in common, and memories. We have all seen what human eyes cannot endure seeing, we all remember what human memory cannot endure remembering. It is a strange twilight journey, out of time, on a macabre farm-cart rattling through a barren, barbaric snowscape, through villages and small towns scarred by gunfire and pillaging, jolting us all away from a past we shall never escape from, towards a future we can scarcely believe exists.

From time to time Samuel turns the horse into a lane or a field as we hear armored trucks thundering towards us. They are filled with Russian soldiers, on their way to the crumbling German lines, perhaps to Berlin itself. Some greet us with wild howls and arms waving. Twice we are overtaken by a different convoy, a complementary convoy, eastbound: lines of ambulance trucks carrying the wounded. Wounded overtaking the wounded. Wounds of different kinds. Will ours ever heal?

The end of our cart's journey is a station platform chaotic with uniforms, bundles and bags, men and women and children. Bewildered, uprooted people. Poles mostly. These children were never among the condemned, the prime quarry for the gas chambers. My own Marika cannot be among them. I have hugged Anna and Natalia who are going north to Czestochowa. We have promised to write. Home has an address. But like people, who knows now which addresses have survived and which have been swallowed up in the devastation?

In the train carriage there is a crush of Romanian soldiers bound for Bucharest on sick leave. I am the only girl. My hair has grown again, in the cracked toilet mirror I even look pretty. The officer with a black handlebar mustache gives me his seat. His name is Karel. We all talk with signs, with smiles, with smatterings of German or Slav. I see something for the first time, something which will plague the rest of my life: because I was in Auschwitz, they are treating me with a mixture of awe and compassion. They are turning me into some kind of secular saint. I don't like that at all. It is not real, it is not me. They tell me about their girlfriends, their wives, their children. From time to time, they dip into their rucksacks, and offer me bread or raw vegetables or even chocolate from their rations.

It is a journey which, in another time, might take hours: now it stretches out into two whole days. Railway lines are disrupted. We stop sometimes for many long hours. Every main station platform we pass is a deluge, swarming soldiers and civilians, heaps of rucksacks and bundles. Standing, leaning, hunched. Most are going home.

Home! I am going home! I am going home!

What is home?

I was taken to Auschwitz by train, with all my family. I

am returning home by train, alone. Trains for me will always mean Auschwitz. Between two train journeys, there and back, my heart was cut out and torn apart.

What is home?

LETTER SIXTEEN
Ronald to Dita

This is fantasy. Why do you haunt me?

It is from my own deepest wish to — well, to *come clean* with you, my dear, that I have to say (and it is really high time I did say) that this entire exchange of letters is illusionary. You see, here I am again, still addressing a letter to you, although of course I know you really are dead. I do know that, because I held you with these my own arms and watched you with these my own eyes and felt you with this my own torso actually breathe in and out your very last, agonized, extremely slow breath. And after that I went on holding your breathless body in my arms. You might ask, had I ever held a dead body in my arms before, and how could I be sure that you were dead, and so forth. That is true, nobody had ever died in my arms before (though I had held a dead body — your father's, just a year before in a rain drenched cemetery in Bad Nauheim. Together with several gray, gaunt figures, complete strangers, I'd wrapped it in its ritual burial shroud, faded yellow flesh in faded white linen). But I was quite sure you had died. That long and very last breath was a frightening chill wind which blew through a house in ruins, its window-panes broken and blind, its doors swinging lifelessly, its corridors cobwebbed, a house already abandoned. I've been in deserted places before — the QE2, eerie and empty corridors and darkened lounge, one night in Southampton; Melbourne airport, during an air-traffic controllers' strike. But these were not derelict, everything was there, restaurants and toilets, only for the moment without purpose. Whereas your body was destroyed. I'm sure I could even tell the exact moment when your over-taxed heart pumped its last spurt into organs wasted past reclaiming, its last dribble of life into your yellowed flesh, mummified past reviving. I knew it many hours before Dr. Margaret Crowley came to sign the death certificate. Your smell had gone, fouled. Rotting rind, decaying husk of fruit. Curves of flesh flattened and parched. The woman I'd fondled for twenty ripe full-bodied years, wrapped in black plastic like a parcel, that same plastic sheeting used for garbage bags, heaved away, out of my life. You disappeared forever, inexorably, behind the red curtains of the crematorium. The curtains closed on the last act, and there are no repeat performances. No, I was sure you were dead. All that remained was the speechless vase filled with ashes they gave me, and it bore no resemblance whatsoever to the woman I knew.

So how can you possibly receive this letter by any kind of mail or messenger service whether heavenly or earthly, still less answer it?

Well, it's been a good and ghastly game of correspondences while it lasted. Some kind of literary sport, absurd no doubt. Or rather, a fashionable psychological-drama exercise in therapy. But now it's high time to call quits. I know, of course I know, of course everybody knows, that no reliable post service stretches beyond the crematorium. After the fire, after the suffering, silence.There is the same problem of posthumous communications in the world of the gas-chambers and the ovens in the camps. I am not such a fool. How on earth could I have received any letters from you at all?

To tell you the truth, your ghost really has its private *pied-à-terre*, compactly, within my floppy computer disc. It is conjured up vividly from the shadowland of eternity first by a switch, and then by a double-click of my Turbo Macmouse. Such are the blessings of microchip technology that nowadays, you see, you don't have to appear moaning at the midnight chimes, to fade away with cockcrow at dawn. But I do have a serious complaint on file, nevertheless. It seems that you do not always have the heavenly good grace to wait for me to switch on my computer, to wait for my spiritual juices to salivate as they hear the Mac's summoning bell. Your need to haunt me, those critical hours, is much more urgent than the mere exigencies of electrical currents. I have to sit, more or less helplessly, and watch your ghost-letters imprint themselves on the phosphor of my screen, feeling a mixture of horror and relief.

The truth is that I just cannot lay your spirit so easily and get on with the humdrum of life. I know too well that your phantom letters will still arrive and haunt my present with their dead but living past. The reason is clear: *you are really two beings for me*. One is the beautiful woman I entered and fused with in the osmosis of loving: she who could shift from eye-bubbling merriment to sudden chasms of seriousness. That being could be mourned with all the protracted pain and guilt that is normal — only, like loving, every mourning is never normal, but unique. My mourning was mine, like my love. But the other being — well, the trouble, *dragasagam,* is that you are the carrier of a myth. The Israelite children Ananias, Misael and Azarias, plucked miraculously from the Babylonian fire. The Jew, the eternal Survivor, the Saving Remnant, the Ark floating after floods onto the dry land of Ararat, and so forth. The survivor of Auschwitz, someone less than one in one hundred and fifty, almost impossible odds . . . You represent the Jew who wouldn't die and disappear. The Jew in every non-Jew, hence the victim and garbage receptacle of history. And the Jew in my own non-Jewishness.

There's the paradox. I can lay your apparition only by admitting it, with its phantom eyes beaming into me my own life-questions, its Auschwitz-tattooed numbers questioning me about my own identity, and its spectral blood flowing with the catalysts of my own life story. Clearly, I must redeem my own life from your ghost. If I do not discover what you mean for me, your letters will haunt me forever.

I lived with and held in my arms a survivor of Auschwitz, someone I loved, but also someone who represented, in spite of herself, a long Jewish, European, and Christian history. Someone who was a victim of perhaps the most terrible crisis in that history. Someone whose suffering was not only personal, but had to be marked like the signpost in a turning point of Jewish and European history. It was inescapably a symbol of unprecedented slaughter followed by renewal, of death and rebirth, of exile and return, casting long shadows back into history.

I see numbers on passports and driving licences. But they do not have the power of the icon I saw every day for twenty years tattooed onto your arm.

Both our lives were trapped by questions, questions which happened to us and hovered around us like harassing guardian angels, questions we wouldn't have thought to seek out.

People have said: isn't it time now, after half a century, to close that particular chapter of history? To come to terms with the evil of Auschwitz? But an Apocalypse cannot be contained within the usual terms of a history book. There's nothing compatible it can fit into. It cannot be enclosed into a 'particular chapter'. When the ink is dry on all the pages of every history book, the fires of Auschwitz still burn unquenchably.

And the questions remain unanswered.

LETTER SEVENTEEN
Dita to Ronald

Mythology and Auschwitz

Don't be silly, bumblebee. This exchange of letters is *not* illusionary. It's *not* just a 'ghastly game', as you say. You're such a wizard with words!

Of course, I do understand why you need to write, and why you're so glued to your Mac computer screen.

You're the same busy book-bee as ever, with your big proboscis, sucking the juice out of computers now as you always have out of books.

You are right when you talk of osmosis. Not all Jews are survivors, as some have been saying. That is absurd. That is dangerous. There remains, invisibly, the electric fence of Auschwitz which still isolates those of us who suffered its horrors from those who didn't. There remains the stench of the chimneys which only we still carry in our nostrils. You did survive something else, a leucotomy, which destroyed your person in a quite different way . . . But *osmosis*. It wasn't just sexual, of course! You also have a very special relationship to the Holocaust because you entered deeply into my life, as well as my vagina. It wasn't only your penis which was sensitive to me. You grew unusual feelers which were sensitive to what Auschwitz was like, and what it was like to survive it.

I've always hated having those mythological costumes hung on me, as well you know. Whether they fit or not is really beside the point. They're not me. They ignore and bypass me. People see the costumes, as if a shop window dummy were inside. Those costumes belong in museums and sanctuaries and history books. Since my own death, I know that thousands of camp survivors are being interviewed on videotape before death claims them all: but their names are not noised abroad. They are destroyed persons who want to reclaim their own lives, just as I did, and not be exhibits on show. The 'professional victims' are those who exploit what should be beyond exploitation. 'Shoah business'! Remember you told me about the waxwork show in London after they discovered Belsen? Cheap thrills and horrors. Do you remember we watched the TV series *Holocaust* together in California? I said then how they had *sanitized the smells,* made horrific feelings *sentimental,* turned it all into another kitsch soap opera?

I suppose it was after the Six Day War that survivors became sacred like secular saints, and Auschwitz itself was turned into a kind of shrine. Like everyone else, I couldn't believe the victory, against such odds, like David and Goliath (you see, bumblebee, I also take refuge in myth sometimes). Relief, relief, relief! The new beginnings, the new Israel, was not to be stillborn. The baby was strong, it was already a giant, the roles were reversed. Do you remember how we rushed to volunteer, (even Colin who was not a Jew volunteered); our first-aid training in Seymour Place; the day-by-day news — first the annihilation of the Egyptian tank battalions in the Sinai, then the scaling of the Golan Heights, then, on the Friday, the taking of the Old City of Jerusalem. It was over before we could help. We flew in the next week to a people dazed by its own feats. Of course the Hassidim said it was *Yud Elohim,* the Hand of God, and the Yemenite in the Carmel Supermarket told us it had all been prophesied in the Book, down to the actual dates and numbers of casualties. But we were more taken with our humdrum, spectacled lawyer in downtown Haifa, who had sweated up the mountainside of the Golan Heights hardly a week before, in the face of brutal artillery and gunfire, and who now sat matter-of-factly in his very dull office saying *Ain bereeya*, *Ain bereeya* — there was no choice. That was his mythology, as it was of most Israelis.

Perhaps the survivors felt safer: anyhow, they broke a twenty year silence and began to talk. Now people had ears to hear with. When I first came to New York, they did not. I was one of the host of silent ghosts whom nobody really believed to have died. Our catastrophe was not interesting. It was even *shameful*! (Yes, we were ashamed of the beasts the camp had reduced us to.) If you began to talk of it, your audience moved on to what really concerned them, your success in their New World. So I buried somewhere, I didn't know where, I didn't care where, the impossible burden of my pain and my memories, as most of us did, and busied myself with becoming a jazzed-up New Yorker, speaking jazzed-up American English, living on Manhattan's jazzed-Upper West Side, dating, working for a new jazz record company with Oran Keepnews and Bill Grauer. We jazzed it up in New York's Greenwich Village, we jazzed it down in New Orleans' Vieux Carré. We hunted down the roots of jazz for our Riverside History of Jazz, worksong and boogie and the old church brass bands of the South. And I forgot my own roots and my own history, and a mist spread over Auschwitz, obscuring its barracks and parade ground and chimneys and blurring all its pain. Even with Agi, who also had the blue-black number tattooed on her arm, we talked only of New York and of men, over our diet lettuce binges.

And Apu, Apu especially, father and daughter, the only survivors . . . Apu was busy only with my future, above all else that I'd find a good husband. Because she alone had come back from the dead, the daughter ravaged but now beautiful again, the sole bearer of his seed, and of all the futures of all his dear ones who had died. The lost life of all that death had to be concentrated into her one life. I

had to have the distilled beauty of every lost beauty. I
had to have the quintessential marriage containing every
marriage that was aborted in the gas chambers.

And the marriage I did rush into was a disaster. You
know about Stanley, of course. Resplendent and insecure
in his naval uniform, on leave from Anapolis for our merest wisp of a marriage and 'honeymoon' — a fittingly lunatic word, which ended as soon as it began with his confinement to a mental hospital . . .

Inside that electric fence of Auschwitz . . . What could
be the language to describe that different world? You may
probe the morass of pain and try to express fragments of
feelings, or some of the camp routines, or incidents you
remember, some of the sights, sounds, smells. But how
do you really convey the altogether otherness of that
place?

The words I know, and the feelings behind them, do
not belong to that different universe, but to this one. Perhaps, if I added up all the words I have had to learn in
my life, they might come to millions and millions: Hungarian at home, in school Czech, Slovak in the streets,
later German, Hebrew, then English. Millions of words.
But still none of them would be much use for talking about
that alternative world.

Auschwitz mocked and turned inside out all my upbringing and all its words. I grew up in a living mesh of
laws and decencies and kindnesses, of heroes and hero-
ines I read about who fought for justice, of writers who
knew evil as tragedy. None of that applied: behind the
gates of Auschwitz right and wrong, loving and hating,
changed places. It was normal, no, banal, for the guards
to whip and torture and kill, senselessly, at random, and
the prisoners to crumple up and die, just as senselessly,
also at random. Dying became the commonplace which
we all came to take for granted. Each morning, the nightly
toll of corpses carried out of the bunker was as familiar
as this world's breakfast cereals. Other prisoners loaded
them onto the cart as if they were so many sacks of coal.

If you want to talk mythology (and that's really more

your way than mine, my bumblebee), you could say that there was a different Genesis, a different Creation, and, Behold! Auschwitz was established on the waters of the deep. Light was separated from Darkness, so that it would never penetrate into it: and Darkness became Light. There was a different sun, a dark one stained with smoke. And surely a different God. And like the other Creation, the one we were brought up to believe in, every creaturely detail was carefully planned, to the greater glory of its Nazi Creators.

You might say, well, after all, Auschwitz was a real place in Europe, it covered some thousands of acres near a Polish village, and so on. The mediaeval Hell had a site too, in the bowels of the earth, which was considered then a real enough place with topological features, even though there were no survivors who came back to speak about it. But the modern Hell realized the mediaeval myth on the surface of our earth, not under it. And right in the heart of Western civilization, nurtured by its networks of trains, telephones, and technology. When mediaeval man talked about Hell, we say, he confused myth with reality. But then modern man, in all his enlightenment, turned myth into reality.

Please write me again soon, bumblebee. There's so much dough of memory we have to knead together, so much of the bread of our lives was only half-baked.

From the Office of Demonology
Templates and Stereotypes

You, Sir, appointed this Office to keep records, *inter alia*, of the eternal underground caverns and of the demons which inhabit them. There is one demonic group, sometimes called the *Nibelungen*, who are masters of mining and casting. Their rings, spears and swords are much prized for their durability and magic powers. We are especially concerned about one of their activities, the casting of stereotypes. The process is known to mankind in their printing presses: an image is fixed in metal, and stamped out time and again without any change.

When human minds are imprinted with these stereotypes, however, their images continue fixed and unchanged through centuries of history and through years of individual lives, regardless of any incoming experience whatsoever. This can produce horrific results. Like the Jewish stereotypes, for example, which bear no relation to real Jews.

The first templates were etched by the Jews themselves: or rather, the first Jewish Christians. These hardened through history into the metal stereotypes, and variations of the originals were also cast. Now we are well informed here about the Covenant with the Jews, some of the paperwork passed through this Office. We were disturbed, therefore, when the first Jewish Christians said that God had broken His promise, that the Jews were degenerate and that the Covenant now belonged to the followers of Jesus, whom they called the new Chosen People, the new Israel. Henceforth, they said, the 'Old Israel' was an outcast from God and from human society.

When the Christian Church became a state power, the stereotype plates became even more pernicious. So St. John Chrysostom, in a Fourth Century casting, said: 'Are Jews not inveterate murderers, destroyers, *men possessed by the devil?* — debauchery and drunkenness have given them the manners of the pig and lusty goat. They know only one thing, to satisfy their gullets, get drunk, and maim one another. Indeed they have surpassed the ferocity of wild beasts for they murder their offspring and *immolate them to the devil.* The synagogue?. . . a house of prostitution, a caravan of brigands, a repair of wild beasts, *the domicile of the devil,* an assembly of criminals.' This was a very persistent metal casting, especially for the new Germanic Christians, who had mostly never heard of the Jews before: even sixteen centuries later, Hitler wrote in *Mein Kampf* that the Jew was *'the personification of the Devil.'*

And then the Crusades. We watched prominent clerics goading frenzied mobs to kill first the enemies of Christ who polluted their own towns, before setting off to kill those others blotting the Holy Land. In the demonic workshops, the mediaeval recastings of the original templates were particularly vicious. The Jew was now also a killer of Christian children, as well as of the original Christ, and he used their blood for his Passover matzah. He was also a poisoner of wells, spreading the plague, hardly surprising in one who was the enemy of the New Israel and the New Jerusalem, the Christian people and their state. Since he had no role in that state, like working the land or joining the crafts guilds, since his only role was to bear witness to his own treachery and the truth of the New Covenant, of course he resorted to the evil of usury — an activity forbidden to

Christians: and this was his subtle way to suck out the lifeblood of the state and its community.

An improved stereotype was cast: the Jew was not only stateless, he was also the Eternal Wanderer. This was first imprinted on the minds of pilgrims to the monastery of Ferrara in 1223, who were sure they saw a Jew who had been present at the Crucifixion and had mocked Jesus. From the Cross Jesus had replied, so a Bolognese chronicler wrote: *I go, and you will await me till I come again.* So this evil ghost-Jew wanders the earth till Jesus returns to it again. He is etched as bony and tall, with eyes dark and huge; he appears and vanishes mysteriously, bringing panic, famine, or plague, and perhaps the end of the world itself . . .

The imprint of this stereotype was deep enough to last even into the age when Jews became full citizens of the state. Soon after Hitler became Chancellor of Germany, Cardinal Faulhaber (who even opposed Hitler's persecution of the Jews) delivered the same myth in a sermon: *'After the death of Christ, Israel was dismissed from the service of Revelation. She had not known the time of her visitation. She had repudiated and rejected the Lord's anointed, had driven Him to the Cross. Then the veil of the Temple was rent, and with it the covenant between the Lord and his people. The Daughters of Sion received the Bill of Divorce, and from that time forth Assureus wanders forever restless over the face of the earth.'*

Naturally, the image of the Jew as God's outcast has justified all sorts of cruelty. We have observed that some cruelty took a common form through many ages: for example, the smells of incense offered to us have frequently been disturbed by the smells of burning flesh, as Jews were burnt alive while at prayer in their synagogues. But we also classify certain original experiments in cruelty. In the time of Chmielnicki in Russia, for example, Cossacks sometimes sealed up all the exits of Jews' bodies, or ripped open their bellies and sewed wild cats inside.

The Protestants have produced their own version of the stereotype of the Wandering Jew: that he will return to the Biblical land of Israel (as written in Paul), as the prelude to the Last Days of the Earth.

The human dealers in the printing-plates of myth, minstrels, writers and artists, increased their circulation by imprinting them onto many different situations, in ballads, folktales and plays. Before the Elizabethan audiences of England, as for the rest of Europe, Christopher Marlow used the same stereotypes for his Jew, Barabas.

He is the rich userer who
filled the jails with bankrupts in a year
And with young orphans planted hospitals.

He is the poisoner — of the food of Christian nuns. And he is the ritual murderer — even of his own child, because she became a Christian. Barabas was even more popular than Shakespeare's Shylock.

We know in my office that the demon plate-makers did not feel unduly threatened by the Enlightenment, by the new secular age of the anti-clerics, which exposed their myths to the golden dawn of reason, and even cast their own new templates. Lessing's Jew, *Nathan the Wise,* for example, glowed with wisdom and humanity: and he was imitated in European culture everywhere.

They bided their timeless time. They knew the impress of their stereotypes was still at work. In the novels of Fielding, Richardson, Burney, Dickens, Walter Scott, Bulwer-Lytton, and so many others, the Jew was still the evil userer, the outcast who preyed on society. Even the ritual murderer. *'I confess I have not the nerves to enter their synagogues. Old prejudices cling about me. I cannot shake off the story of Hugh of Lincoln,'* said Charles Lamb, seven centuries after that imaginary ritual murder of an eight-year old boy, and the massacre it bred.

We talk, Sir, of the casting of new plates. But it is mostly a matter of reworking the original templates, adapting them to the changing modes of society, religious, economic, political.

We may instance the stereotype of the Jew as greedy, as

the malicious userer. In the nineteenth century, a host of French writers, including Balzac, maligned the Jewish capitalist, nouveau-riche and unscrupulous, who was moreover an *international* financier. The Jew who preyed on society was now part of a worldwide Zionist conspiracy to sabotage Christianity, government, and the economy of the world. We observed that the forgery, the *Protocols of the Elders of Zion,* the alleged minutes of night-time cemetery meetings of Zionist leaders planning to take over the world, continued to survive for three generations. It was publicized in the United States by Henry Ford and others, even after The Times exposed it in 1921 as a forgery made with the approval of the last Tsar of Russia.

The stereotypers adapted their imagery . . . While the Jew in the past was excluded from Christian society because of his religion, now it was because of his race. And the myth of the carnal Israel became the myth of the race of Israel. Four centuries before the German Nuremburg laws of racial purity, even the Spanish Inquisition was obsessed by *purity of blood.* After the expulsion of the Jews from Spain in 1492, it demanded to see genealogical charts to prove that an aspirant to any position in society did not have the blood of a Jewish convert. In nineteenth century France, Jewish racial inferiority was a theme of Gobineau, and of the best-seller *La France Juive* by Edouard Drumont, which became a textbook for Adolf Hitler. Ernest Renan wrote that 'the Semites never had any comprehension of civilization'. Wagner wrote of the Jew as the 'protean demon of humanity's decadence . . . the born enemy of pure men'. His English son-in-law, Houston Chamberlain, claimed to prove that Jesus himself was an Aryan: the Jews had forged his genealogy. The entire Bible was the work of Aryans, he claimed, misappropriated by the Jews.

Thus the Jew was stamped with distinctive features, because of his race, which made him always an alien in the country of his birth, no matter how fluent and distinguished he became in the language and culture of that country, no matter how loyal.

The officials of the Christian churches were imprinted with the revised version of the ancient stereotype. Thus the Civilta Cattolica, the official newspaper of the Jesuits in Rome, declared in 1897: 'The Jew was created by God to serve as a spy wherever treason is in preparation . . . anti-semitism will become, as it should, economic, political, national . . . Not only in France, but in Germany, Austria, and Italy, Jews are to be excluded from the nation. Then the old harmony will be reestablished and the peoples will again find all their lost happiness . . .'

In the 1930s, Hitler was questioned by two Catholic bishops about his anti-Jewish policies. He replied that he was only realizing what Christianity had preached for almost two thousand years.

The Nazis imprinted the old stereotypes onto celluloid. The eternal myth became the Nazi film *The Eternal Jew*. And the power of the image on the big screen surpasses the power of all the media of history. Image of Jews migrating: image of hordes of rats. *Jews are rats who infest with plague.* Image of Jewish butchers hacking meat with knives. *Jews are sadistic butchers.* Jews dressed in fine Western clothes. *Jews only assume the outer clothing of Western civilization in order to infiltrate, destroy and possess it.*

Our Office has noted that separate stereotypes for the Jewess were cast. Dating from the original templates, she was pure like the Jewess Mary (Miriam in Hebrew) the Madonna, she was loving and penitent like the Jewess Mary Magdalene the harlot, she was beautiful and erotic like Shulamite of the vineyard, the heroine of the Song of Songs. *Dark but beautiful.* Like the Virgin herself, who had Black Madonna statues in many churches.

This stereotype proved very durable. In its prints, the Jewess was seen in good light, even though in reality she was martyred alongside her menfolk.

There are several plates of the Eternal Wandering Jewess. She is the immortal Herodias, as old as Eve the earth mother of mankind, protecting her offspring through endless generations. She is the pure daughter of the faithless

Jew, like Abigail, the daughter of the villainous Barabas, the Jew of Malta. She is a fallen angel of heavenly beauty who pities the suffering Ahasuerus, bringing him goodness and everlasting faith. But she is also the eternal Salome, wily and seductive. She is a sex symbol. She is not only pure like the Madonna, she is a courtesan like Mary Magdalene. She is *La Belle Juive,* the embodiment of feminine power and enchantment.

From the Archangel Head Office

Memorandum to the Throne Chamber

In view of Your concerns and overall designs for the human planet, Sir, we feel you should know our consternation at the above Report from the Office of Demonology: since one of the primary concerns You have leased to my Office since the Sixth Day of Creation has been with human freewill and human responsibility. The demonic stereotype plates analyzed in this Report would make poor imprints if not for a notable degree of human cooperation.

Human guilt is, of course, secretive and complex, and we have to monitor it extremely carefully. We have watched individuals become both the spokesmen for, and the inciters of the masses. Thus was Augustine, or Chrysostom for the fourth-century Church: thus were the clerics of the thirteenth century: thus were Drumont and Gobineau for nineteenth-century France: thus were Hitler and Goebbels for Nazi Germany. Then again, some groups become agents or symptoms of greater communities, like the incidence of a disease in one member of a family: so was Nazi Germany with regard to Europe.

However, evil is not some involuntary disease, and we have no hesitation in this Office in filing Auschwitz and the other death camps as absolute evil. And we must cross-reference this file with the manufacture of stereotypes which preceded Auschwitz and made it possible.

Above all, Sir, is our concern for the polluted conscience of mankind, for those tangled cobwebs of guilt, which provide, as it were, the grimy and grainy surface on which those stereotypes of the Jew can be readily imprinted. For the Jew has frequently been chosen, if not by you, Sir, then by mankind itself, as the carrier of its conscience and as the scapegoat of its guilt. Our Office Lexicon defines 'scape goat' as a 'proxy replacement'. It is the wrong victim.

We have observed, Sir, that the individual Jew or Jewess has soul-searing resistance in accepting the sacrificial role imposed on himself or herself by the choice of others. Naturally, Sir, these persons would like to know more definitely how far you yourself, Sir, are involved in that choice. If at all. To such persons, your silence, in these circumstances, is very disturbing.

LETTER EIGHTEEN
Dita to Ronald

The palace of my childhood

In Kosice we lived in a palace. Yes, really a palace. It was
called *Jacob's Palace.* Jacob was a famous architect in
Kosice, especially as a restorer of historic buildings —
which abounded in that mediaeval, once royal city. Jacob
had built that house for himself. It was a replica of the
Rákoczi castle at Siebenbürgen, with neo-Gothic turrets
and windows of beautiful stained-glass. It reared up mag-
nificently over a green park, right next to a bridge over
the river Hornád. From the window of my own room, on
the right side of the building, looking at it from the front,
I would watch the greeny swirl of the river below me.
You know, *dragam,* 'paradise' was a Persian word for a
park created out of the wilderness for the delight of princesses. So was that Kosice park for me: a green paradise
separating our home from the hubbub of the town. I loved
to linger on the bridge, on the way home from school, to
watch the ducks waggle their tails, moorhens and mal-
lards, or the solemn pageant of mandarins, with their tur-
quoise pate and fantastic orange-brown side-whiskers.
The palace itself was divided into apartments. We came
through the rotund entrance hall with its stained-glass
windows into our own, on the ground floor. It was enor-

mous. Apu also had an office there, with his personal secretary. Kosice had been bombed in 1941, no one was sure
exactly by whom: but the palace remained untouched.

In that same Jacob's Palace, incredibly enough, the
President of Czechoslovakia, Dr. Edvard Benes, had his
home (the official Presidential Palace was, of course, the
Hradcany Castle in Prague). We used to see important
black cars with chauffeurs draw up outside. Benes lived
there throughout the war, although by then he had resigned as President. After Kosice's and my own liberation by the Russian armies, I was not the only one making my way back to that Palace. The Czech government
in exile from London, and also the Czech party leadership from Moscow, both arrived at the same time in Kosice
in January 1945, and came to Benes' apartment: and it
was there that they drew up their plans to form the new
communist post-war government.The 'Declaration of the
Kosice Government Program of the National Front of the
Czechs and Slovaks' was made here on 5th April 1945; at
that time Kosice was the seat of the government and of
the Slovak National Council.

That government would not rule Czechoslovakia until 1947. And Benes would die in 1948 — the same year as
the great Jan Masaryk, the writer-statesman who was the
leader of a humane Czechoslovakia (he was pushed from
a window, almost certainly murdered by the Communists), and the same year that Israel was recognized as a
state, after two thousand years, by a fluke benign con-
stellation of votes in the new United Nations.

But Apu and I wanted nothing more to do with the
death that stalked Jacob's Palace. Long before Benes'
death, long before the Communist government, we had
left the ruins of our past, making first for the New World,
then for the Palestine soon to become Israel, another new
world, finally back again to New York. New world after
new world, new and new again . . . We needed the new,
we both wanted to believe in the new. The old was too
horrible. We were cripples, really. In our minds, in our
imagination. In order to live, we needed to dream of a

new world. Of a tomorrow somewhere which didn't carry all those memories of family, of work, of school, somewhere not polluted by the terror of the transports and the smoke of Auschwitz.

So the future of our personal lives, as of the life of Czechoslovakia, both were decided under that same Gothic roof of the palace in Kosice. Father and daughter were reunited in a deserted apartment covered with dust, haunted by the ghosts of our murdered family, even by the ghosts of once living wishes and dreams. We were oppressed by the furniture, by pictures and books, cutlery and crockery, lace and silver heirlooms, all of which, like us, had lost their *raison d'être*. While in the apartment overhead, politicians debated the future shape of the country which had been our home, which had been betrayed and dismembered.

Apu had made desperate efforts to locate my mother Bella and the rest of the family, hoping against hope that they were alive somewhere. I was life from the dead: and he for me. You have to imagine the offices set up by the American *Joint Distribution Committee*, stuffed with files and distraught people. Like half-alive, half-dead sardines in a can. But not in orderly lines: just a tangle of lost and anguished people waiting for any kind of news of their relatives. 'I know you, weren't you living in Kesmarok? Did you know the Feldman family? Have you seen Zita or Wanda?' 'You're from Palace street, aren't you? You must have known the Kordas, have you seen any of them?' 'Where were you? Auschwitz? Treblinka? Maidanek?' All of us there are macabre leftovers from a catastrophe, all of us are living in an unreal time that is also a leftover time after the end of the world. Among us are wandering groups of children whom the Office has to care for, orphans, severed from their parents, many of them paralyzed from trauma, pale, unable to speak. Would Marika my little sister be among them, could she still somehow, miraculously, be alive? . . . For weeks, Apu is meeting every train which pulls into the station, scanning every face to recognize someone he knows, asking questions. He has no idea, as none of us could have, who is still alive. But I cannot see him, or anyone I know, on that teeming platform smelling of steam and sweat when my own train puffs into it, one summer morning, whose brightness promises to clear away every cobweb and nightmare. Soldiers and baggage spill onto the platform. I don't know what to hope for. I see in the melée a man dressed in blue serge with a white Star of David on his armband, wide Slav-Jewish nose and thick lips, blue eyes penetrating steel spectacles. I speak to him in Czech, I tell him my name and where I've come from, and he takes me to the makeshift office, besieged with people, bursting with files stacked on files. And a woman with thick glasses and a green-specked scarf round her head actually finds my father's name . . . But no one else's.

I am walking down the main street, dazed, with unsure steps as if on glass, and everything is both familiar and strange at the same time. It is an eerie *déja vu*. In spite of the clear sunshine, the loggias and arcades of the buildings seem to rise out of a mist, the mist of a dreamlike past. I see and I don't see the Dessenffy Palace picture gallery, the Forgach Palace, the Town Hall. And now I'm crossing the park itself, there's the river Hornád and there — home? The Gothic Palace looms up like some fairytale castle of princesses, real only for the space of a picture book story. But the beating of my heart is real enough, and so are the pains in my legs.

It is Apu who opens the door. A very thin Apu, with a grisly stubble. The flames I used to watch inside his eyes have been damped out of existence. But he shouts hoarsely, 'You are alive, Ditukam, you are alive!' And we are hugging each other with our stick-arms, and our tears leak and dribble from dried-up eyes that have forgotten how to cry.

That evening, all the stones and streets of Kosice seem to be bloodstained in the sunset.

Apu has survived Auschwitz himself, by luck, by his own bull-like tenacity, and by the *chutzpah* I adored in him. He hid a diamond in his anus before the deportation. It's as if Apu had inherited an instinctive behavior for survival which linked him with distant forbears like the Jews expelled from Spain in 1492, who also hid gold and silver in their anus, and even swallowed it because their stomachs could not be searched in the guarded ports of embarkation (though legend has it that their stomachs were sometimes ripped open by robbers . . .). Four and a half centuries later, miraculously, Apu's diamond was not discovered in that brutal searching which was part of the rite of welcome to the Concentration Camp. In that sub-world of grisly barter, he dared to offer it to the head *kapo*, a trade-off in return for work in the kitchens, one of the most prized jobs. Some warmth, some scraps of food instead of starvation, at least a postponement of death.

In the weeks that follow, Apu goes to the station by himself, sometimes we go together. To wait, and ask, to wait again, to ask again. To cry, sometimes. Who else might come back? But of our family, no one else comes back. Father and daughter, we are alone.

Apu left Galicia as a boy, and in Kosice he developed a rich coal and wood business, drawing on the fertile forests and mineral deposits of the Spis Ore mountains. He owned horses and high-sided wagons, carrying his merchandise all over the city. Although there were several coal merchants in the city, all Jewish and competing against each other, Apu outclassed them in energy and business acumen. He owned a plot of land and a sizeable store, as well as his office, partly in the town centre, and later at his own flat. He had very black hair (when you knew him, *dragam*, he was already grayish); he was dark-faced, darker than creole, Mediterranean. He was Anyu's opposite. For my mother's skin was as white as if enveloped in the foams of exquisite soaps — this from our writer friend Erwin Soos: *'As white as Aphrodite,'* he said, *'stepping out of the waters.'*

You met Erwin, didn't you? Did you know that in the short-lived Hungarian commune of 1919 under Bela Kun, Erwin's father had been a chairman of the directorium, the governing body of the soviets of soldiers, peasants and workers — after the Russian model — and he had been executed, along with the entire directorium, in August 1919. Bela Kun's name was a corruption of 'Cohen'. Many Jews were prominent in the socialist revolutions after World War I, not only in Russia, and many were murdered, like Kurt Eisner in Bavaria, or Rosa Luxemburg in Berlin. Erwin was three years old when his widowed mother managed to get them out of Hungary, carrying just a basket, to Kosice, where her brother lived. She was 'Aunt Helena' to me, as my mother was 'Aunt Bella' to Erwin. And the two women were close friends.

My mother and father were opposites in every way. Anyu was a well educated woman who had been a teacher. She was an intellectual who could absorb books and ideas like blotting paper. Her mind was as fragile and refined as a Meissen figurine; this was Erwin's poetic metaphor, of course. She was handsome, with hair rather reddish, eyes lucidly blue and transparent, but arresting. People said I had the same eyes, the same white body speckled by the sun, the same fastidious cleanliness. Perhaps intellect too. Marika my little sister was also blue-eyed, tall for her age, and as fair as a viking. Mother and daughters, we all looked so Waspish and Aryan — something I'd never thought about until the first anti-Jewish laws were passed, when we had to sew the yellow star on our coats, were forbidden to go to the cinema or theater (and Kosice was so rich in culture) . . . Whereas Apu was clearly Jewish and foreign. When Jews were forbidden to own businesses, he arranged a Gentile 'front', a friend and partner behind whom he secretly operated. Apu's tough resilience was as natural to him as his nose. He would enter Auschwitz equipped to survive where survival was designed to be impossible.

I was their first child. I was chubby and pretty, assertive and talkative. On the whole they were carefree years, the thirties, although I was sometimes disturbed by the tension between Apu and Anyu. Then came the tragedy of the baby boy who followed me. I'm sure that my grandfather (a very religious Jew) and Apu himself valued a son more than a daughter. So their grief was intense when my brother died as a baby, a 'cot death'. Anyu and Apu blamed each other. Had they done enough? They could have afforded the best doctors. Anyu remained melancholy and restless for some time, until that spiritualist session at Helena Soos' house. I still don't know what to make of all that. I believe it affected my mother more than Apu who had his feet on the ground. Erwin wrote of the event in his first novel, which was published in 1936 when I was ten years old. This is what happened: The medium was an illiterate washerwoman. She scribbled things on a pad of grayish rough paper, like packing paper. Sheet after sheet. Nonsensical doodling it seemed. But it was written from right to left. No one could make sense of it. Nevertheless, my mother (Aunt Bella to Erwin) took it all home, and showed it to her father. My grandfather managed to decipher some words. It was, incredibly, Hebrew. He went to the next session. He suspected some fraud. Everybody did, even Anyu, who needed desperately to believe, in spite of her rational intellect, that she was receiving some word from her dead child. But now there were coherent and readable texts. Messages. Nagyapu, my grandfather, read them. 'I'm alright. Don't worry. I watch you. I love you.' All in Hebrew. Erwin had held these pages in his own hands: but I never saw them. All I am sure of is this: from that time, my mother's anxiety left her. And soon she became pregnant with her third child, my sister Marika.

Kosice was a cold but healthy city on the eastern spurs of the Spis Ore Mountains. The northern winds blew from the Tatra Mountains, and it was cool even in summer. Nevertheless, each summer we moved to Kesmeret in the Tatras. Near Kosice spread the ravines, crevasses and caves of the the Krast plains, crowned with fantastic castles and châteaux. It was a royal city, dating from the thirteenth century, with all the insignia, the dignity and prejudices of an old royal city. It had been Hungarian up to 1918. There had been no Slovakia. That's why we still spoke Hungarian at home, Slovak on the streets, but

Czech in college, or with officials. When the Hungarians left Slovakia after the treaty of Trianon in 1920 (two-thirds of Hungary was parceled up between Czechoslovakia, Yugoslavia, and Romania), there were no Slovak teachers or lawyers or any professionals left to run the country: and the Czechs supplied them. I grew up loving the new Czechoslovakia. It was an enlightened democracy — we had twenty-seven political parties while I was a young schoolgirl in the thirties! The questions were: who was Hungarian, who was Slovak? not: who was a Jew? Anti-semitism wasn't noticeable until about 1939. That was when Czechoslovakia was stabbed in the back and betrayed. In March of that year, a month after my thirteenth birthday party (one present was the silk scarf I wore on the photo you have of me), the shadows fell; sometimes quickly, sometimes stealthily, but surely. That depended on the government: henceforth the Hungarian government. When the Germans marched into the Sudetenland, the Hungarians also reoccupied Kosice and southern Slovakia.

We became officially Hungarian again. For that reason many Jewish lives were saved. We had quite a long breathing space, compared to the rest of Europe. Five years later, when I was eighteen, the Nazis could look at the map of the continent and see their 'Jewish problem' solved — except for the political island of Hungary. In March 1944, a month after my eighteenth birthday, the war was already lost when the Nazis finally got their way in Hungary. Eichmann had to come himself. The Hungarians had gained land in the north, east and south through their alliance with Germany: but they could not extricate themselves when the tide turned after the great winter retreat of 1942 to 1943. The Regent, Admiral Horthy and his feeble ruling class of landowners were no match for Germans like Eichmann. When Horty issued his Manifesto saying the German Empire was near defeat and Hungary was withdrawing from its allies, the Arrow Cross took over immediately, well prepared with guns and uniforms for this moment. The Nazis themselves came in March

1944. But Eichman came to Budapest in person, even when the war was nearly lost, to set up the ghettos and to begin the deportation of the Jews to the death-camps.

Meanwhile, the Jewish men feared their 'conscription' by the Hungarian army for the so-called labor camps, the *Munka-szolgálat*. Rumors had it that they worked in appalling conditions at the Russian front building trenches and forts and risking Russian fire. And worse: they were used as human mine detectors, which meant they were often maimed or killed . . .

On one dank autumn evening when we were all sitting together in our living-room, and I was looking through the lace curtains at the Hornád river now pockmarked by fallen leaves, a gendarme delivered a summons to Apu in the hallway. I know the living-room lights burned throughout that night, not for the first nor the last time; I saw them when I went to the toilet, early in the gray-mist morning. A haggard Apu left us a few days later before dawn while Marika and I still slept. But true to himself, he had made his plans. My mother and Joel, his business partner, were bribing a high official in the War Ministry, so I would learn later. Twice they travelled to Budapest. Two months later, when the park was white with the winter, we rushed to open the front door for him, but he was so much more haggard, and I had my arms round his chest before he took off his coat and even as he was lifting up Marika to kiss her . . . So you see, when you were in the Spanish prison, I knew something about the power of bribery . . .

But this frightening backcloth to my adolescence does not prevent the tender and fierce loves of a young girl's heart. I lose it more than once, but to no one as passionately as to Petr. He is seventeen to my sixteen, rugged and fair-haired, the son of a Jewish father and Catholic mother. (He is to die, together with his father, in the gas chambers of Auschwitz, transported there from Terezin.)

But what can we know of such a future as we cycle together in the country, as we watch, hand in hand, the hundred-foot high Helany geyser spurting cold water. It is unique in the world, Petr says, knowledgeably. As we kiss moistly (and precariously) beneath the giant colored stalactites of the Domica Cave, as we glide through it by boat on its underground river, the Styx ('let's cross it together and hide in the netherworld,' Petr jokes). We fondle each other above the Silica gorge while its forty-foot frozen waterfall curtains beneath us. Oh the sweetness, the first wild taste of flesh smelling of the wind, that spice of intimacy! It was hardly savored before it was swallowed up and brutalized.

Petr will get a place to study law at Budapest University — remarkable, because there's a *numerus clausus* for those of Jewish descent. But his lawyer father has influential friends. We write each other letters, fervent love mixed up with political chit-chat. Yet within a year the blaze becomes a glow, and Petr finds a blond student to be his mistress. I cry most of the night, looking out of my castle window at the Hornád, like some mediaeval Lady weeping for her knight errant. Surely, this is the end of my world!

The Hungarians are as anti-semitic as the Germans. But they need the Jews they revile. I don't know if you realize, *édesem*, how the Jews in Hungary were almost the only middle-class: doctors, lawyers, journalists, businessmen. Budapest was nicknamed *Judapest.* So their restrictions upon us come cautiously, step by step. Early on, they introduce a quota system. That means, for me, that getting into University will be almost impossible.

Apu says that Prime Minister Kallay is protecting us from the Germans, that things are much worse everywhere else. Now it is March 1944, five years after the carving-up of Czechoslovakia, and things are changing rapidly. It is a month after my eighteenth birthday, a lavish affair by the standards of that time, a new white linen dress embroidered secretly by Anyu for me, *mákos* — poppy-seed cake, and marzipan, my favorites, food hoarded over months . . . Horthy is being given the choice of a German occupation or German-approved ministers, and he has to choose the latter. Masses of German 'advisers' are swarming into our country. We are bombarded by a terrible barrage of anti-semitic railing on the radio, together with eulogies of the Nazi Führer and of the glorious Third Reich. The 'advisers' have several offices in Kosice. The black Arrow Cross uniforms appear on the streets as never before. The Arrow Cross is the Hungarian fascist corps set up by the Germans and modeled after the SS. Soon I see the SS themselves for the first time in my life. I see the death's head sign on their black caps, over their black leather coats, as they drive through the streets in their black limousines.

Black, black, and more black.

It seems suddenly that life has lost its spectrum of colors and is turning black. Black seems like the absence of color. I cannot really understand this non-color of hatred. I'm innocent, I suppose, in spite of my eighteen years. No saint, of course! Jealous sometimes, resenting things, rebellious. Quite normal and understandable. But nothing like this tidal wave of impersonal hatred which now surges on every side of us, in which everyday sanity seems to be drowning.

Black, black, and more black. And the culmination of all black will be the blackness of the smoke from the Auschwitz chimneys which turns the blue sky to black with the ash of burnt human beings.

LETTER NINETEEN
Ronald to Dita

Bombs and the end of childhood

It's hard to bear the pain of your story, *Ditukam.* Your
return to Kosice, and your house and park of ghosts. Like
moraine in the memory, left behind by the great glaciers
of the war. Like barnacled once precious objects washed
up onto beaches, after the storm-waves have retreated.
Beaches full of homeless people looking for home again.
What an age of homelessness we live in! True, we all first
experience home and homelessness with the first taste of
our mother's breast, which is both given and taken away.
But I wonder if history ever before uprooted such masses
of people, ever saw such a scale of exodus, such devastation of cities, such human lostness? Did the days of Attila,
or the Thirty Years War, see such bizarre journeys of survivors through cruel landscapes, farm carts washed by
the tide of a vast Eastern army lusting for vengeance, such
as you describe?

  I too experienced an exodus, but of a different kind: I
was part of the huge evacuation of three million children
out of the reach of the Nazi bombs. I experienced two of
the homes of my childhood reduced to smoking rubble
by direct hits. And I also saw the huge conflagration of
the City of London, its second Great Fire.

I grew up in the tremors of the same global earthquake that would consume all of us.

But I would never be taken to Auschwitz.

I never had to wear a yellow star, as you did. You spoke of being frightened in the streets of Kosice: for me too, there was a territory of *goyim* I feared at the end of my childhood street, where I was abused and beaten up one night on the way home from *Cheder*, the place of Hebrew studies. My father told stories of the killings and looting of Jewish homes in the Poland he had left as a boy. The East End of London was literally a battleground of fascist blackshirts and communists. Sir Oswald Mosley held huge Fascist rallies in the thirties, and the communists often chose the same time for their own, deliberately, to confront them. The Fascist meetings in London's East End echoed the contemporary rallies in German towns, and the rank and file blackshirts paralleled the SA with which Hitler won his street battles. So I saw the early stages of a homegrown Nazism which in England could never reach its Final Solution. Crowds of hundreds, growing to thousands, would surge out of houses as the Fascists marched past, screaming antisemitic slogans. I was ten years old when a crowd of blackshirt hooligans terrorized the Mile End Road, opposite the house where I was born, violently attacking any Jews in sight, even children, breaking windows and devastating Jewish shops, looting and scattering their goods along the street. I saw the wreckage for days afterwards.This was the week after the famous march of the Fascist Party through the East End which Mosley had called for in October 1936. The streets were full of policemen, on foot, on horse, in cars — six thousand were drafted to the East End. Thousands of men and women, Communists, many ordinary decent people, Jews and non-Jews, barricaded the streets with overturned carts, prepared themselves with bricks and broken bottles, and with stones they actually broke off from the pavements, to prevent this march. When Mosley finally arrived in the afternoon at the Fascist rallying point near the Tower of London, the Home Secretary telephoned orders for Mosley to disband his followers. He did so, saying, 'The government surrenders to Red violence and Jewish corruption. We never surrender!'

For the boy I was, there was still a simple polarity to everything: black or white, good or evil, and now communism or fascism. Those were the days of the *God that Failed,* before people were disillusioned with communism and with the Soviet Union. Many of the adults around me volunteered to fight in the Spanish Civil War with the International Brigade. Some were killed, and others returned home wounded and crippled.

I grew up in the foreboding of a cataclysmic war to come.

A cartoon in the newspaper used the map of Europe to show the Nazi wolf with Czechoslovakia in its jaws, after the Germans marched into the Sudetenland. In Kosice you were living within easy reach of the wolf's front teeth. The London parks were being scarred with trenches for air-raid shelters. We all lived in an electric atmosphere. And one day, incredibly, we were given gas masks in cardboard boxes, children and adults, and shown how to put them on. We goggled and giggled at each other through them, smelling the stink of the rubber, hearing the hiss of our breathing. But it was more than some kind of macabre game, it was also terrifying. I used to creep into my older brother Mac's room when nobody saw me, and sit stunned with horror before the deformities in a book on his shelves called *NO MORE WAR! PAS PLUS DE GUERRE!* There were only photographs inside, page after page of grotesque monsters who had once been men, whose faces gaped with holes, with missing cheeks, with vanished jaws, with mutilated fragments of nose or ear, even lost pieces of cranium. There were still more horrible ogres, with sticks of metal shrapnel protruding through their flesh, from an eye socket, out of the side of their head. These pictures may have come from the First World War, or from the Spanish Civil War. No matter to a thirteen year old boy . . . There was also a book on First Aid, and I was glued to the gruesome description of choking and burning, the effects of mustard gas. We were all frightened by the talk of bombs. The Prime Minister, Stanley Baldwin, warned that German bombers would always get through, and we knew they had poison gases to drop like phosgene and mustard. We heard of Guernica, the Spanish town where the Fascists tested their new warplanes against defenceless civilians. And England had few defences at that time.

That was also the time of a personal trauma in my life. I won a scholarship to an exclusive English 'public' school. Henceforth I had to become an English gentleman in black jacket and striped trousers, and to disown the rough-hewn coarseness of the East End (and all the vitality that went with it). The City of London School was actually a healthy mix of classes (as Kingsley Amis, a Prefect when I was in the Fourth Form, once stressed). I was awarded several other scholarships, so that my father used to boast, not quite truthfully, that he was actually making a profit on me. In fact, he was to become *nouveau riche* enough over the next few years to spend every winter with my mother in Cannes or Monte Carlo after the War. He was an immigrant from Poland who'd come to this country before the First World War scarcely knowing a word of English, roughly a contemporary of Isaac Wolfson and Charles Clore whom he knew (he introduced me to Sir Isaac, a short man in a Dickensian top-hat, in Great Portland Street Synagogue one Day of Atonement), and he envied their infinitely greater wealth and success (*inter alia*, Clore owned Selfridges, and Wolfson endowed the Oxford college which bears his name). These were all poor Ashkenazi Jews from the Eastern ghettos who were strangers both to the great Germanic culture of Central Europe and to the mores and breeding of the assimilated and established English Jews — the Sephardic Montagues and Sassoons, as well as the German-Jewish immigrants like the Rothschilds and the Warburgs: and at first, consequently, they were resented as much as helped by their fellow Jews. The rough and tumble ferment of the East End of London was the catalyst, the high-pressure cooker, which gave these newcomers their mettle and vim. I have childhood memories of my father's master-tailor's workshop in the yard of our house, where he was king (my mother ruled the house), and of his fellow immigrants — Joe the cutter, Phil the tailor, Sid the machinist, and the others who worked for him. When he later became manager of a very large factory in Little Portland Street near the BBC, each of these went West with him to become heads of the Departments of Cutting, Tailoring, Machining, and so on, one on each floor of the building. But their loyalty to him and his concern for them remained as personal as before, in spite of the size of the factory, in spite of its rows of machines and its systematized mass production. What a contrast that was to the present day organization man, with his loyalties to abstractions!

My mother was the eldest of nine children, who all lived in the next house but one in the same street. So my childhood was nurtured in an extended family, a *Grossfamilie,* four aunts and four uncles, more than a dozen crammed into the one room kitchen-dining-room-playroom-washroom, and overflowing onto the hot pavements in summer alongside dozens of other street neighbors. The street was an extension of home, and I was streetwise before I became bookwise. My mother's father had escaped, alone, over the border from Plotsk, hiding from the Cossacks, in the savage anti-Jewish pogroms at the time of the Russian-Japanese War, leaving his wife and three daughters (my mother among them) to follow later with a single battered trunk containing all their possessions. Survivors survive differently. My grandmother continued to see catastrophe loom everywhere; the whole of her life was an emergency, and she thrived on it. I remember my grandfather as the opposite, avoiding fuss. Perhaps this was also to do with his failing heart. He died when I was a boy, after three years in bed. But my grandmother lived, tough and gnarled, into my teens, still speaking only Yiddish, a fabulous oddity from another world to her anglicized grandchildren.

At first my father's Jack-of-all-jobs, whose name was Jack in reality, drove me every day to the school. The journey through the City of London became symbolic for the sensitive boy. Out of the familiar smells and noises in the multicolored grimy side-streets off Whitechapel, heading in the direction of that mythical region of wealth, ease and flawless fabled Englishness which was called *the West End* (as if it were *Life's End,* a goal as well as a geographical area), through the City and its symbols of financial power, past the grandiose palace called Mansion House. Here lived the invisible, awesome City Fathers, the financial sun-kings, who had founded and now watched over the City of London School itself. And they watched me too, month after month, wearing the oversize school cap which bore their coat of arms, in my daily journey through the London traffic jams. Watched me in my painful, shocking rite of passage, like ancient gods awaiting their sacrifice.

For they did, indeed, demand a death — as well as offer a rebirth. My death, of course. But also the death of the entire East End, it seemed to me, with all its boisterous life-giving bluster and struggle, with its raw, sonorous and complex vowels, suddenly seeming ugly and slovenly, forced into a newly refined, clipped accent. I studied Latin and Greek, traditional humanist training for a gentleman. I learned modes of behavior which turned my background on its head — I had to efface instead of assert myself, to understate things instead of paint them lushly, and above all, to beware of showing my feelings but maintain, in every situation, a stiff upper lip. Such was the ethos for the scions of the Rulers of the Empire, which in fact would be dismantled within a decade or so.

I still have the photograph from my first year at that school. There I sit, a plump little prig with severe eyes, a teacher's toady. Of course, I have the seat of honor right next to the tall elegant Mr. Marsh, the Form Master and our teacher of classical Greek, whose rarified Oxford accent was both charisma and terror to me. He was undoubtedly the messenger from those dark City gods, sent to initiate and supervise me.

Almost half a century later, after the City of London was bombed and rebuilt, I would celebrate its history in a musical pageant with text by Ursula Vaughan Williams, stretching from Roman times to the evacuation of 1939. It was commissioned for the City of London Festival and performed in St. Giles Cripplegate where Shakespeare's parents were married and John Milton buried, a monument church of the old City amid bleak modernist blocks, confronting the gaunt Barbican Arts Center across concrete pools.

In the great Evacuation — early assembly at the School, labels for us as well as for baggage, chocolate and cheeserolls hoarded in the gas-mask box, the special train from Paddington, one of the legion of trains mobilized that day — we joined together with Marlborough College, one of the privileged bastions of class, founded originally for the sons of English clergymen. So I absorbed Anglican Christian liturgy, singing Stainer and Parry in the Chapel choir, as well as playing Bach on the organ.

But strange to tell, since we were a London school, special trains ran back and forth between Marlborough and London every holidays. There were long holidays, almost five months in a year. Parents wanted their children next to them and took the risk of the bombing. So it was that I experienced real explosions and real fire and real deaths — in London. My first childhood home was razed to the ground, our No. 21, where my parents were raising three sons, together with its tiny backyard we used to fill with sunlit water from the yard tap and pretend it was a pool; along with No. 23 where lived my mother's family — grandparents and eight uncles and aunts; even the entire street and a good square mile of the Whitechapel Road, all vanished in one night's black magic, replaced by jagged walls and debris, a whole lost universe of my earliest childhood.

Our second house, my mother's pride with its Chinese

lacquered drawing-room and its palatial red-tiled bath-room, also received a direct hit. We were sleeping in the basement shelter opposite and further up the street. (But I slept blissfully, tasting a cocktail of danger and eroti-cism: I had my arm around my love of that time, bosomy, husky-voiced Pearl, who lived down the street.) A terri-fying noise woke us, an ear-splitting boom followed by thunder rumbling close by. The shelter shook violently. But no one was hurt. When the insistent high-pitched All Clear of the siren pierced the daylight, we surfaced dazed into a different street. The sky was the same, gray and speckled with barrage balloons like airborne whales float-ing in a foreign sea. But my home was now once again rubble. No game, no hearsay, real bomb rubble. Bits of burned brick, grotesque twisted metal, stone solid or flaky, charred wood still smoking, broken glass glittering on the street like morning frost. A stink of cinder and soot. Air Raid Wardens in their steel helmets had already cor-doned off the place with ropes. I was deeply shocked. The war had now, literally, come home to me.

And just around the corner, in the main Mare Street, there was another huge promiscuous heap of rubble. The walls of buildings on each side seemed shaved off by a giant jagged razor, leaving exposed the privacy of bed-rooms, bathrooms, family kitchens. Beneath the debris lay several bodies, among them a friend from my own class at school, called Cash, crushed and dead. By the time I ar-rived, I saw no scary sights of mangled bodies; only lumpy gray blankets on stretchers carried into the ambulances. Air Raid Wardens, everyday civilians in their workday suits, passers-by and neighbors were looking for survi-vors, digging with spades and even clawing with their hands, like the frenzied cats who clawed the rubble look-ing for their snug-holes, or their owners. Firemen still hosed the smoldering dust and debris. Later that morning, in Whitechapel and Stepney, where the tenements had been savagely bombed, I saw women wandering dazed and aimless, carrying cases and bundles of belongings they had snatched from the dust-smoking debris of their homes.

After each night of bombing, people emerged into a changed landscape of ruins and smoky masonry and tangles of fallen telegraph wires, out of their Anderson shelters, out of the bowels of the tube stations (which also became permanent shelters for the homeless; they had next to no toilets and were horribly overcrowded compared to the ease of the rich in the West End hotels; in March 1943 Bethnal Green, a shelter for as many as ten thousand, would be the scene of a disaster caused by panic, not by enemy bombs, in which hundreds of people were crushed to death). Groggy, they made their way to work, on foot, begging rides from those who still had fuel for cars, feeding on rumors: this bus was still running, but not that, this tube train was the best bet . . . Complete strangers could be as helpful as old and trusted friends. Shared catastrophe made that possible, even normal.

The armadas of the German mainland began their devastating raids three months after the collapse of France.The figures speak. On the clear night of Saturday September 6, 1940, three hundred and twenty bombers, protected by six hundred fighter-planes, throbbed over the East End: that night had been turned into day by the fires of the preceding, audacious, daytime bombing, by two hundred bombers.Then fifty-seven unremitting nights of bombing flattened the riverside dockland stretching east from the Tower of London, with its network of railway yards and warehouses: and the East End shuddered from thousands of wounds gaping to the sky, wounds filled with the rubble of once large buildings, even of entire streets. Only slowly would the weeds creep over those scars, as if to hide them.

Later, in the June of 1944, we would see the unmanned flying bombs low over the rooftops, droning until their engine stopped suddenly. Then we would hear their frightening whistle as they dived, the last-minute warning to hide from the glass window-panes or run to the shelters before the explosion. But in the following September there would be no drone or whistle warning, just the earthquake of a twelve-ton rocket bomb.

Images are reliable keys to unlock our personal histories, aren't they darling? I remember that time through many images, but two remain the most potent. One is of the cliffs and crevices of wrecked buildings, of the bomb-hollows in a street like giant mouths with decayed or destroyed teeth, the cavities filled with a debris only partially covered, as if from shame, by the first of the weeds. The other image is of the great City of London in flames.

After the bombing of their house — and because the East End Dockland was such a prime target, my parents decided to stay in a hotel in the West End of London, first the Regent Palace by Piccadilly Circus, then the Mount Royal near Marble Arch. And it was from the top of the Mount Royal, between Christmas and New Year's Eve of 1940, that I saw the City of London blazing from the German fire-bombs. It was a grandiose spectacle, and a horrific one. Searchlight beams criss-crossed the sky as usual, but their fingers of light were dim compared to the vivid, garish sheets of flame across the entire horizon, flickering upwards from a glowing red base as if from a gargantuan brazier of burning coals. In the City's history, this was the second Great Fire. Although St. Paul's Cathedral survived, miraculously, its majestic dome towered now, sublimely and surrealistically, over a rubble wasteland of skeleton structures smoking like some sulphuric hell, towered like a monument over a graveyard of precious buildings, including many Wren sister churches, a few only gutted of their insides, but most burned completely to the ground.

And gutted alongside them were the buildings of my own childhood, the temples filled with the fantasies and longings of childhood.

The battles of Romance against Reality. Of dreams and desires against necessities. Doesn't the path of every adolescent wind its way through that same battlefield? Yours did too, *Ditukam,* though your reality was horrific beyond belief . . .

But oh, there was fierce, burning romance at Marlborough!

I must have told you about Treacle Bolly? That was a thickly wooded fringe of the Kennet, the trickling stream flowing out of the Thames, glinting with stones and the gray-black trout which darted or poised immobile like underwater sculptures. In summer, Treacle Bolly was dark and lush, a rustling, buzzing womb of leaves and insects. In winter, a sparkling wonderland of motifs all custom-designed by the frost. And when we followed the wild-flowered banks upstream, the woods would finally give way to the steep green sides of the bare downs. It was then, overhead, that the great White Horse would loom mysteriously out of its prehistoric antiquity, sometimes half-veiled above us in the wisps of morning mists, sometimes monumental, resplendent and divine in sunlight, sometimes ghostly and ominous in moonlight. That chalk god was a beacon for German bombers and had to be veiled with a camouflage net. It was still full of magic energy as it hovered over my own walks alone by the Kennet, or over our group's passionate moonlight talks and readings of Keats, Swinburne, or Dostoevsky. We loved Treacle Bolly. It was a place to find secret idols, away from the school, a place to find ourselves.

I've told you about that 'group', *dragam,* you remember? We were all contemporaries, with contempt for the insensitive, conforming products of the school system and a passion for literature and music. We met sometimes at night, when we were not supposed to be at large (once we were caught and penalized with 'lines' by Kingsley Amis, our prefect). Most of us would make our mark in later life: Louis Zinkin would become a renowned therapist; Malcolm Pines would found the Institute of Group Psychology; Guy Williams-Ashman would distinguish himself as a biochemist, 'Horse' Macnaughton-Smith (his older brother Michael, the poet, would be killed in a bombing raid over Germany) as a mathematician. We were bringing each other up at Marlborough, sharing our discoveries about life and thought and books. With Louis, as you know, I remained close at Oxford and in later life until his recent premature death; otherwise, the 'group' scattered.

That was before the days of co-education in the British 'public school'. I could appreciate the quasi-monastic concentration, but I was also full of a healthy sexuality, and I managed to find both profane and sacred loves. The latter love lived in the town, a delicate beauty, a star of ice. I saw it melt only once, when one of her two brothers, both at the School, was drowned in a Swiss lake on holiday. It never melted for me. My more sensual longings had to be satisfied with pick-ups from the town girls like Gwen (plump and blouse-bursting) or Elma (waif-like and cherry-lipped). Otherwise, I was learning sublimation, mostly into my composing which dated from childhood, and was now a stylistic brew of a delicate Chopinesque champagne, a full-blooded Lisztian red wine, and a heavy Romantic port reminiscent of Rachmaninov.

And the War? One day rich American G.I.'s with nylon stockings and chocolate in their fists took over the blacked-out town of Marlborough and its prettiest girls (some of whom they took home as brides), and barred me from the fern thickets of the Savernake Forest I loved, which now became an impassable ammunition dump. My School had its Officers Training Corps, in which I learned to blanco belts and puttees and to aim a Lee-Enfield rifle. I also learned 'strategy', which always differed from paper to practice. One 'Field Day' when I led a platoon defending the thousand-foot high Martinsel Heights, the enemy typically failed to appear as planned. We shot our blanks in the air and went home, bedraggled by the rain.

The truth was I found all that preparation for killing other human beings really monstrous. I knew I would have to be a conscientious objector if I were called up to fight: but I never was. I was deferred at Oxford, and the War ended. I was very lucky, then, to meet another, quite different 'group', long past their adolescence and their schooldays, who had their own battles with the terrible realities of the war. Out on the London Road towards Savernake Hospital were camped several soldiers who were conscientious objectors. They had been drafted into the so-called Pioneers, whose tasks could vary from behind-the-lines camp chores to stretcher-bearing. They were here vegetating, waiting for some kind of assignment.

I visited them often, and they befriended me. Wülff Scherchen was the son of the great conductor (whose *Handbook of Conducting* would one day be my textbook). He was a communist who wrote fierce intellectual poetry, which he read to me. He confided in me about his love for his girlfriend P, whom he might have made pregnant. He also spoke of his friend Benjamin Britten, another pacifist, who was writing to him from the United States. (I would meet Britten years later at Aldeburgh, and he would give me some valuable advice about my composition.) Wülff was a Prussian, tall and angular, both steely and gentle in turn, and he influenced me deeply. I told you of my communist days, didn't I? Much of my adolescent milk was the Marxism of the previous generation, of Spender and Auden and MacNeice, the generation which also produced the spies Burgess and MacLean and Blunt.

Ken, who was no intellectual, spent his time painting in oils. And there was Roland Gant who would soon make a complete volte-face, catapulting from this non-combatant corps straight into the commando parachutists, from a blunt refusal of the sword onto its most dangerous cutting edge. After the War, he would became a distinguished publisher and author.

The pacifism of these adult men confirmed my own, which I wanted to squash in myself as the romantic unreality of adolescence — squeamish according to the macho Army Officer traditions of the School.The Pioneer Corps into which they'd been drafted was an alternative, frequently, to the humiliation of Wormwood Scrubbs prison. That's where Michael Tippett served his sentence as a conscientious objector. Benjamin Britten and Peter Pears, who had both been allowed to continue making music, gave a recital at the Scrubbs in 1943 for which *Prisoner No. 5832 Tippett. M.* turned the pages . . .

If I was unlucky in the disruption of my home, I was

also lucky in my adolescence. I could experience the brutal reality of the Blitz while still cocooned in a country chrysalis of great beauty. I was fortunate to have some adult teachers and mentors who were both brilliant and nurturing of my own growth, while at the same time I enjoyed a rich and rare fellowship in the group of my peers. The moth was now eager to spread its multi-speckled wings, to fly in and out of some bright flames, but at its own peril.

LETTER TWENTY
Dita to Ronald

The brick factory and the transports

I am frightened now to be on the streets of Kosice, and I never cross the park alone. There are fascist louts lurking on street corners. Sniggering, looking for Jews to taunt and abuse. When any of the black uniformed Arrow Cross are around, it's worse still. Then there are physical beatings, and sometimes brutal rapes of women. These incidents never get into the papers, but we hear the accounts every day. Even in the center of town I see an old Jewish woman being beaten and kicked by four or five louts, laughing and smoking cigarettes, one of them in the black Arrow Cross uniform. She lies bent up and moaning at their feet. I'm cycling home from school. At home I collapse and cry in Anyu's arms. Apu says, 'It can't last forever, *dragasagam.* The allies are winning. It's a matter of months only.'

Within a few weeks, Jewish shops and offices vanish: some are taken over by strangers, most of them are just boarded up. Apu says that Jewish bank accounts are frozen. There's a curfew, we can't go out after dark any more. We can't go to public places, to the cinema or the theater, the tennis courts or swimming baths, and we can only use the trolleycars at certain times. It's really frightening.

They have taken away Apu's car. They came one afternoon from the Post Office and took away our telephone. Now Anyu has to dismiss Kamila, our cleaning lady, who is almost one of the family: that's because a non-Jew can no longer work for a Jew. As Jews we can't travel any more, unless we get a special permit.

The most hateful day for me is when we all have to sew those yellow stars onto the front lefts of our coats. I feel branded like a pig. Stigmatized. But for what? Am I really, born with Jewish blood, some kind of genetic freak, as they're saying? Am I really doomed to pollute human society unless isolated like a bug? This is all such incredible nonsense! And yet all around us, there are so many 'reasonable' people who now turn their backs on us. They cross the street to avoid us. Anyu has one non-Jewish friend, a Dominican nun, a teacher, who still comes to see her at the Palace. But the official Catholic Church doesn't lift a little finger to help us. They're more concerned that Christians (even priests) whose parents were born Jews, or who are converts, have to wear the yellow star also. Their concern is really quite selfish: they just don't want to be associated with a people who are marked out for hatred. What kind of Christians do they think they are? And it's hitting me at school. Eva and Irma and Truda are cold-shouldering me. They don't say anything, they just avoid me.

We have a terrible sense of being trapped, like caged animals, animals in a circus, or even animals in a slaughterhouse, waiting upon other people's decisions for our future. 'So where can we go? There's nowhere to go!' my mother is saying to Aunt Helena. This is one day after school, I can hear them from my room. 'All we can do is wait, and pray,' she answers. 'The Russians are advancing quickly, they'll be on our doorsteps in a matter of weeks.' 'It's so hard to believe they'll be here in time,' my mother says. She sounds despairing, which is not like her at all. 'Listen!' Aunt Helena is speaking very quietly and firmly. 'The war has turned. Ever since Stalingrad last year. Now Italy's surrendered and out of it, the Germans have their backs to the wall and are being bombed around the clock.' We hear the war news from the BBC late at night, the Hungarian radio is not to be trusted. Anyu lets me stay up sometimes to listen. The BBC is like an oxygen line to people who are underwater — and among sharks. And just as precarious. We could be killed if we were caught listening. What it means to us, that unemotional voice of a disembodied messenger who reports of desperate fighting and the movements of vast armies of men and tanks, all in a few clipped cold sentences, while we sit helplessly! We are trapped by timing. The Soviets have to reach an insignificant little corner of the world, Kosice, before the whole of our world finally collapses and we are deported to nowhere.

I never return to school after the Easter recess. Towards the end of April we are ordered (in the newspaper of the Jewish Council, and by a circular from the city police) to prepare for 'resettlement'. Where, we don't know. But the papers promise decent work and living conditions, and we want to believe them. We are living in a fantasy world, we have never heard even a wisp of a rumor of any death-camp. We are to be assembled temporarily in a brick factory, we are told, until the transports are ready.

So, on the very same day we hear that the Red Army is actually massing to break into Hungary through the Carpathian Mountains, we must pack to leave. I look at my meager piece of luggage, and then I look around at all the things that make up home for me. The immoveables: my heavy oak desk, a present from Apu when I entered the Gymnasium, my red velvety armchair, my friendly mahogany bed, the Persian rug with its exotic ultramarine blue. From outside, through the window, the plash and babble of the Hornád's waters. Then the endless moveables to choose from: schoolbooks, three heavy dictionaries and a set of encyclopedias, novels, school exercise books; my tennis racquet and hockey stick; skirts, scarves, sweaters, shoes, my embroidered white linen party dress with the red ribbons — such a luxury in wartime . . .

The night before we must leave, I see Apu and Anyu sitting in the dining room through the open door. Apu is hunched over the table, his head in his hands. This is the first time I've ever seen him so bent over. It frightens me. Anyu is crying very gently. I creep away without disturbing them. I'm sure that they have more to leave than I can imagine. Intangible things, like Apu's business and all its connections, their life savings and their insurance, their once rich life built up painstakingly with all their plans for its future, for my future, for Marika's.

We are woken up abruptly at five in the morning by the bell. There are two gendarmes, *Csendörök,* really mere kids of nineteen or twenty with guns. Their Hungarian is coarse, from the gutter, and their eyes are greedy as they look round at the sumptuous heavy furniture on the Persian carpets, at the crystal chandeliers, at the rings we wear and the fur coats we carry. 'Always so rich, aren't they, these Jews,' one sneers to the other, 'Where do they get it all from?' They show Apu official papers they carry, but they are also patting their guns. We are shocked out of the heaviness of our sleep. Marika is crying, shaking her mass of brown curls violently. Anyu picks her up and holds her till she quietens. We are clutching our bags, and stumbling away from the warm smells of home, through a town sleeping and indifferent. When Nagymama suddenly totters and trips, one of the louts laughs and pushes her. Apu shouts at him, and he pulls out his gun. There is nothing to be done. We know where we are being taken. It is the brick factory. The airless, smelly factory rooms are stuffed with a countless mass of people, bedding messily on every inch of the floor, overflowing into the huge paved yard stacked with red piles of bricks and cut through by railway tracks. We are stunned, though far worse traumas are to come. Now living human beings are to replace the dumb bricks waiting to be loaded onto the freight cars. But where to?

Bricks are fired to make them hardy and robust for the housing of life. But the fires of the crematoria are for dissolving life, dead bodies into dead ashes.

We are nearly all elderly or young, women and children, and the old suffer the most. Men in their prime have been conscripted into the deathly *Munkaszol Gálatosok,* the Jewish auxiliary battalions of the Hungarian Army on the Russian front. We are lucky that Apu is here with us. We don't know how long we have to wait. We live in a confused limbo where days pass quickly into weeks. The food Anyu and Nagymama have brought disappears soon enough: otherwise our daily ration is a little bread and two cups of soup. Anyu always gives extra food to Marika, sometimes to me also.

In the crush of people we find some we know. Gyuszi, my father's secretary, who is not much older than myself. After two days in the factory, I wake up from a nightmare sleep, bundled up on the dirty floor, to see my friends Elena and Rebecca! I kiss their drawn faces! These two sisters and I have shared so much: day-long hikes in the Tatra mountains, double-dating, dancing, growing girls' intimacies like first menstruation and secret passions for boys . . . Suddenly all these things are overshadowed here, they seem phantasmagoric. But our feelings for each other remain real. We can help each other in this dark place, we can stay together. But it isn't to be. Only three nights later, they will both disappear . . .

I help myself to keep on top of things by bustling about. I organize games for the children every morning in one corner of the yard. The Hungarian police guards allow this to be our 'territory', after Apu spoke with the officer, whom he seems to know. Marika forgets her tears, so do the scores of other children. Play is a protection. Eyes laugh again. Imagine: this macabre yard, a place of tears, is echoing with the laughter of children! We scratch markings on the stone pavings and play hop-scotch, 'It' games with holding hands in circles and who is 'out', word-games. We play with the toys we've brought with us: dolls, spinning tops and skipping-ropes, puzzles . . . *édesem,* you must try to imagine how, even as we play in our corner, the rest of that yard becomes a setting for horrific and bizarre scenes. We see frightened people arrive with their bundles and bags, brought by the police to Kosice from smaller, neighboring towns and villages, and then hustled and stuffed into the overcrowded brick factory buildings with us. There are sick and lame and crippled people pushed along ruthlessly or carried in on stretchers. We see women in wheelchairs and blind people. The guards are now emptying the hospitals. No one is to be spared, not even the sick and the deformed. Another day our play is disrupted by several trucks with a human cargo of madmen and madwomen, mentally deranged people. The body gestures of some are stiff and slow, of others wild and uncontrolled. Some faces are vacant, some are screwed up and intense. Some are drooling and slobbering. The guards unload them savagely with sticks and with jibes. Can you imagine such scenes out of hell? Enacted in front of children who can only stand and stare in astonishment. It is beyond all our crying, all our laughter. We have never seen such things. Nothing in our lives has prepared us for this fearful springtime in the brickyard. Our playing is not just interrupted. Surely it is being murdered forever, our childhood with all its toys and playthings.

People are brought in during the day, every day. But only under the cover of night do freight cars clang and thunder into the yard to take them away. Every night the overseers come with lists, hundreds are taken, some sobbing, a few even screaming, but most are quiet and resigned. They believe the lies about resettlement. Apu tells me that the railway track from the brickyard crosses a main street in town before it joins the main line. The gendarmes don't want their human transport to be seen or heard during the daylight hours.

We arrived at the brick factory well dressed, and hopeful for some kind of future. In three weeks we are reduced to hunger, dirt (even my fastidious mother, Bella), and despair. The few latrines cannot accommodate so many, and the factory stinks of excreta, in spite of the cleaning rota. All around us we see adult human beings, our mentors and models, become beasts. But this is not true of my family. Apu reassures me always, and I can still believe him: 'Ditukam, we shall all stay together. The war is nearly over; maybe a month or two only. Take care of your sister . . .' At night I am drugged into sleep by his strong-sweet brown eyes. Eyes I also see blazing with anger. He is a fighter. I know in the brickyard he tried to bribe the gendarme louts for more food for us. Not that it worked.

Our turn comes at last. A damp cold three in the morning. Hustled and shoved into the yard. Not freight cars, not passenger cars, but cattle cars. *So we are not just bricks, we are beasts.* Crush of bodies. Torches. Some screams. Confusion. The Hungarian Arrow Cross *nyilas* searching our baggage. Our clothes. Even our bodies. Jabbing and jeering crudely, hurriedly, and thoroughly. Looking for valuables — before the Germans get them, I realize. Wallets, purses, earrings, necklaces, bracelets, pendant from Nagymama (but not the one I found and wore after the war, the gold one with a circle of rose-jewels, remember?). Into the cattle cars. Pushed in. Goaded in. Beaten in. Maybe seventy in each. Maybe many more. One bucket of water. Doors closed, clang of bolts. Final, irrevocable. No air, stifling, squeezed tightly, hot, sweltering, fetid, suffocating. Apu holds a sobbing Marika over his head, to breathe.

Outside, beyond the weight of wooden doors on those cattle trucks, securely hidden from us as we from them, the dear kind people of Kosice do not storm the heavens with shouts of indignation like thunder, do not beat and hammer on doors with clenched fists, do not cry loud and fierce their outrage that such injustice should come to pass on their ancient, royal and holy Hungarian soil. On the contrary, they turn on their pillows as the trains clang by; perhaps a few are wakened, grunt and shrug, and then certainly sink back swiftly into their disturbed sleep.

LETTER TWENTY-ONE
Ronald to Dita

The operation on my brain

I shared the doubtful distinction of being a patient in St. Andrews Hospital, Northampton, with the great poet John Clare. But he spent a significant part of his life there, almost twenty years. He entered St. Andrews a century too soon to receive the simplified label of 'schizophrenic disease', and to undergo the routine dozens of insulin-induced comas or electric shock convulsions of my time: or, failing that, a common enough prefrontal leucotomy, which would probably have destroyed his poetic imagination, along with many other qualities which are specifically human. Why it did not destroy mine is a mystery. You know, *Ditukam,* how very angry I have been that this unnecessary and dangerous slicing of my brain was ever permitted and performed. But also how grateful that it didn't (in the end, and after much suffering) impair for life my humanity, and my creative imagination. That I would later become an academic and an artist of international standing, and what matters more, a person capable of caring relationships, was not due to that operation but in spite of it.

In 1950, the year I entered St. Andrews, there were at least two million people confined to mental asylums, and most of these looked like the survivors of the Nazi camps, hidden from the world until stumbled upon by the American and British armies in 1945: naked on moldy floors, treated like pigs or cows by 'nurses' who were often enough recruited from the jails in lieu of their sentences. 'Euthanasia by neglect', one journalist had written in 1946, in contrast to the deliberate extermination policy of the Nazis.

In that respect I was lucky. Like William Tuke's Quaker Retreat Asylum in York, and in the wake of the reforms at Salpetriere in France, whose director Pinel looked on mental derangement as the extreme end of a spectrum of hardly perceptible gradations between 'normality' and 'insanity', St. Andrew's had avoided the overcrowding and neglect of most of its contemporary asylums. No doubt this was due to its wealth: it was the most expensive mental hospital in Britain, as well as one of the largest. It was an ironically elegant setting for so much suffering and pain. Its original Georgian building had been modernized and enlarged, and it stood in a hundred acres of parkland greenery, with a neo-Gothic chapel designed by Sir Gilbert Scott shaming the nondescript stone outhouse for the arts and crafts of what came to be called occupational therapy — a legacy, along with the occasional dance for patients and staff, of nineteenth century humanitarianism.

It was recommended to my distraught parents by the renowned Dr. William Sargant, a tall, handsome White Knight figure, the champion of the new physical treatments which, it was hoped, would give psychologists the same prestige as their medical colleagues; a man who was liberal with the assurances everyone wanted to hear, patients as well as their relatives. But in some cases, as in mine, only the relatives had ears to hear, and the patient was certified in order to be given treatment against his will. I could not have imagined then the great surge of protest in the next decade, especially in the United States, against such involuntary commitment of the mentally disturbed, and against the monstrously crude leucotomies of which I was a victim along with countless thousands of others all over the world.

My memories of that time remain intense and vivid, although I have to distinguish my first few weeks in St. Andrews, which had the alien feel of a powerful dream or trance, the time I was labeled 'psychotic', from the two or three months following when I'd surfaced back into my conscious self: again, the times before and after the electric shock treatment: and, more radically, before and after the leucotomy.

The suffering I experienced was real and terrible, but it must be understood relatively. For the question is, how much was an 'I' there? I have suffered a quota of life's pains since that time — family conflicts, the pain of wasted years, bereavements, or the great anguish of watching you wither and die of cancer in my arms: but the 'person', myself, has been *there* to understand, to experience, in the end simply to bear; and 'I' have been enlarged in doing so. In St. Andrews that 'person' came and went and then came back again. Now 'I' existed less, and then more. Now 'I' was standing, so to speak; and after the savage assaults of the electric convulsions, 'I' collapsed temporarily. And finally, 'I' took much, much longer to emerge after the leucotomy.

It's difficult to mention in the same breath your own sufferings in Auschwitz, which were far more terrible, not only because it was intended to be a place of destruction and not of healing, but because 'you' were more there to experience it than 'I' was in St. Andrews. But were you, really? Because the mental effects were similar. You wrote how you were stripped of yourself, your own will, your own past, your own face, your own name. I was also stripped of myself, as was everyone who underwent 'deep sleep' treatments, or insulin injections, or electro-convulsive therapy, and above all leucotomies.

The first I saw of St. Andrews was its old bath-house with its waterpipes and faded white tiles, where the traditional hot-cold water shock treatment had been given, before the days of drugs and ECT. Since I was violent with myself, for my own safety I was locked in a padded cell. The door had a little round porthole through which I would see the faces of nurses. It was opened only to bring me food. Nobody tried to communicate with me. I was in that cell for perhaps a week, a time in and out of time. I remember my intense feelings of guilt, of fear, and sometimes despair; or else a marvelous sense of release and of wonder. I was trapped within visions of strange half-human monsters and of cruel sacrificial rituals of appeasement, which seemed to encompass and alleviate the pain and the guilt of all men everywhere and at all times. I read primitive mythologies today and realize how I was reliving them there in my solitary psychosis, universal myth of yesterday in my modern madness. I can see method-in-madness even in one rite I resorted to near the end of my psychosis. God was the god of all that was despised and rejected: and to become one with him I 'took communion' and ate a mouthful of my own excreta. A repulsive twisting of a truth which can be understood . . . Among the mythologies of the sane, I think of the Egyptian god Khepi who appeared as a scarab. The scarab lives in excreta, in the dung out of which emerges new life. Aristotle taught that fish were first born out of dead and putrefied algae, living insects out of inert slime.

But my night ended, and the means of its ending might be taken as a justification of William Sargant's own theories. I remember the mental hurricanes whereby I exhausted myself to the point of collapse: and it was in this way, by convulsion and collapse, that the mania effected its own cure. For cure it was, and by the very means that Dr. Sargant analyzed in his book *Battle for the Mind.* Thus, for example, he pointed out that the most reliable cure for the hysterical dancing mania which followed the Black Death in the fourteenth century was to urge the dancer on until he or she collapsed from exhaustion and lay on the ground as if dead. And then, very slowly, the dancer would recover and even return to work as if nothing had happened. The mental tempest seemed to have created its own cure.

But as you know well, I did not, of course, walk out of St. Andrews as if nothing had happened. I surfaced to the sounds of the Brahms Clarinet Quintet from a radio in Ward Four. I had loved that music since I was a boy, and in that bizarre setting it now replayed for me a tapestry of rich meanings. I am sure, as so many have known since Pythagoras or Plato, that music has a special power to reach the mind's deepest centers, to concentrate and to heal. The psychologist Oliver Sachs, for example, writes of a man who 'floated' without any sense of 'time', or memory, or power of recognition, yet who became 'anchored' and recollected whenever he listened to music.

In Ward Four, as I returned to my own senses, I awoke to witness a heartbreaking Hell, if Hell means the rule of dark unconscious forces. The faces and bodies of most of the patients around me, along with their minds, were possessed and contorted into strange gestures and grimaces, and their speech into scarcely intelligible cries and moans, sometimes even drooling. The night nurses gave out a sedative every evening, before the lights were turned out, peraldahide I think it was. During the night the drug wore off for several patients: they awoke, moaning, craving more from the nurses, for that Lethe drink of forgetfulness. I have an indelible memory of the same man, a tall man with black bushes of eyebrows, groveling on the floor, whining and begging, his dark eyes rolling, until the nurse gave him yet another dose. And this pitiful scene was re-enacted night after night. The nurse was a corpulent middle-aged man, whose manner, like most other nurses', was hearty and perfunctory with patients as if they were all alike, some kind of strange animal species beyond communication.

But I was not in Ward Four many nights. I was moved to a sunlit, spacious ward facing South, its windows overlooking a serene lawn which billowed luxuriantly down to the golf course, for all the world like some exclusive country club.Two of these wards were winged symmetrically on either side of a central building. Since I was more or less back to sanity, this should have been the time for

some talking. I needed ears to listen, to understand the
threat of that other world which had opened up inside
myself, so that I would know it was understood. I needed
people to tune in to my wavelengths, to help me cross
those crevasses between that nightmare inside myself and
the world outside. The world I once knew had collapsed
around me like the buildings of a city in an earthquake.
Now it needed rebuilding, reclaiming. Without that hand
from the other side of the crevasses, I remained trapped
and isolated.

But there was hardly any attempt at communication.
The nurses remained perfunctory. To them patients were
not individuals, but branded together as a class: irritat-
ing and sometimes infuriating, incomprehensible, often
quarrelsome and complaining, and their job was simply
to keep their cool and leave judgements and treatments
to the doctors. As for these, the demigods of the system,
they made only brief and routine rounds of the wards (in
some state hospitals, I hear, these could be six months
apart) with impersonal formulae of few words: 'Improv-
ing, I see?' or 'And how do we feel today, then?' and 'Did
you enjoy your breakfast?' without caring much about
my answer, or anybody else's. After all, their faith now
lay in so-called objective diagnoses which jam-packed all
mental disturbances, in all their human complexity and
variety, into a few neatly labeled compartments: and in
the new physical techniques, which were themselves
impersonal, often speedy, and comparatively cheap. Almost a conveyor belt process back into some social norm,
without the need (not to say the time and expense involved) to delve into a person's latent conflicts — or treas-
ures. St. Andrews has a record from that time of one patient receiving almost one hundred insulin treatments —
and that was not so unusual. From being merely prisons
or places of confinement, mental hospitals had now become centers of technology where humanitarian intercourse was incidental. Humanity had to take its chance.
Patients tended to become numbers and objects, no longer
suffering persons. Typical was my most frequent day

nurse, Nick, a bright-eyed young man in his twenties, who was off-hand, immature, and coarse. 'Off to the lav again, are we, Ron?' Because he had to escort me there. 'You're gonna just love wolfin' down this puddin'!' — as he brought me a supper tray. 'Nah then, no fuss today, eh?' Typical, because like his more mature seniors, like even the doctors themselves, he had to protect himself against so many grotesque human beings, against the suffering and effort of really entering inside their lives.

As I found myself in a row of beds, *Ditukam,* you have to imagine my fears, sometimes panicky, my feeling of helplessness, my sense of dependency on this fortress hierarchy of authorities which seemed so impenetrable: from the nurse orderlies to the higher-up, but still junior, doctors who regularly, for no apparent reason, and without needing to give any explanation, would carry out bizarre operations on other patients — putting long tubes down their throats as they lay in a coma (to bring them round and avoid irreversible brain damage in insulin treatment); or wheeling them away into the screened-off annex at the end of the ward, to bring them back heaving and panting violently for breath, ruby-faced and monstrous, to lie coiled and moaning after a crude shock of electricity: finally to the inscrutable and transcendent doctors who rarely appeared but controlled everything from behind the scenes. Since these were all, I imagined, voluntary patients, why was there so little communication? Why were there always locked doors and the constant rattle of keys, for voluntary patients? The atmosphere was filled with suppressed violence. The row of lavatories had no doors. You were exposed as you sat, and patients would stare at you, some vacant or wild-eyed, as well as nurses. The lavatories at my school, Marlborough, had been similarly open — there, presumably, to watch for masturbation or homosexual practices. Here it was to watch for violence, or simply for depressive inactivity — a patient stuck, paralyzed by a force beyond his control. Was the severity of the male nurses so necessary? I am sure they themselves were frightened of the violence, and no doubt of the treatments themselves which were still fairly new. It is terrible to watch the wild convulsions of a human body after it has received powerful electric shocks. There were stories from the past of severe bruises, of bones being broken, even the spine. Nowadays, even though the electric shocks are much milder, most hospitals have completely forbidden such treatment.

None of my bones were broken when I, too, received a prescribed routine course of six electric shock convulsions. But my spirit was broken, even before they began: else I would have protested more vehemently. I was still, then, in name at least, a voluntary patient.

The head nurse was a Scot called Jock, a solid tower of muscle, a grim regiment in reserve, in spite of his jocular talk on the surface. His favorite phrase to me was, 'Com now, Ron, it's fer yer ayn good'. This before he wheeled me into the annex, before the nurses greased my temples and stood ready to hold me down to prevent injury, before they put the rubber in my mouth to prevent my biting my tongue in the coming convulsions, before they put the electrodes on from behind, before the searing flash and the immeasurable chaos of black abysses from which I would clamber up — oh, so painfully, so slowly, and so desperately. In the days between these sledge-hammer blows to my brain, I was the defeated boxer who reels back to his feet again and again. Trays of food and drink came, I washed and went to the open toilets, I drifted through the dayroom among stupefied or jittery patients unable to concentrate on the radio, the cards, a book, or each other: and wonder of wonders, a stream of quite amiable and meaningless chit-chat with other patients flowed in and out of me, just as the food and drinks did. I had become banal. For a time. Is that the goal of the electric shock convulsions, I wondered, to reduce humanity to banality? I had been shocked up to the surface of my soul, and I floated there like a seagull on water which rippled placidly while underneath half-forgotten sea monsters coiled themselves in the depths of the ocean. A limbo time, a chapter temporarily suspended from my book of life.

Not altogether, though. I would come to between shocks, tentatively, vaguely. Sometimes in the streaked light of the dawn through the curtains I would lay in bed terrified, yes, *Ditukam,* sweating with fear, that today those unapproachable authorities had decreed for me another ordeal of electrical shock. As breakfast time came, I waited anxiously for my own tray. If it didn't come, that would be the sign. They wanted no risk of vomiting as my body convulsed.

Weeks passed and, one overcast morning, Jock brought me my clothes. Dr. William Sargant, he said, had driven down from London just to see me. In a comfortably furnished office of the main Georgian building, Dr. Sargant sat gracefully, legs crossed, and casually offered me a cigarette. I was uneasy, stiff, and I refused. 'You know', he began, 'you don't want this sort of thing happening again, do you ?' I made no answer. He continued, very persuasively, 'I've seen this operation done many times, and the effect is quite extraordinary.' I answered: 'I've heard that it impairs the faculties that really matter, that it makes you a sort of vegetable.' 'Not at all,' said Sargant: 'there may be some temporary confusion, but after a while that disappears, and so do all the mental disturbances, all the pressures and anxieties.' I answered: 'In any case, I feel well enough now. I want to leave this place and get on with my life.' After a while, he said, 'Well, perhaps you'll think about it.' The brief interview was at an end. He had asked me nothing at all about myself, how I felt or what had gone on inside me or what was going on now. William Sargant was the apogee of generations of organic theorists of mental disorder who regarded all the talk of their patients as symptoms and never as sense. He nodded cursorily to the nurse, who took my arm very firmly and led me out and back to the ward, and I felt I was a criminal who had just faced his judge. An understandable confusion, since Sargant did make the judgements and had the power to execute them, whereas I was a social outcast about to be branded.

Two days later my mother appeared with Mac, my older brother. Her face was taut and tearful. She had lain awake in bed night after night, torturing herself, 'What had she done wrong, how had she failed?... 'Mac told me that Dr. Sargant had recommended a prefrontal leucotomy. Mac was six years older than me, quite a gap for children. As a young boy, I'd looked up to him, his paintings, his Left Book Club socialism, his pacifism: I became the artist and scholar he might have liked to be, he became the worldly businessman I despised as a young man but later envied. We looked alike and had similar temperaments. You know, *Ditukam,* that it was quite late in life that we finally resolved the tensions between us. There in St. Andrews I repeated to him what I'd said to Sargant: 'I don't need to stay here. I certainly don't want my brain tampered with.'

I recognized the look of guilty accomplices in their eyes. William Sargant must have persuaded them, however reluctant they were. He'd argued, firstly, that the operation would prevent any recurrence; and secondly, that the effects on my intellectual and imaginative abilities would be negligible. How else could my tormented mother have agreed to have her darling son 'certified' — legally deprived of all civil rights, made totally powerless to make his own decisions — so that his skull could be forcibly pierced, and the brain which she had borne in her womb, the precious castle of his mind and imagination, cut into against his will?

In the preceding decade, of the thousands of people who underwent the leucotomy operation, only fourteen people had been ill for less than two years prior to surgery whereas over forty percent had been ill for at least six years.Two-thirds of the patients were chronic, lifelong schizophrenics. But I had been diagnosed as mentally ill barely a few months before!

I did not know I'd been certified until the very morning of the operation, a Saturday.

'Com now, Ron, it's fer yer ayn good.'

I was drugged against my will, I had no strength or

right to struggle. Fear made my hands sweaty and my throat dry. The fear of a living vegetative death, the worst fear possible for a human being: to lose his memories, his creative will, his core of consciousness. The fear of becoming one of those inane zombies I saw continually through the windows shuffling around the lawn and sitting on the benches, sunning their gray hairs, vacuums without thought or passion or memory. They all seemed to live long, and I was a young man in my twenties. My brain was 'me', unlike any other part of my body. You can amputate my foot, even invade my heart or my lungs, and I will still be myself. But mutilate my brain, and I am no longer my self.

The dark amnesia which followed was never conclusive. They say that slicing the brain is painless, because there are no nerve-endings (then why was I anaesthetized?). Yet I know that a body-mind sub-soil experienced the pain of that violation, of that slicing of synapses and nerves by the knife, just as it did the violent electric shocks: and that pain would scream to the surface in nightmares. Fifteen years later it was experienced again consciously in a deep therapy session with Kay. Twenty-five years later, after I'd talked about the operation with F., a scientist friend, I had to stagger, literally, into the men's room of a pub to be alone, my head in my hands, because the memory of that pain seared suddenly through many layers of new growth and adaptive living, and burned nakedly again.

But I felt nothing of that when I awoke in the St. Andrews ward, flooded with summer sunshine. For days I floated on a tranquil hazy sea, as once again food came and went on trays as naturally and unquestionably as day followed night. I was child-like, jelly-like, dependent. My identity had disappeared, it had drowned. I had become the vegetable I had dreaded: and the perfect vegetable, because I did not know it.

But then islands appeared in the sea. Islands of memory. At first a small atoll, one here and then one there. Later much larger islands, and, strangely, they were joining together to form coherent land-masses. My past life was re-emerging, gradually, like a legendary Atlantis from the ocean depths. And with it an identity, a self, 'myself'. And *time* came back. I mean much more than the planetary times of days and seasons, of growth and decay of plant and animal tissues, the times for nourishment and for excretion. I mean the human time, which opens up the moment to fill it with meaning and purpose. Time which loads and stuffs the flow of yesterdays and tomorrows.Time which is transient and precious, because it is comprehended. Time which is tragic. Time which means the life before death, and the death in life. I even remembered the words of a Shakespeare sonnet, *How shall summer's honey breath hold out against the wrackful siege of batt'ring days . . . Where . . . shall Time's best jewel from Time's chest lie hid?*

I remained in hospital for several months after that operation: but it took many years to get well, years of faltering and starting again. Recently, I saw the film of Janet Frame's life (*Angel at my Table*), how she was wrongly diagnosed, spent eight years in hospital, was given hundreds of ECT shocks, how she was spared the leucotomy although her mother had signed the authorization. I wasn't so lucky! In fact the long process of re-claiming my past, of learning to walk again psychologically, took some eight years anyway, which was the time Janet Frame spent in hospital.

I feel sure the operation ought not to have been done. Partisans of the operation estimated that one in three were 'successful': but the statistics have never been accepted as objective by its opponents. Even supposing that I was one of the blessed minority, the risks were horrendous. The crude surgeon's knife damaged the surrounding areas of nerve tissue, and that damage was usually irreversible. I was one of innumerable victims of that professional optimism about the operation — and of professional ambition. But, miracle, my heart today has grown whole again, and it goes out to all those casualties of the battle, that *Battle for the Mind* of which Sargant wrote, who live out the rest of their days in a living death but have no monuments.

I might have been, throughout all these forty long years, a Sleeping Ugly imprisoned within the vegetative sleep of one of the failed leucotomies, the majority. I would never be awakened, so I would never know I had been deprived of my forty years of life. Forty irreplaceable personal years, of loving and tasting and knowing that I loved and tasted, interwoven with forty irreplaceable years of public human history! In Oliver Sacks' *Awakenings,* Leonard comes to himself after forty years of unawareness caused by *encaphalitis lethargica.* He sees himself in a mirror. He is shocked and sad to recognize the lined middle-aged face which has replaced the boy's face he once knew. Poignantly, he realizes he does not know what year it is. He can never know what he might have been and done. But he has a simple gratitude for the gift of his returned awareness, for life itself . . . I am one of the survivors of the St. Andrew's leucotomies, School of 1950, as the other poor specters, ambling vacuously around the locked and barred hospital wards or their lawns, are not. I am grateful too. But I have also been very angry.

There is a thin line which separates everyday reality from the world of the imagination — that other reality, superor sub-reality. It is a hairline, a line built of ghostly particles, of nanoseconds. For the heightened sensitivity, for the original and exploring, usually an outsider in society, for the poet and artist who lives by meta-phor, by metaphrase, by marrying two realities, that line is easily crossed. For him those realities may be not merely fused, but sometimes confused. And that is madness.

I wrote you about John Clare, *Ditukam,* at the beginning of this letter, who was also once in St. Andrews. But I am also a pygmy among many other giants who entered in and out of madness at some time: from Robert Schumann to Frederick Nietzsche, Dean Swift to Percy Shelley, Ben Johnson to Lord Byron, Cowper, Goldsmith, Blake, Melville, Coleridge, Rousseau, Pascal, Tasso,

Nijinsky, Virginia Woolf, Robert Lowell . . . Perhaps their brains, like my own to some degree, inherited a more complex wiring than is ordinary, and were therefore extraordinary in synthesizing unexpected connections, in experiencing a gamut of emotional extremes. Perhaps their brains, like mine, were periodically flooded with the volcanic energy of manic storms, leaving behind a flotsam of original ideas . . . If you imagine them all transported to St. Andrews Hospital in 1950, the majority, no doubt, would have had their brains bored and sliced against their will, and would still perhaps be shuffling among the other human ghosts across the green lawns.

I doubt how many of the pathetic and deranged patients I had contact with in St. Andrews were men of that calibre; but each, nevertheless, had his own special qualities, however submerged and splintered by his 'illness' (whatever that may mean) and by the institutional harness and muzzle he was confined within. For the two months before I was released, I had two constant companions in Ward One — which was as close to a hotel with private servants as you could get there, in spite of the ever-dangling keys. And one was indeed a young man of a very rare sensitivity, intellect, and perception. Slender, with a large overhanging forehead, he was a sculptor who had also been associated with Eric Gill's community, and had found himself a 'voluntary prisoner' in St. Andrews after twice assaulting his mother in fits of temper. The other, an elderly grayhead of an aristocratic family who comically insisted, from time to time, that he be addressed as 'Honorable', had clearly given up on the troubled world outside, and had settled for St. Andrews Ward One as his permanent home.

The only human — and humorous — exchange I had with a nurse in all my time in St. Andrews was in Ward One. He was cleaning out the grate, and found there a screw among some other odds and ends. I said there were plenty of those loose around here. He laughed with me, not at me, and said that if he had had any say in the matter, I'd have gone home a long time ago.

Archangel's Central Office
Report on brain surgery

Archangel's Central Office to the Throne Chamber

Since, Sir, You made them in Your image, it's hardly surprising that sooner or later they would find out how to get to the inside of things. Of course, I don't imagine, not for a second or an aeon, that You wanted those secrets to remain forever on the classified list, closed to their prying. I mean, naturally, those hermetic sources like the power in the nucleic particles out of which You formed the myriad galaxies: or the serpentine maze of enigmas called chromosomes by which mankind may give birth to their own images, loaded, these too, with the same audacities and diseases. Some, as You well know, have ascribed men's very discovery of such cabalist powers to the patronage of Beings opposed to Your Lordship, indeed Beings who from the Beginning are out to thwart You. Since we intercept their messages from the Resistance hell-holes and possess the keys to all possible codes, we do not doubt that such Beings influence men (and women too, though not as exclusively as was once believed on earth) to misuse their newfound powers. However, Sir, in any case, and in spite of the partiality you have long been credited with, I submit humbly that we are dealing with new toy-technologies in the hands of fumbling and often fanatical infants.

I am thinking of a report which has just reached my

desk, of which, Sir, I enclose for You a summary. Their own brains have for men always been as impervious a mystery as the chemistry of the stars, or the arcane core of the oak's acorn. Yet are they now learning to fathom and to blueprint all these hermetica. In particular, their brain-probes and brain-maps are as crude as once were the first explorations and charts of their newly discovered continent of America. The continent of their own brain is still largely unknown to them in any significant detail: hence they have scant theoretical basis for the mutilation by surgery of those subtle and vulnerable areas where, as they themselves would once have described it, their soul would seem to reside. The aim of such surgery, of course, is to cast and cut out the devil — to resort once again, Sir, to a metaphysics of myth not necessarily dear to such surgeons. Unfortunately, from our reports, the soul itself may be unquestionably maimed. (The philosopher Nietzsche, he who, You will remember, announced Your death to his contemporaries, also said to them: *Be careful lest in casting out the devils you cast out the best thing that's in you.*)

Since certain such doctors have believed, with a fanaticism that my Office has filed alongside the religious fanaticism of the Reformation period, that they can now remodel human character by slicing and severing the pathways and synapses of the brain, they have indeed appropriated areas of what was called *morality* by giving these areas the name of disease in the same sense as diseases of the body. Thus they would operate on the brain of a husband to cure his cruelty to his wife, or on the brain of a child to cure its rebelliousness or lack of concentration. In the United States, it was reported to me, a million dollars was given in 1967 for a program which intended to cure rioting in the cities by brain surgery on a very wide scale.

Such soul specialists are called *psyche-atrists.* They have no doubt been envious of the body-atrists, or doctors, who have achieved speedy and worldwide easement of bodily disease through drugs and surgery. Some psy-

che-atrists used to remove teeth or intestines in the belief
that disturbance of the soul was caused by an infection to
the brain. Of course there are malfunctions of the human
brain, as there are of the human heart and liver. But it
remains nonplussing for modern psyche-atrists when
they discover their scans reveal healthy brains in sick
souls, and sometimes sick brains in healthy souls.

Since we were present on the Sixth Day, Sir, this Office
is well aware of the mystery of breath-in-clay which is
man and woman. It is a mystery which reflects Your own
oneness and Your own infinite complexity together. But
since You have made man and woman the special charge
of this Office, we are naturally concerned to see that oneness trivialized, and to see human complexity — from
tunneling to stargazing, from self-meditation to the artificial probosces which penetrate the universe, all the intricate and invertible spectrum of human caring and jeal-
ousy, desire and murder, creativity and despair — all con-
densed into formations of electrical nerve impulses or of
chemical transfers.

Report from the Angelic Ministry of Health and Morality

Among the new techniques for transforming human
states of soul or psyche, none is as irrevocable as surgery
of the brain, which mutilates its nerve fibres and synapses.
I submit this Report, Sir, in three divisions: (1) the nature
of this operation and its history; (2) its effects; and (3) its
use as a means of mind control or brainwashing . . .

(1) In 1936 the Portugese Egaz Moniz used a steel cutter,
or leucotome, to cut the nerve-fibres linking the frontal
lobes to centers deep in the subcortex of the brain which
regulate emotions. His enthusiasm for the relief it brought
to some twenty suffering people inspired two American
surgeons at Georgetown University, Freeman and Watts,

to take up his work. They developed the so-called standard leucotomy. A burr hole was made in each side of the head above the ear. Into these the surgeon inserted the cutting instrument, and swept it through an arc to divide as much white matter as possible. It was a very crude operation: post-mortems found great variations in the positioning of the cuts. Most people, within the medical profession, as without, were horrified. Yet in the heyday of belief in the operation, between 1944 and 1960, some 200,000 leucotomies were done in Europe and North America. Tens of thousands more were performed in Japan and India, three or four brain mutilations each hour: the patients usually wheeled in fully conscious, anaesthetized in a flash by an electric shock, then the braincells behind their eye sockets crudely destroyed by a trocar, an instrument like a little ice-pick which was tapped by a surgeon's mallet.

(2) But by 1960 the number of operations had dropped dramatically, because the ghastly consequences were intolerable, particularly for the psychiatrists who had to care for the poor victims. Compared to the monitoring of the after-effects of new drugs, the post-operative evaluation of a prefrontal leucotomy was superficial. Yet most neurosurgeons were by now quite aware that the benefits of the operation were tarnished by serious side effects: emotional instability, outbursts of aggression, the clouding of the intellect and the dampening of all initiative. This was known even twenty years earlier. However much prefrontal leucotomy might relieve patients of their acute depressions or psychotic obsessions, however successfully it might cure their schizophrenia, it was clear enough, neverthless, that there was a price to pay: the price of their humanity. And hence the worldwide reaction against this operation.

In fact, the effects of frontal lobe damage were known for over a century. In 1848, an accidental explosion on a Vermont railroad drove an iron bar through the left cheek and out through the front of a construction worker's skull.

His name was Phineas Cage, and he went on living with a three and a half inch tubular channel running through the frontal area of his brain And his character changed strikingly. He had been reliable, hardworking, and likeable. Afterwards his physician, Dr John Harlow, described how *the equilibrium or balance . . . between his intellectual faculties and animal propensities, seems to have been destroyed. He is fitful, irreverent, indulging at times in the grossest profanity . . . obstinate, yet capricious and vacillating . . . A child in his intellectual capacity and manifestations, he has the animal passions of a strong man.* In fact, a sort of Frankenstein's monster.

For the purposes of this report, Sir, we have made a thorough survey of human hospitals, and we find that patients who willingly enter a hospital for treatment of some physical illness cannot then be made involuntary patients: that is to say, they cannot be held against their will, even if, in the opinion of a doctor, their life is at stake. In the case of the so-called mental illnesses, however, *a voluntary patient at the hospital is as much 'confined' and has as little freedom as a mentally alert trustee in a jail or prison*: these words are taken from the 1971 decree by the Supreme Court of Utah in the USA. For it can never be known for certain whether a patient enters, or remains in hospital voluntarily, or under the threat of force by the psychiatric and legal authorities.

To be sure, Sir, there is some distinction between mind-control, as practised by terrorists or in some totalitarian countries, and treatments therapeutic in intention. However, the physical treatments given to political dissidents in police states, and to hospitalized persons who do not conform to some norms of 'mental health' in so-called free societies, is essentially the same. In so far as the so-called voluntary mental patient has a quasi-prisoner status, my reporters suspect a moral wrong reminiscent of witch-hunting.They refer to the thin line, Sir, between well-intentioned if sometimes misguided therapy, and social and political brainwashing, which usurps the human rights of the subjects, as does slavery.

They have drawn my attention, as I draw yours, Sir, to the ruthless and unnecessary misuse of these physical treatments on innocent people — electric shocks, drugs, and prefrontal leucotomy — in the Toronto hospital of Dr. Cameron, which was financed by the USA Central Intelligence Agency. That agency gave Dr. Cameron *carte blanche* to discover how political brainwashing was achieved quickly and efficiently, and failed to prevent the patients under his care from becoming his guinea-pigs. Even Dr. William Sargant, the idealistic pioneer of these methods, was so disturbed by his visit to Cameron's Institute in May 1960 that he strongly disapproved of what was being done to the patients.

(3) It is a source of concern to this Office that Nazi doctors shared these attitudes to patients in Auschwitz, Bergen-Belsen and Dachau, places that would become the testing grounds for inhuman experiments on a scale hitherto unknown. Those German doctors found comfort in the knowledge that certain eminent colleagues across the Atlantic as well as in Britain believed, for instance, that criminals were born with distinguishing physical characteristics, that they should be sterilized, confined to ghettos and allowed only to marry among themselves: and that eugenics should breed a superman of superior intelligence to control them. Dr. Cameron saw nothing wrong in such proposals, which admittedly stopped short of Hitler's Final Solution, although most of them were embodied in the Nazi Nuremberg Laws.

We need scarcely emphasize, Sir, that this Ministry has witnessed many forms of cruelty practised under a mask of moral concern either for the good of the victim or of society as a whole. We are disturbed, therefore, to discover a familiar crusading enthusiasm in many of those who see the possibilities for mind-control in the new 'treatments' of the brain — chemical, electrical and surgical, in the service of socio-political ends.

LETTER TWENTY-TWO
Ronald to Dita

Growing limbs again

Disease was the most basic ground
Of my creative urge and stress:
Creating, I could convalesce,
Creating, I again grew sound.
(God speaks these words in Heine's *Songs of Creation*)

It took years to open up the wells of my life again, as you
know. To make sense of the broken fragments of my 'I'.
An honest 'I', an authentic 'I'. Drifting in a hinterland
somewhere between a no-one and a someone, I struggled
to distinguish a bewildered 'I' from the shifting play of
roles on society's stage, which most people affected and
demanded of me. Elaborate games of masks, so it seemed.
I'd learned to play some of them back in the hospital at
St. Andrews. I remembered, and I was ashamed of, those
dozen daily little compromises, the dishonest smiles, the
small-talk to doctors and nurses that would win me their
approval, their seals of normality, their rubber-stamp of
authority to release me. When you are branded with being mentally distorted, you sniff out the comforts of 'normality' as do moles their holes, and you take refuge in
them like schoolboy toadies.

I lived in many kinds of pain, less or more consciously. A pain of bewilderment which blankets everything like that *cham sim,* the desert wind we both knew in Israel which turns sunlight black. Again, the painful feeling of having betrayed myself, of having sold my birthright for a pottage of conventional approval. A pain seared with fear, and a suffering which was secret. After all, I bore the invisible stigma of the one stigmatized legally insane by his society; and even more, the one who has had a *brain operation.* Wasn't he still the village idiot, even if the village was now global? Had his devils really been exorcized by the knife-slice through his brain?

For people's unspoken dread of mental breakdown and insanity is of a different kind from their fear of physical disease, even of epidemics like the plague or AIDS. That is why they would like to reduce it into a quasi-physical disease also, a matter of objective chemistry and brain structure, and hence make it more manageable. For all that, insanity still remains of a different order. The distortions of the mentally disturbed are distorting mirrors held up to society. At the very least they are questions, questions which exist in their own right even if you suppress and neutralize their source by declaring it 'insane': and at most they are real threats to the basic assumptions, norms and manners which make a society cohere, and against which a society closes ranks to protect itself morally and intellectually. A society has to define itself. For one society's sanity is another's insanity, and the sanity of one time and place is the insanity of another. What's considered real and what illusion varies. The spiritual upheaval I entered into, my 'vision-quest', has been far from unusual in most peoples of the world for most of its history. But it is very strange to our own materialist society and to the hierarchy of St. Andrew's, from the male nurses to the doctors, who represented that society to me as surely as the orders of clerics and priests once represented the general world-view of the mediaeval Church. I suffered in my pain and loneliness from my inability to communicate with those nurses and doctors. But then even the very *language* of any society colors and selects what it chooses to see as real. And the kinds of experience I'd been through had to be force-filtered into a vocabulary which denied them any 'objective reality', where another culture would have been more at ease with them.

Do you remember the painting of a dream I did at that time? A self-portrait with my head swathed in stained bandages? But the bandages could not contain the drippings from the wound. Bright red drops of blood seeped through the linen, down into my eyes, so I could scarcely see, and down into my mouth, so I could hardly talk: and mingling with the blood, leaked yellow-white drops of tears.

Do you remember the recurring dream from which I always awoke into a kind of paralysis of horror? I was in the hands of doctors, whose leader was recommending for me a reliable surgical procedure, that my feet and my hands and fingers be cut off one by one . . . And now I have had the first of several operations. There is no blood, no pulp of flesh, only a clean sterilized cut and a chill of horror. One of my feet has been cut off, and the doctor is saying that the next operation will be more expensive.

Expensive? Not in money. There is no doubt about the dream's meaning. My feet are my means to walk through the world, my hands and fingers to manipulate its objects. They are my instruments to reach out to people, to embrace those I hold dear, to give and to take. My most intimate tools to create, to probe, to fondle and feel. But it is my mind which needs hands and fingers to feel with, and it cannot feel without them. It is the mind which suffers when limbs are amputated. Thereby it is itself amputated.

The limbs of a tree wither without its outer sources of earth and air. But it is also dependent on its own inner sap to unfold its branches and leaves. I searched for my own earth and air, my human context of family, of community, in which I could grow, to which I could respond and become wholly myself again. But how aware I was of that human sap within myself in those lonely hours when I fought my own despair! You know about that, don't you, my love? I discovered my own tenacity, maybe inherited, maybe a legacy from my childhood and adolescence. I learned about my own persistence, again and again prodding myself out of paralysis into some creative work, which of its nature had to be done in solitude, or else into reaching out across an abyss to some person in whom I knew there was understanding. There are two different portraits of me from that time, both by Charles Lutyens, the grand-nephew of the architect Sir Edwin, with whom we shared a 'unit' when we first went to live together in the community. I look at either portrait now, the oil painted in 1964, the charcoal drawn ten years later, and I see the same determined eyes, the same obstinate thrust of chin, the same intensely pursed lips.

I had much to respond to in the community which I joined and lived in for many years: our 'chosen family'. Set apart from the usual social judgements, we had the understanding that all men are maimed in some way, and that 'normality' is a shifting mythology. We started from the fact of our own inner anxieties, and from these grew our understanding of each other and of the world outside — and with that understanding grew a language to express and to share, a language different from the usual articulateness we'd learned from schooling. We lived within an inner landscape where the norms of society were highlighted and questioned, and we learned to take each our own stand as a person within that landscape. The landmarks in that landscape differed according to our differing backgrounds, German, Czech, Irish as well as English, Christian, Jewish, Oxbridge or 'working-class', our differing personal histories, our differing professions. And the real-estate property we developed in common was merely a setting for our psychological property in common: an understanding each of his own and each of the other's predicaments.

It was living within this landscape that I rediscovered my own obscured resources, and tested abilities I no longer believed in and had to learn to believe in. The ability to give and receive love. You, especially you, know about that, don't you? Beginning with loving myself . . . The ability to compose music again. I relearned the craft — don't you remember, darling, my variations for you on the tune of *Happy Birthday* in twenty different styles, from Palestrina to Stravinsky, from Machault to Mozart, from Bach to Bartok, all such convincing forgeries! And I found my own musical voice. A voice which could be powerfully simple — how you loved my music for children, the *Basket of Eggs,* the *Streets of London, My Animals,* the opera *The Wolf of Gubbio* to Peter Porter's text.

Out of the mouths of babes and sucklings . . . *The art of children really should be taken far more seriously than are the collections of all our art museums* said Paul Klee, if we are searching for the primal bases of expression: *That is how far back we have to reach in order to avoid facile archaizing.* I worked with hundreds of children in dozens of schools through the program on the universals of music I directed for the Social Science Research Council from London University. And that was a unique elixir for turning my baser metal into gold.

The world of children I entered does have its own rites and language, which seem to be international. Nevertheless, it is an embryo of the adult world. And this foetus is not yet confined by the tangle of boundaries, the mesh of rules, the latticework of insiders and outsiders, which define the universe of adults. I mean social mores, but I also mean the canons of musical technique belonging to particular musical systems and styles. Modern broadcasting, TV, and recordings expose children to dozens of such differing musics. My quest was for the basic musical operations which underlie and form *all* musical systems, however different these may be on the surface. And I believed young children's music-making would reveal these universal operations clearly, no doubt because they were inherited, given. Noam Chomsky had parallel insights into the 'deep structure' of spoken language, as much a Babel of tongues as the musical: and I presented my work at the MIT in Boston (among many universities), where Chomsky himself was a professor. Apart from my own experience with children, I was encouraged by the school founded by Leopold Stokowski originally in New York and then moved to Santa Barbara in California, where children were free from the traditional training in the canons of one particular musical system. When I heard and saw the music they created spontaneously themselves, I was thrilled that their chants, their songs and instrumental music were all formed through the series of elementary and universal musical operations I had myself isolated in the entire history of music known to us.

It was a long journey through those landscapes: you might say, it was my own march out of the gates of my private Auschwitz, towards liberation. A strenuous journey, with my own sore and diseased limbs. And beside my own footprints in mud and snow were those of some treasured companions who supported me. But none of them so close as you . . .

But — gates of my private Auschwitz? Isn't that ridiculous? How could anyone give the same weight to these things? The Nazi concentration camp, and a prefrontal leucotomy in a mental hospital? Between a system set up to destroy for the sake of destruction, and a novel experimental system of destruction in order to heal? Of course they can't, and of course I don't. But 'the rebuilding process is the same' as Bruno Bettleheim said, himself a survivor of Dachau, whether 'the traumatization is due to the Nazi holocaust or to having been forced to exist in a most private hell.'

We each experienced, in different ways and to different degrees, a fearful isolation, a childish dependency, a systematic destruction of our beliefs and our identities, our selves and our self-respect. And we each had to learn to trust again in a world overshadowed by those different traumata. That was a learning with a backpack filled with whys — more whys, I suppose, than many other people: why did I survive Auschwitz, when my family and so many died? Why was there an Auschwitz anyway? Why did I not become a vegetable like most people who had leucotomies? Whys never to be answered conclusively. Whys which were a burden we'd often gladly have done without, wouldn't we? Except, except . . . that's who we were, darling, and in the end they turned out to be whys which made us more humane, and our lives more meaningful.

Most of life seems full of trivialities, doesn't it — shopping and cleaning and income tax and weather reports . . . And only at times do we find we've climbed some higher peaks where there's a view of a landscape of sense and value. I suppose that's the meaning of the myth of Sisyphus.

We were sometimes, a few times, on those peaks together. When we savored something very precious, all the more precious because it was salvaged. Something beyond naming: our life, our selves, our own pulsating being.

LETTER TWENTY-THREE
Dita to Ronald

The joy of living

Oh my bumblebee, you do make such a buzz with words! Just like you used to talk. But, well, you do find the honey.

Yes, of course I know what you mean. It even happened once on a literal peak — the *Mesa Verde* in the Rockies. But we could never find the right words to talk about it.

We called it sometimes — well, the sense of just being alive. But it's not 'just', it's the opposite of 'just', it's everything. Or we called it joy. Something different to pleasure. The pleasure in food or sex, satisfying an appetite. Even the wonderful pleasure in music and art — though that's closer. The joy isn't joy in anything or of anything. It's not loaded or clogged up with anything, it's not entangled with anything. It's something like fun, like play. Like children's play. It feels fantastically free. It feels that everything is all right, marvelously all right.

I used to wonder if animals could have that kind of feeling also. That was after those scientific experiments with the rats we read about: the electrodes in their medial brains, the animals pushing levers day and night to give themselves IT, some wonderful feeling, the experimenters weren't sure what it was. The fact is, the rats never sat back satisfied, like after food, but pushed their lever till they were exhausted. Could even rats be mystics in a Skinner box, we used to say! It's nonsense really. Could they be slaves to a divine experience like all the hippies and the Ginsbergs and Huxleys and Lehrers, who were then using their own levers of pot, mescalin, LSD . . . with all their senses bowled over by colors and sounds and touches like a revelation, and transported into ecstasy beyond the senses? No, that wasn't for rats, I'm sure.

But yes, you're right, it is like artist's play. Sometimes, anyway, when you break through to it, after all the work. You spoke of ecstasy from your days of solitude and monasteries. Meditation. Emptying your mind of humdrum things. But it can also come quite unexpectedly, without working for it, and without pushing any levers. Don't you remember that hazy, half-crazy, summer day in Hyde Park? The time Penny was visiting me from the States. I was in such a turmoil, you and I hardly knew each other, but should I give up my job and all my life and friends in New York to come to live with you in London? And work with Kay, bringing up the camp and all that terrible pain again? I looked down at the number tattooed on my arm, then overhead where the branches of leaves were swaying like sails in the breeze, and I just dozed off in the deckchair. Well, really, maybe it was more like a trance. And then there was IT. THAT. Out of the blue. A wonderful and oh! so tranquil sense of being alive. Of joy . . . Intense. Calming. And then I just took your hand and pressed it. Remember? You must remember that.

When I was sick with the cancer and thought of my dying, I sometimes remembered that feeling, like the taste of a very pure juice I'd once drunk but I couldn't quite recall. A memory buried somewhere even inside my tumors, inside my fevers. And I even thought that if dying would give me that, then dying wouldn't be so bad.

But about the levers . . . The drug thing. We were both skeptical, weren't we? Escape, trips. Reckless, unreal. The most addictive thing in the world, the easy way out of the world, like the rats transcending their Skinner box. And really dangerous too, damage to the brain. This was brought home to us, quite literally, in the community, when Frank's son Luke became hooked. Don't you remember how shocked we were one evening, leaving the Underground at Piccadilly Circus, to see Luke doped and dazed leaning against the tiled wall with other addicts? It went on for years, it ruined his life, in and out of detention and treatment centers, prisons really ...

I think we each had terrible things happen to us, but I also think we've been lucky.

LETTER TWENTY-FOUR
Ronald to Dita

Communities I lived in

We met in the CHOFA community, *Ditukam*, our 'chosen family', we married within it, we lived our life together in it, and you died there, metaphorically in the arms of the community as well as literally in mine.

But I myself also had a long history of living in other communities of one kind or another. Most of my adult life had been a search for a community in which I could live a whole life, and overcome the fragmentation I experienced within myself, and my aloneness in trying to become whole. Since my own fragmentation was a sensitized mirror of the fragmented society of the modern western world, you could say I was a victim of that society, as you were a victim of a political movement which tried to overcome it.

It was the life-blood of the CHOFA community we lived in to open ourselves to change. We lived squarely inside the modern world, its problems and the marks it made on us were our daily bread. But it was not surprising, was it, that the first communities to which I was orientated — the monasteries, Eric Gill's community at Piggotts, the Taena community, were all in fact artificial and deliberate recreations of past societies. They had reversed the direction of their clocks, and they nestled within bygone traditions which they highly idealized, paradises lost and now to be regained: mediaeval monasticism, the mediaeval craftsman, the pre-industrial village.

I was looking for myself, and for my communities, in that dislocated twilight time which stretches from the late teens into the late twenties. There was for me no clear social rite of transition into the adult world, such as boys in primitive societies undergo with so much fear and awe. My growing pains were solitary, and the communities I sought out were also sequestered from the world and marginal to the then 'society-at-large'. There were many such communities springing up in the late fifties and throughout the sixties, on both sides of the Atlantic, filled with young people in some kind of rebellion and seeking alternative styles of living. You knew some of that generation in New York yourself, didn't you? So that although my own experiences seemed to be a personal volcano in a personal landscape, yet, with hindsight, they also belonged to the wider vistas of the rebellion of youth in Western society, from California to New England, from Berkeley University to the Sorbonne in Paris.

Many of these new communities gave political thought and action a pride of place. In this they were reflecting our century as a whole, with its Marxist and Communist Utopian visions igniting countries in every continent of the globe, its Mao and Castro and Che Guevara, its Falangist *Long Live Death* in Franco's Spain, its German Reich of a thousand years in Nazi Germany . . . But in spite of my earlier communism, I believed that political vision was only one dimension of life, and certainly not its main axis. And the succession of communities I lived in reflected a journey to find that axis within my own psyche.

It proved to be a circular journey, in retrospect, as were the quests of mythical heros. First phases upwards, into mountains and rarified air, later phases down again into the human turmoil of the valleys from where I'd started.

My dreams are a record of that reversal. Dreams of descent. I was a skier down the frozen slopes of a mountain, which turned to a luxuriant green nearer its base. Green for fertility. Or I was a pilot bringing in a plane to land, out of a blaze of sunlight, which turned into the artificial necklaces of a city's lights glowing in the night. And people waiting to greet me, people in need of each other, even, it seemed, of me.

My first communities were monastic and austere. Parkminster, a Carthusian order: a long period at Aylesford in Kent, and then again at the Carmel monastery in Lyons in France. Aylesford had been the site where St. Simon Stock had founded the first Carmelite house in England six centuries earlier. It was dominated by the missionary fire, which I resented, of the Irish priest Malachy Lynch, who clearly identified himself with his ancestors who had once carried 'the Faith' back across barbarian Europe to Rome itself. I have a clear picture of him like a modern Noah on a man-made raft of an ark, literally riding the flood when the river Medway overflowed its banks, rescuing people, pigs, and hens marooned on the upper floors of the buildings and the hillocks around. The same river had just turned as red as the Red Sea: but the cause was waste from a dye factory, and not the Hand of his Lord . . . I went to the Carmel in Lyons at the invitation of a Jewish convert from South Africa, Friedman, who was en route for Mount Carmel in Israel — Lyons was the center of the ancient French 'province', and in our Carmel we lavishly entertained the Cardinal Archbishop 'Primate of Gaul'. His Palace was on the top of Fourvières, the old Roman forum which dominated Lyons. On Easter eve I accompanied Friedman to that same Fourvières into a women's Carmelite Convent — a very rare thing for a man who was not a priest to do. Friedman officiated at the Holy Saturday rites for the nuns, and the fire leapt and danced to his chanting, the primitive god which had been tamed. At the University I learned from Gelin about the pre-Christian Jewish communities he called *Les Pauvres de Jahweh;* and from Henri de Lubac — as later from Teilhard de Chardin, a far-flung vision of religion which belied the narrow sense into which the word Catholic had become confined.

Within the *couvent*, the daily two hours of silent meditation made me realize that the leuchotomy had not damaged within me that precious power of 'contemplation'.

Steps of the ziggurat, rungs of Jacob's ladder, ascending chakra centers of Buddhism, progressive 'mansions' of the Carmelite Teresa of Avila — call them what you like, they describe the same experiences. Time and again I entered what Teresa described as the 'fifth mansion'. Metaphors just stammer . . . I imagined entering into a cavern containing an immeasurable underground lake, drinking its indescribably sweet waters, which overwhelmed me with a sense of relief and peace, with a kind of concentrate or essence of compassion. In the everyday world, that concentrate is always diluted and polluted.

But that world jolted back, and with it my search for a community.

Piggots was a community of artists living in the shadow of Eric Gill. Gill had followed in the footsteps of William Morris, and like him idealized a pre-industrial culture of craftsmen, and a mediaeval village of universal faith and ritual which conveniently overlooked its hatreds and its outbreaks of witch-hunting. Eric Gill was a potent charismatic cocktail. On the one hand he believed in the grand hierarchy of the universe, visible and invisible, and he expressed this in his monumental and impersonal sculpture — over the BBC building, for instance, or his *Stations of the Cross* in the Byzantine edifice of Westminster Cathedral. In person, on the other hand, sandaled, smocked and red-bearded, he tyrannized anyone who disagreed with him and demanded that even his son-in-law call him Master. He committed incest with his sisters all through his life, abused his own daughters and the wives of his friends under the very eyes of his wife, and expected every model to sleep with him.

At that time I responded to his idealism, to his condemnation of the enslavement of men by machines because of the profit motive, or of the way culture had become something 'added like a sauce to otherwise unpalatable fish', and the artist a fantasy-ridden hermit or a pet of the rich. I too longed for a community where the creativity of every member is valued, and not only 'fine art'. You remember we were in Bali, don't you? On the way back from Sydney — they'd just extended the airstrip, and ours was among the first big jets to land. Before the coral beach became a parade of luxury hotels. You were actually in tears when we talked of how this living mosaic of culture was about to be destroyed by tourism. The Balinese people have no word for 'artist', everyone is an artist in Gill's sense of 'maker of things' as in his Utopian mediaeval world, not just the musicians, dancers and painters.

There were a number of antecedents for Gill's communities, like Abramtsevo in Russia on the industrialist Mamontov's estate, established in 1874. And Princess Tenisheva also set up an artists colony modeled on Abramtsevo on her estate at Talishkino, near Smolensk, in 1893. But one important modern English offshoot was the Taena community in the Cotswolds, where I went to live for three years.

The Taena community, like Gill's, also tried to build for itself a time-capsule from the past. It truncated itself, as far as it could, from the modern world outside, with all its competitiveness and racing technology, and returned to farming the land and living close to the natural seasons. Like the Gill community, it had many artistic people — George an architect; the bearded gruff Cornishman Douglas, a sculptor; gentle Lou and Margaret, both potters; John Crocket, painter and theater director; Ronald, a man of letters and music — and it had a hankering too, in the footsteps of William Morris, for an idealized mediaeval past.

I first heard of Taena from Bede Griffiths, when I stayed at the Benedictine monastery at Farnborough where he was a monk. He had a simple breadth of vision: he was a student of yoga, and he would found an ashram in India where he would live until his death in May 1993, revered by many young people from the time of the 'hippies' to the New Age. In his book *The Golden Thread,* which he was writing at that time, he described the parallel experiences of the major religions. Another leading light of Taena was Sri Aurobindo, the Cambridge revolutionary turned mystic, who also founded an ashram. His writings influenced us at Taena; among them, for example, his vision of God as Mother, the feminine power which could transform the strife and over-rationality of a patriarchal world. The midwife of Taena, so to speak, was the Jungian analyst Tony Süssman, with whom its leader George had worked: and Jung's teaching of the universality of the numinous archetypes which lie beyond religious dogma fertilized the soil in which Taena grew.

In Taena we tried to set back by centuries the hands of our clocks; to immerse ourselves in those rhythms of seasons and animals which the galloping growth of artifice and technology had obscured. We sought to compensate for the scientific intellectual objectivity which had split and desacralized both men and nature. That hard-edged objectivity, clinically sterile, whose abstract face is the plastic and stainless steel of the modern city: that objectivity which had estranged us from the organic stuff of birth and decay, which is smelly and slimy and sticky, like the sweat or semen or excreta of our own bodies, which had become despicable.

Taena had been founded by a group of pacifist conscientious objectors during the Second World War, who were allowed to farm the land as their war service, and it had developed into a community of families with their children, and several single people. It was loosely attached to the Benedictine Abbey of Prinknash, just up and over the hills, and sometimes Abbot Upton came down to eat with us, a man whose down-to-earth wide range of talk belied his single and simple inner eye. We met to recite the 'offices' — of psalms and readings from the Bible — which followed the sun and punctuated our day as they had done the Benedictine monks' for many centuries. Yet to these we added regular periods of silent meditations as in an Indian ashram.

However, like the Gill community, and like a hundred other communities across the USA which had turned their backs on the modern world, Taena relied on electricity for everything from lightbulbs to the latest milking-machines for the cows, and bought its food in the town, using the amenities of high technology while at the same time condemning its effects. Our concern for 'ecology' (the word was hardly known then) would become fashionable and worldwide two decades later.

We were mostly of middle-class backgrounds, and some even from top private schools, as George Orwell had been, although at that time Ron made a point of deliberately destroying his Christ's Hospital accent with coarse, if musical, diphthongs. (That would become usual in the sixties, and still later merge into the 'radical chic'). But of different background was Robert, a *house* painter, or Richard, a stooping gauche man of a childlike trust who was doomed to die young of uric acid poisoning in his blood. That was one of several tragedies which we shared. Connie, George's wife, would die of cancer, as would Sean. And Ron and Hilary's first-born pink-cheeked Ben would be killed in a tractor accident.

Inevitably, Taena was a tiny world, putting back its clock, radically limited by its isolation. The exigencies of milking cows and farming cut me off from my musical creativity, even, paradoxically, from the richness of human relations too — because the idealism and the rules by which we lived could obstruct them. So that when out of the blue, Carmella walked through my cowsheds, my daily environment, dark-haired and dark-eyed, she became my Beatrice to lead me back into the creative hell of the larger world. It was she who first introduced me to Kay and to the community in London growing up around her in which you and I would one day live together.

I remember the day when my mother arrived without warning to see how I was living, driven by her chauffeur in the Daimler through the cow dung on the farmtrack.

She'd kept her distance, allowing me my own life, though a distance still limited by the beating of a mother's heart. In World War Two she'd fought her own war to preserve the family — and within it myself, snatched from her by the alien authorities of the English public school system: it was a war she'd lost. She'd tried to bridge the distance to Oxford bearing the gift of a fur for my mistress Margaret, and the surprising olive-branch that she could become my wife, though non-Jewish. She'd appeared suddenly at the Carmelite monastery at Aylesford. Always waiting in the wings, she'd been called to the Cistercians at Caldey to take charge of her severely disturbed son, and then, cruelly, had agreed to a brain operation. Once, when I talked of my loneliness without a woman, she offered to give herself to me, her body, if she could. My father sat in silence between us, at the dinner table. I did dream of her naked once, and I was whipping her with hatred, not desire. An Oedipal dream? But what I'd always wanted from her was not her body, but an *understanding* of my own concerns, so different from hers. And now she was at the Taena community, trying again, and failing, to understand this complete *bouleversement* of my life: rich into poor, urban comforts into country roughness, Marlborough and Oxford into milking cows, intellectual into manual, prestigious into humble, Jewish into apparently non-Jewish. And it was unbearably painful for her.

A week later, 'There's a little parcel for you,' said Lou. The huge package was taller than myself. It was a giant and expensive radiogram (so-called then, before the days of hi-fi): like a monument, really, of her caring for me, but grotesque in the circumstances.

And the day I left Taena, likewise, she sent the Daimler and the chauffeur for me. After three years, I stepped literally and abruptly out of the dung of the cowshed into its luxury leather and plush. I did wipe my feet first, but this was not to wipe off my past. These were the first of many steps, not into luxury, but back onto the streets of the everyday world I'd turned my back on.

I can see what I had in common with the hippies and the beatniks of the following decade. Nevertheless, that counterculture, as it came to be called, stole from the establishment against which it rebelled not only its electricity and its motor engines, but also its fast-food, quick-fix, high-stimulus mentality. It needed mescalin or other drugs for its psychedelic ecstacies. It was impatient with the lackluster drabness of life which stretched between the fixes, the troughs for which religious disciplines were once developed. Therefore it lapsed easily into the cynicism of the Seventies. Thrown back on itself, it became dependent on 'kicks' or 'experience'. In *Howl*, Allen Ginsberg wrote compassionately:

> I saw the best minds of my generation destroyed by madness, starving hysterical naked,
> dragging themselves through the negro streets at dawn looking for an angry fix,
> angelheaded hipsters burning for the ancient heavenly connection to the starry dynamo in the machinery of night . . .

The counterculture rebelled against all social authority and mores, almost indiscriminately, without replacing them: what would become of the difference then between the saint and the criminal? It wanted to destroy structures, but that would have destroyed every kind of society, even an anarchist society. The counterculture was swallowed into mass merchandizing and 'radical chic'; and its protests into its own psychedelic drug-taking.

A violent outcome was predictable. The riots on the streets of Western cities were contemporary with the Red Guard Terror in China, the other side of Maoist idealism: so had the French Revolution begotten its own Terror, as had the Bolshevik in Russia. Mick Jagger (my neighbor in London) and the Rolling Stones advocated violence in the sixties (as in their *Street Fighting Man*), in contrast to the flower-power of the Beatniks. Their music festival at Altamont near Berkeley became a riot: a black man pointed a gun at Jagger, the Hell's Angels stabbed him to death, three more people died and hundreds were injured.

The Beatles, in contrast, ignored the shadow side of their idealized LOVE which in *The Yellow Submarine* (a favorite anthem or hymn of the counterculture) magically transformed the evil blue Meanies into wonderfully luxuriant flowers — but all in the twinkle of an eye. A childlike twinkle which was the prerequisite of the quick-fix culture. Yet neither the Beatniks, nor the Meanies, nor anybody else can be transformed instantaneously.

If at all.

It wasn't that easy . . . My epitaph, you remember? It just wasn't that easy . . .

LETTER TWENTY-FIVE
Dita to Ronald
The spider's web

I've a vivid childhood memory — I must have been four or five — of being fascinated by a spider's web being woven between two corner tendrils outside my window. I watched the spider working at it, glinting silver in the sunlight. It didn't hesitate, it was never in doubt. I was amazed how the design grew so large and so intricate, but through the same simple back-and-forth motion, repeated over and over again. Something so simple growing — by repetition — into something so big and wonderful. It reminded me of my mother's intricate necklace — also glittering, which was formed by graded loops of pearls nesting inside each other, and joined together by a jewelled line on her breast, just like the 'lateral' of the spider's web.

The fly I remember was tiny, a baby. It struggled to free itself from the sticky web in spurts of desperation which became fewer and more feeble as I watched. Yes, I did watch, *édesem,* and I remember the feeling like horror. But I only watched the spider's first bite . . .

In a very vague way, I believed as a child that there was a good and wonderful God. That's the general sense of what I was taught — by my mother especially. And I could apply his wonderfulness easily enough to the wonderland of designs that delighted me everywhere. But about his goodness I had doubts. Serious doubts, for a child. Like the time my Suzie was butchered by the wheels of a car. Suzie my gray striped cat who came and went so independently and proudly, whose green eyes understood me when I talked to her (Suzie in Israel, nearly twenty years later, was called after her). I never thought about the red pieces of meat in the butcher's shop. But when I saw my beautiful and nuzzling Suzie's insides squashed and red and spread over the street . . . that was unimaginable horror.

I suppose every child paints its own picture-book of the wonderland of designs. And it gets mutilated. It gets blotched and blackened. That's part of growing up, isn't it?

But not so brutally as my picture-book was mutilated.

Do you still have my little sketchbook with the maroon cover? My portfolio of colored drawings? They might have been left lying on the red lino worktop under the skylight in my tiny studio next to the bedroom where I died. Or maybe in Fulbourne, in our *Rosemullion Cottage* with its tangles of wild flowers which were themselves as old as the cottage, all of three centuries, and maybe much older.

You know, don't you, my darling, what that sketching meant for me. Perhaps escape, a kind of refuge. But really I was trying to discover once again the picture-book of my lost childhood. That little sketch-book helped me breathe again.

You were always more abstract, weren't you? Of course I was fascinated also when you showed me — so excitedly — how the same 'operations' (as you called them) worked in the designs of nature, of art, as they did in music. *Repetition:* petal-shapes, the spirals of chestnut flowers, the angles of the veins of a leaf, the hexagonal cells of a honeycomb. *Centering:* the petals of a sunflower or rose opening and closing around the heart of its calyx; the arms of a starfish; the bird's nest; the spider's web.

Transposition: branches, leaves, the clusters of flowers or fruit, all transposed in space so variously to form the different beauties of trees. *Inversion:* leaf veins again; the rich designs on butterfly wings mirrored in symmetry; in fact symmetries as common as peas in a pod — birds' wings, deer's antlers, all the bodies of fish and animals and ourselves . . . These were like universal principles. You were always seduced by universals.

But really I was more concerned to capture on paper the magic of things before they disappeared, things that were always changing and different from moment to moment. How a particular petal was bending over. How a specific leaf was curling. The way a stalk was swaying in the breeze. Every grain and every texture was *special,* skin or scale, husk or peel. Universal principles or no, what I wanted to sketch was each time unique. And it was a unique rapport between the leaf or petal or grain and myself who was discovering it. Oh, so much *wonder,* such fascination, such entrancement, that was my way to unearth and reopen the private wonderland picture-book of my childhood . . .

LETTER TWENTY-SIX
Ronald to Dita

The community we lived in together

Do you remember my God of Excreta, a god who haunted my madness? The God of everything repulsive, overlooked or thrown out. With whom I wanted to become one, by ritual communion? A sane insanity, after all. Truth in madness. The traditional God of Shit is He who cared for the despised and rejected, for the buried and unfulfilled: and this peculiar care was a more valuable attribute than His much blazoned omniscience and omnipotence and so forth, which allow the amazing processes of particles and stars and organisms to unfold, breathtaking beyond belief, yet remote from the cages of our own predicaments and touching us little in our day by day struggles and lovings and blockages?

That was the attractive thing about the CHOFA community we lived in, and you died in: it cared about the *shit*. About wasteland which could be reclaimed. About what was disregarded and discarded by our mothers and fathers and families, and by the societies we grew up and worked in. And about what we abhored and spurned ourselves within our own psyches.

It tried to do that, even when it failed. And both its success and its failure had much to do with Kay, her mag-

netism, her penetrating intuitions as a therapist, but also
with her own personal problems and ambitions which
were never fully worked out within her, and so were
played out in the arena of all our lives. But how can we
talk easily of her who in a sense both made us and ruined
us? Even after her death, the strength we found in our
own fibers without her presence derived from insights
and training she herself had given us. She had inspired
our communal living in the first place, starting from the
simple question: *Can people really live together?* But *really* live together, that is closely and nakedly? Without
subterfuge, without the masks of idealism and of abstract
common causes. Therefore the means to answer this question lay not in political activity, but in the new insights of
psychology. She spoke of our being 'revolutionaries, yes,
but of men' — not of political and social institutions. We
did, in fact, develop outward forms of living together,
didn't we — 'units' of families and single persons sharing kitchen and bathroom, common rooms, 'playrooms'
for the children. But these ways of living never became
institutionalized. We remained particular persons living
together, and the nerve center of that living, the psychological axis, the hub of any practical problems, was always 'therapy'. *Therapon* was a powerful word for the
ancient Greeks, much more than our *therapy* today. A
therapon was both friend and servant, someone who gave
understanding and advice in troubles, took risks for his
friends even to the point of death. We tried to be *therapons*
to each other, unravelling threads of our histories and
problems in one-to-one sessions, in the weekly psychological groups, in the special mini-groups formed to explore and resolve the tensions within a single 'unit' of
living: even when we met on the stairs or in each other's
kitchens.

There was no question about Kay's charisma, was
there? We were both irradiated and burned by her presence, what she herself called 'being-there', or 'da-sein'.
Years before we met her, in Berlin, before she'd fled to
Israel, she'd been an actress. I think she'd acquired then a

repertory of facial expressions, secret tricks of the trade. Yet the face we knew was hardly an act. It expressed her vitality, her awareness, her genuine concern. Eyes piercing or reflective, a compelling or coquettish smile, head bent sideways and upwards. Words sometimes as quick as darts, although English was her learned language: but most typically she stretched out her words so that they stretched you with them, like a rack. They were sticky like a spider's web. Life-enhancing, or a trap? They were both. Of course she'd had her share of psychological training — originally with Anna Freud: but her therapy was a hit-or-miss art, her insights intuitive, but she voiced them with a force not easily resisted. The atmosphere was hazy with her own illusion that she was just one equal voice among the rest of us. In reality, she had to know and dominate everything: and that was the flaw she would never admit to herself or to us.

Kay had been married to a Jew, and was passionately concerned about Israel, where she had lived, as a refugee from Nazi Germany, and raised her children. The daughter of a Protestant minister, she had become a Catholic. I was attracted to the way she brought together both Jewish and Christian traditions with modern psychology. The target of her therapy was an 'authentic' person, born inevitably in anxiety or *angst*, who could find their own voice and life. She brought round the concept of *angst* a full circle in its meaning. For Kierkegaard originally, *angst* could recall us to a life lived in a relationship with God. Without that relationship, *angst* serves to remind us of the agony of existence in a world from which God is absent. But for Kay the realization of our personal freedom was always a paradox because it was dependent not only on other human beings, but on an unknown God. 'I am not my own Creator' was one of her refrains. And as for Kierkegaard, religion had to be rescued from the encrustations of its official guardians. In this, she was reflecting the Protestantism of her father. But we all had a variety of backgrounds and beliefs. Sometimes we read together the Old or New Testaments (as we did authors as diverse as Erich Fromm or Teilhard de Chardin — you remember?), we explored interpretations which were windows on our personal problems and relationships.

In a prominent position on her desk Kay placed a signed photo of Cardinal Bea he'd given her. Bea was the leader and inspiration of the Vatican Secretariat which officially opened the musty doors of the Church to the truths in other religions in its 1965 Declaration, but in particular sought to undo the savage injustice of centuries by removing its absurd charge of guilt upon all Jews of all time for the crucifixion of Jesus, and by changing the insidious teaching and liturgy which spoke of the perfidious Jews. What Bea was doing on the world stage of history, opening the way to a genuine understanding between peoples of different backgrounds and traditions, Kay thought she was doing concretely in miniature, person to person. For in fact, as she stressed, neither the Jewish nor Christian traditions had ever demanded universal love of 'humankind', but rather of flesh and blood individuals.

Our visitors frequently reflected Kay's preoccupations: the Benedictine Abbot of Jerusalem; Victor White, the Dominican author of *Soul and Psyche* (a disciple of Jung, with a crucial difference: if a patient saw a pink elephant, or a pink cherub, it mattered to Victor whether the elephant — or cherub — existed); Bruno Hussar, the Jewish Christian who established the center in Ein Kerem where Jews and Arabs could mingle as friends; Ivan Illich, with his profound sense of 'conviviality', and of the ways in which technology becomes self-defeating; R.D. Laing, who listened to madness and was himself thought mad by his colleagues.

I went to live in the CHOFA community in 1958, two years before we met. Different men and women had become associated through their work with Kay, but what they all had in common was a search for some value in their lives which they had failed to find elsewhere. This was not a 'religious' search in any narrow sense of the word. The members had a variety of backgrounds, Chris-

tian, Jewish, agnostic, but very little formality of alle-
giance. They knew that they didn't know, as Kay said. It
was in 1963 that we decided to live together literally, under the same roof, and we moved from a number of separate apartments into the big adjacent houses where you
and I spent our married life. The architects among us
joined the houses together with extensions to form a single complex, comprising the unit apartments and common rooms we needed to reflect our lifestyle. Together
we watched the separate gardens bury their fences beneath a single quilt of grass bordered with flowerbed and
paving-stone, even transforming that corner heap of
builders' rubble into the gracious curves of a mini-mound.
If you only saw what your eyes saw, it was just another
'housing development' in a 'desirable area', a smallish
one at that. It had taken a year to track down these houses,
hunting in pairs through the London labyrinthe. How did
we pay for them? With a mortgage. We were young and
searching, our careers were fluid. When Kay died in 1973
— eight years before you did, my dear, we were seventy-
seven people, including thirty-six children. Many of us
would make our mark: directing the building of a nuclear power station, for example; or a petro-chemical company; or one of the leading publishing houses; or giving
away the British Empire, as we joked — Roy prepared
the independence agreements for the Commonwealth
Office; or conceiving and producing renowned original
television programs; one of us was a well-know actor who
played in the première of John Osborne's *Look Back in
Anger* at the Royal Court Theater, and later in Peter
Brook's improvised reflection of the sixties, *USA;* another
actor among us premièred Edward Albee's *The Zoo Story*
at the Arts Theater; there was a leading engineer who
became a therapist; a nurse; two professional artists; several teachers from primary school to University level.

'Concerned, caring, sharing, committed' and so on:
words meaningful forty years ago which have now been
cheapened by popular psychology, and sensational chats
on TV. So many words which for us are the shells of once

breathing creatures. We know that we can never trans-
late into words our own experiences of the groups. They
are part of our secret, as all the members of that community carry the secret of their own experiences, and each
one's experience is different. Quantitatively, I suppose you
and I have taken part in about one thousand psychological groups at CHOFA: and myself without you, before you
came to England and after your death, perhaps fifteen
hundred. The quantity in itself tells little, except the passing of the years. The clock-hours have nothing to do with
understanding — understanding of the damage in ourselves and in others, of our burdens, of the problems of
trusting, of authority, of competition, of careers, of sex.
Understanding of the pain and problems of an individual
or a relationship, reflected in the mirror of the group, leading into unsuspected awareness of ourselves and of each
other. Sometimes with anger, with resistance. In the end,
the groups were cleansing, as well as revealing, as well
as reconciling. In the blood-families we were born into,
such clarification was rarely possible.

I think of days, hours even, dense with the inner
events of relationships, both ongoing and new: relationships with each other, between parents as parents,
between parents and children, among the children
themselves — for every problem is a family problem of
some kind: and also our relationships with those not
actually present, I mean with our own parents and
blood-families, some of them dead — in the lives of
several people like yourself with the brutally murdered; and we tried to clarify our lives as we lived
them together, as we had lived them in the past, and
also as we were living them outside of CHOFA too,
among other friends or professional colleagues.We got
to know each other more intimately than is usually
meant by that word. Living together day by day with
the purpose of exploring beneath the surface. If there
was an outburst, what lay behind it? Why did we often
resist becoming closer? We got to know the real geog-
raphy of a person: high tides of buoyancy, depressions

in which we can no longer see our own values. We tried to care for each other as we really were, in our struggles and aspirations, not for the mask we thought we were or would like to have been. That honesty, in the end, was the only glue that held us close together — a psychological glue, not one simply of shared possessions or interests. That was all the *work* (as we called it) which was lifeblood for both you and me, each of us a destroyed person.

Kay had been fascinated by the kibbutzim in Israel: and one of her sibylline sayings was that we were building up the person and not the land, which had been the basic need of the kibbutzim. If we were 'revolutionaries of persons, and not of society', then the way into real communication with one another began with the way into ourselves. In her own words, 'the inner noise had to become audible.' Again, 'the question Who am I? alternated with the question Who are you?: and by a to-and-fro between these questions, a 'we' is created, and within this 'we' is contained my weaknesses and strengths, and yours.' And it was this 'we', based on mutual *under*-standing (her stress, again), which was the basis for a life together rather than any oughts or shoulds or ideals. It had nothing to do with any kind of institution, any external command or prohibition. 'The 'we' embraced a community of differences — in age or development, in gifts or education, in profession or income, in religion. And when a person realizes his own true value, these differences do not lead to destructive competitiveness.'

So-called 'mental illness' is always related to the ever fluctuating norms of a society. To use again Kay's words, 'we were as well or as ill as society is today — but with this difference: that we faced our illness.' Whatever that might be. We never gave the concept of 'mental illness' a chance to become a tool to reify a person as a case or object, at the expense of the person.

You didn't know Jane Flower: she died before you joined the community, before you and I met. She had Huntington's chorea, an inherited and terrible disease to live with, because you watch helplessly as the brain and its faculties waste away, and like Altzheimers or muscular dystrophy, it is incurable. Jane played the piano and had been a school teacher. When I first saw her, the disease had already made its cruel inroads into the coherence of her speech, into the coordination of her movements. But there was still a *person* there, and that person we involved in every way we could, calling her out continually without any mollycoddling, to fight against her fear or apathy, to express her angers. And to the wonder of physicians, the disease was arrested for several years. Jane was for us a paradigm of the power of human relationship over a diseased brain.

And myself? Why didn't I become a kind of quiescent vegetable as did the majority of victims of prefrontal leucotomy? I revived and was revived, and meanwhile I imagine that my brain must have re-routed some of its million-fold circuits, perhaps taken over other synaptic trails as new thoroughfares for its mutilated functions; or even, like the insects and reptiles who grow new limbs to replace their lost ones, it may have repaired its severed communication lines with new brain-cells. These are all plausible theories in what still remains a dark area of knowledge. But the only truth clear to me in that dark time, the only truth which I had to accept, was that incisions had been made through the prefrontal lobes of my brain, that area which is the seat of human foresight, creativity and responsibility; that the damage done might have permanently impaired the faculties which made me particularly human and, above all, particularly me; that I had no way of ever knowing what I might have been without those incisions; that what I was now, after those incisions, was all I had to start with.

In a dark time, the eye begins to see . . . My life grew along with my neuron circuits. I became a loving human being among a surrogate family who knew who I was and what was the road I had traveled, and why. Who sang my music too, from nursery rhymes to motets and settings of Rilke or Teilhard de Chardin. Whose children I loved and scolded and worried over as if my own flesh. Children for whom I wrote music-dramas, especially for them to perform together (I felt a kind of betrayal when one of them was later televised on the BBC), for whom I composed their own tailor-made private piano pieces and duets when I gave them lessons. I would later become a composer, a university professor and a researcher. But the music-making of those years was my seed-bed and greenhouse.

The community had its share of natural catastrophes — two deaths from cancer before your own, my love, and another one since. But we had our failures and drop-outs too. You and I experienced the wrench in our own 'unit', when Jim and Jacqueline with their two children left CHOFA altogether, after our living together with them for almost as long as our entire marriage. You remember the months of unresolved tensions between us, which the mini-groups could not resolve? There was another unit which also fell apart. And, six years after you died, Daniel committed suicide, after years of fighting his depressions. In the empty unit, while Margot was away. A suicide quiet and even tactful, infuriatingly tactful, as Daniel well knew how to be in his social life. And a bitter defeat, of himself, of his wife and children, of all of the community! For all our understanding of his depression and its psychological origins — that murder of his family by the Nazis when he was a child, his suicide remains a cruel rejection of his wife, above all, but of the rest of us too who were his friends in a sense rarely to be experienced. For some, this way of living was a solution and a success: for others it did not work.

And we come back again to Kay, and to her charisma which was a double-edged sword. For she was herself a victim of her own charisma, of her own special powers. Why did she have to play so dominating a role in groups, rarely contradicted? Why did she come to be jealous of every relationship in which she did not figure as the primary instigator. Why did she develop so exclusive an 'inner circle' of confidants? Why did some of the children so resent her fascination, why did they feel that their own sense of themselves in their own family was denied them when their parents returned from groups and seemed aligned against them? Why did some parents, too, feel that they had denied their own authority with their own children in this way?

Let me tell you what I think. Kay felt deeply for the risk of our lives after we had bought the common houses and committed ourselves. The reason why she intervened more and more in the details of our lives was in order to ensure the success of our 'experiment in living together', which she had initiated and for which she felt totally responsible. Yet she was mistaken in these feelings; we were more capable without her than she gave us credit for. She overemphasized her own importance and thereby diminished her own importance. You and I were aware of this, weren't we — as we all were. It was in spite of her, as well as because of her, that we wove the richness of our personal lives in and out of the common life.

Do you remember the first shockwaves on that day when we were sitting by our kitchen window, the beech tree outside silhouetted against hazy clouds, when Nigel came from downstairs with the news that Kay had died? It was as if a magnetic pole of our world had disappeared — even though we'd talked of her death, all together with her, in groups, more than once.

Now we had to cement the process of distancing ourselves from her personal power — and yet preserve our gratitude for all that she had inspired. Some of us had to work through resentments we had harbored against her but not expressed. Some felt they had prostituted themselves to her for a love they had been deprived of all their lives. Some felt they had betrayed friends by leaving them undefended against Kay's sometimes misplaced anger. We began groups again, but without her leadership. And what is remarkable, without any leader at all. We had the means and the insight, which she had given us. And the groups have continued for the twenty years since her death, without her, as has the community. We accomplished the difficult task of demythologizing Kay without discrediting her rare healing touch.

CHOFA was our cocoon, into which we came out of our different catastrophes. You were 'hatched' out of that cocoon into a premature death: myself into another form of life, outside. Yet I reconnect easily with that community family because of the history of shared life and intimate exchange: a life which seems to have been cut out of the cloth of my own soul.

Recently I dreamed of a lovely enclosure, and I knew it was the CHOFA community. There was a crystal stream, and lots of chattering children playing beside it. Children mean fresh and open eyes on life, don't they? A gray-haired man appeared who confirmed to me that the ground was rich in very valuable archaeological things. I felt very contented. I knew that many strata of wealth lay in that community ground, veins of gold, and that they could be mined for the rest of my life.

LETTER TWENTY-SEVEN
Dita to Ronald

Community life

Daniel's suicide shocked me very deeply. He too came from Czechoslovakia, like Jan and Frank. So there were four of us in the community who sometimes spoke Czech with each other and had some feelings of belonging through language and nationality, although we were so different, and I don't mean just Bohemian-Moravian-Slovak. The others had escaped the concentration camps. But their parents and families had been murdered by the Nazis. They had their own ways of coping with what could not be coped with. Daniel himself was haunted by his depressions. I recognized them although he hid them, and I was frightened by them, because I knew there was something inside me to resonate, something deeply painful, dark and bewildered. Beneath the surface you knew and loved which, in some ways like Daniel's, could be bubbly and warm and outgoing (and how warm he was to you, his *Ronniebach!*). Not that I had anything of his finesse of words, his fabric of charm that was so skillful as well as so disarming. He was a victim himself, he was himself sucked into a vortex he couldn't control. And it's my fate to understand that vortex only too well. As you have said yourself, darling, wasn't my own cancer also a vortex, a physical one, a similar legacy from the Nazis, hiding behind all the rest of my life, lying in ambush for its own hour to strike and finally triumph?

There are wounds which are too terrible to heal, which must remain open. I know that, and I've lived with that knowledge. I've been lucky with therapists, and I've been lucky with a rich life and with loving friends, luckier than many other survivors, I suppose. But therapy has only made me aware of my wounds. It has helped me live with them, that's all. I say 'that's all', and it sounds belittling . . . But that 'all' is a very big 'all' indeed, a huge 'all', the 'all' of an all or nothing situation, life or death. I mean that the popular idea is that you dig It all up and then you experience the terrible pain, and then you are *cured.* Once and for all, *cured.* Like an inflamed appendix that's been removed. But you know, or you know if you've been through the Nazi camps, you just can't be cured of some wounds.

If it had not been for Daniel, you and I would never have met. I visited him in London because I knew his sister in New York, and that is how I met you, and Kay, and everyone else around her. And it was through that meeting that I gave up my New York fizzy jazz world, Riverside records, all my friends, the lot. Not only because of you, *édesem,* but because CHOFA took the lid off questions about what mattered, and seemed to promise me some meaning for all I'd been through. But Daniel was the first link.

Yes, our groups always turned out to be worthwhile, though I was often fearful and reluctant to begin, as were many of us. There was no way we could have managed our lives without them. Sometimes they were superficial — like cleaning our teeth regularly, Kay would say. But in the powerful and dramatic groups you felt you were being turned inside out so that your entrails were show-ing. I remember one of my first groups, where Melanie who was German (she would also die of cancer) described how she had been pregnant and desperate and couldn't get into a hospital in Berlin to give birth, although there seemed to be complications. This was in 1945. Hitler's capital was now choked with rubble from bombs and shells, and those hospitals still standing were full of wounded and dying, both civilians and soldiers, every age, some of them Hitler's boy soldiers of thirteen. And this was the same time when, hundreds of miles south of Berlin, I was dragging my swollen feet along German country roads, one of the column of swollen feet under the noses of German guards and guns. In that group twenty years later we had a strange meeting, Melanie and I, the German and the Jewess. We could embrace each other as the stereotypes peeled away like the petals of an artichoke from its heart. Each of us an innocent victim in a different way, each caught up in terrifying mass movements and mass murders far beyond our control. That group began a friendship which lasted all the years of living together. And you know, too, how close I became to her son Eric, and Alan also, her second son. Alan was hard to understand. As a little boy he was strangely withdrawn, as if lost: he loved to listen to music by himself: he would creep upstairs into our kitchen and appear behind me suddenly, so that I jumped, and then just talk to me nonstop. I cried bitterly, you remember, when he died so suddenly and mysteriously in that dancehall, a teenager caught up with sniffing glue and some wild kids . . .

I'm rambling, sometimes you liked that and sometimes you couldn't stand it. I'm being your *dilinos* again, your scatterbrain, remember? But I have to ramble now, I'm flooded with so many memories of life in CHOFA.

Memories not just of big events. Like our own New Year celebrations, which always began seriously — before the hugging and the dancing into the early hours and the food and wine — with each one reviewing what had gone on inside themselves, how aware they'd become of this or that, how this awareness had modified what they wished for the future. Or the birthdays, which again were always serious and 'clarifying' as we called it, as well as wonderful fun, because we really learned, I think, the freedom to celebrate each other and our own being alive, really to laugh. Or the nightly readings and meditations, where we squeezed our own juices out of passages from the Bible which had become dried-up. Or how we worked together in groups through our anger and our grief after the deaths from cancer; first Sean's — a few years after he'd had one lung removed — and then Melanie's, with a tumor in her brain, when we took turns to sit with her, her eyesight gone, until — it was an Easter Sunday — she finally died. Or that ritual burial of my soap with its RJF imprint, a ritual which meant so much to me.

I mean that I'm flooded with memories of so many small things, of everyday living. I really like your dream about the rich archaeological strata. But you know, *édesem,* when they find things in a dig, or in the wreck of a ship sunk to the bottom of the sea, it's not just the jeweled goblets and the great casks of silver coins that matter, it's the little things, like tiny pieces of broken pottery, that you put together to give the everyday picture and the real feel of how people lived.

But I've a big bone to pick with you. I thought you'd long been cured of your old school tie chauvinism. How come you had less to say about the women than the men? Most women had degrees and professions which they left to concentrate on bringing up their children. Willingly. And you know how much value we gave this task, a value not usually given to it in these times when women want to throw off what they regard as a yoke, and enter the world dominated by men. The women at CHOFA shared the upbringing by means of a rota or schedule, so they never suffered the isolation of most mothers. But that also meant each child had a rich web of family adults so that, as Amy said on the Thames TV film about us, 'You could go to anyone with your troubles.' You wrote about the authority of the parents being sometimes undermined by Kay, and that's true. But it couldn't really destroy that wonderful crisscross of relationships which enriched both children and parents in our 'extended family'.

And how I was enriched by it! Of course, those of us who had no children took no part in the rota; we had our professional work, as Rosemarie her dancing, Gwen her library at Kings College, or myself my ceramics. But I too was a proxy mother to the children I couldn't bear myself. I knew most of them from birth, even before, because I shared the excitements and the troubles of the pregnancies and the actual deliveries, and I babysat and changed their diapers, and I worried over them even as their childhood slipped through our fingers so quickly. All the gurgles and peals of laughter, so much laughter, all the shouts and the sobs, blown across the garden to our corner and captured in the beech leaves outside our window. They're still caught there in my mind. Alongside their mothers I had joy and anxiety from the children. How can I forget the time when Joel as a toddler in our own unit tumbled down the whole flight of stairs, maybe twenty stairs. It was Jacqueline's first baby, neither of us could believe in the resilience of babies, who survive earthquakes and houses collapsed from bombing. Jacqueline and I were both so frightened, and afterwards reassured together. Joel was one of my special loves, and later Ellen his little sister also — for you too, *édesem* — remember you dedicated *A Basket of Eggs* to her, your first published book of children's pieces? Her name was in print before she could read!

Some of the other children became special as I taught them pottery, and we worked together with hands or on the wheel. I shared in the parents' worries as well as their pride — the children's jealousies, their feelings of inadequacy, their school set-ups. And then into their late teenage all the choices of colleges and careers: Adrian to become an architect like his father but his brother Ian to do art history at Cambridge and wind up in computers, Suzanne, an architect's daughter also, to do architectural landscaping at Manchester, Martin to teach handicapped children, Gerald to Imperial College but his twin Malcolm trying to become a tennis pro, Amy to art school in Dublin but then onto the stage and TV like her father, her

brother Tom, whom you taught, a composer, James into
ecology, like his father, at Bristol, but then his own path
into radio and TV reporting.

Space wasn't the problem it might have been, was it?
We gave up space to live that kind of life. Like sharing
the kitchen, and cooking and eating together. Like doing
without a separate private bathroom. Of course that had
to have its problems. As when Jim objected to my hanging my wet laundry there. As he was angry also when I
took it on myself to paint the toilet — he called it a slap-
dash job, and he didn't like the yellow either. But the issue was, we hadn't talked about it first. This was a practical side to the 'learning to live together'. We usually
found that practical things weren't so hard to settle if we
first sorted out the tensions and attitudes behind them.
Sharing table and bathroom helped to bring us closer. Or
I'd put it differently: it forced the issue of how close we
really wanted to be. Of course we shared things at many
levels: like theater and films and music and books. But
sharing such physical necessities as kitchen and bathroom
always brought us back and down to a kind of bedrock of
sharing that most 'friends' don't have to face. That is what
made CHOFA so exceptional and worthwhile, but also explosive.

Among the 'big things' I remember, my darling, I
haven't even mentioned one of the biggest things of all
— the day of our own marriage in 1963! You remember
how careful we'd been, how we'd both tested it out by
living in separate rooms. The deed's done in a few words,
but you can never know for sure about a marriage until
you've actually lived it, and worked at it, and for years
too. The time of our marriage was another springtime of
life for each of us, in our late thirties. Both you and I have
been lucky enough to have many springtimes. Some steal-
ing over us so that we hardly noticed them, others bursting with the energy of new sap. Have we needed them
more than most people, perhaps? At that time, the community had just moved into its new common houses, you
had just begun your new lecturing job at the college, I

had just begun to fulfill my dream of being a fulltime potter — and we were discovering each other. Ah, we didn't have a marriage but a whole dayful of marriages! A basketful of rituals! All in my new sky-blue suit and under my new black umbrella hat which you loved. A smiling day, across Richmond Park, past the year's frail new crop of fawns, to the civil ceremony in Kingston; through London to the Christian marriage mass in the crypt of Westminster Cathedral; then the ancient Jewish benedictions, in the very common room we used for our groups and so haunted by them . . . At night the party in the common room reserved for celebrations. Some wild dancing too, Rosemarie the professional dancer with Stephen leaping and twirling up onto sofas and tables, your brother Mac and his wife Sonia kicking out their legs *à la Russe* . . . Our own private gala of dance and drink and merriment, all swirling around a still and unforgettable moment of seriousness, when Kay said that you and I belonged together, myself the victim of Auschwitz, you of a more personal upheaval, of a leucotomy; we could understand and help each other because the effects were similar.

LETTER TWENTY-EIGHT
Dita to Ronald

Why your silence?

Why haven't I heard from you? Why this silence?

I remember your silences. Sometimes because you were wrapped up in your own thoughts and feelings. You could be very self-contained. Other times it was aggressive. But I also recognize your silence now. This time, *you're covering up something, aren't you?*

What's happened?

You're with another woman, aren't you? You don't want to tell me. Partly because you're frightened. Partly because you don't want to hurt me, you still want to protect me, even though I'm beyond your protection now.

You've got married again? You have, haven't you? Tell me about her. What does she look like? Is she beautiful? Attractive? Sexy? Is she like me at all? Yes, of course I'm jealous. You and I were just trying to do something about our love-making when I discovered my 'lump' and within a few months there was no body left to play with, fore, during or after.

I'm thinking, do you still ejaculate too soon? You always were quick off the mark, weren't you? Always in a hurry to gobble everything up, even me when you already had me. Because you'd been so deprived, wasn't it? Gobble-de-dook, fits and froth, and it was boiling over and spilt milk again. What a waste! Of course I was angry sometimes, but still, aaaah! how I loved that penis of yours, my little king, perched on two golden orbs, too quick to crumble, crown and all! Nowadays people have implants, don't they? Automated sex machinery. Prolonging the thrusts of love, as pacemakers prolong the beats of the heart. You haven't done that, have you? Come to think of it, implants would work for dead bodies too. Imagine, intercourse between corpses to catch up on what they missed before their souls left them! A ghouls' paradise! Provided, of course, that their bodies haven't been burned to cinders and ashes like mine. So we couldn't ever catch up, could we?

You and me — whom you insist on reducing to a ghost in your computer like a neutron particle.

LETTER TWENTY-NINE
Ronald to Dita

My new life

The reason for my silence, *Ditukam,* is that it's so hard to lay your ghost. To free myself from your haunting my new life and, yes, you are right, my new woman. And now that I'm in New York — it was *your* New York, though I'm making it mine, I see your ghost everywhere. Not surprisingly — you had your apartment there, I saw you in West 73rd Street, carrying carrots and sweet potatoes in a brown bag. From the A & P supermarket, I'm sure. Then again in the Verdi Square on Broadway (Triangle really, like all New York Squares) to which your old street forms a tangent. Three times. Once you were cashing a cheque in the munificent bank-palace which reigns over the Square. Later you were standing very still below the stone Verdi on his pedestal. For a foolish moment I thought you'd been transfigured yourself, like the petrified characters from his operas surrounding the composer. The third time I was working in the Ansonia, the other side of the Square, which was itself full of other ghosts like Stravinsky and Caruso, and though I didn't actually see you in the flesh, I heard you. It was your voice without any doubt. First you were moaning, as if you were in pain, deep moans, belly moans, horribly disturbing,

and they splintered all my fragile musical ideas like breaking glass. But after a moment you were laughing! That
hearty contralto laughter, with a silvery edge of lace.

It's you all right, no question. I ought to be angry with
you, really. . . I have to exorcize you from New York, again
and again, as well as from my bed.

No, Miriam is dark-haired, you're fair. Or were. Yes,
she's beautiful, and yes, she's sexy. It seems almost inces-
tuous, since I was introduced to her by David, your lover
in New York whom you left to marry me in England (and
we became friends instead of enemies). I hope you'd ap-
prove of Miriam: I can't tell you how rich a life we've
built together, and how much she means to me. Our story
began when David took me to a musical soirée given by
a pianist whose career he thought I might be able to help
in Europe. I was welcomed by a woman whose energy
overflowed like the inner tides of New York itself, bubbling into her eyes, which seemed oversized like everything else in this city, from skyscrapers and stretch limos
to crime. First sight, second sight, far sight, hindsight, they
were all encapsulated there, and she has said that she
knew at once. She'd spent fifteen fulfilling but single
years, enclosed in music and in circles of friends like the
circles of the sound waves she made herself, not expecting to find someone to love and be loved by.

Myself? I was two persons. One person threw himself
into this new relationship greedily, hungry for life to hum
and drum along the fibers of his nerves again, for only
yesterday they'd been paralyzed as your healthy body
shriveled into death, and they wanted to be cured of their
own mortality. Into one week only, he and she already
compressed a mini-history.

The other person — well, how could he discard so
quickly, overnight, not just a skin, like a lizard in spring,
but what seemed to cling to his bones like his own flesh ?
In the B.H. era (Before the Holocaust), when you were a
child, my squirrel, did you ever play with zoetropes, those
circular toys with pictures around the circumference, discs
which you spun around, or else those flick cards with

pictures at the edges, so that the pictures fluttered together
— now separate, now merging into one continuous moving image, then separate again as you slowed down the
spin of the disc or the flick of the cards? That's like the
mystery of loving and bonding. Two people who are really quite separate, fusing together into a single motion
of living, into a unique private civilization. When one of
them dies, it seems that bereavement makes the world
stop spinning. Then is the separateness highlighted as
never before: and the fusion that is now lost forever ago-
nizes the memory.

Back to Person Number One who had recoiled from
death like a spring, and boomeranged into life's ocean
currents. (Boomeranged, because he had still to return, of
course, to his mourning for you. To these ghostly letters.)
In London, he had embraced a beautiful Bulgarian architect . . . And now Miriam, like a witch or goddess of mythology, flew across the Atlantic's entire three thousand
miles (on a Jumbo Jet, not a broomstick) carrying an en-
chanted pecan pie baked by her own hands. Now he, our
foolish hero, exhausted by acrobatic juggling of his two
newfound women, made a confused decision. New York
was too much of an upheaval for him, he said to her. She
was brave: 'I don't expect I'll meet anyone else now. But
I'll survive . . . ' He invited her for one last dinner together.
In a Greek restaurant in Soho, they sobbed away the
evening. A bewildered waiter came and went with *me-
sas* untouched but well watered.

So began my own tale of two cities, commuting between
New York and London. New York teemed with new life
for me, and my dreams responded with time-proof symbols. Deep into one night I was transformed into a dark-
skinned woman, whose hair was a mass of writhing
snakes. And there were scarab beetles crawling all over
me. I woke up frightened and excited by these ancient
symbols. The snakes of mythology slither through the
earth carrying the secret of hidden energies. As the snake
has twin fangs, so those powers may work for good or
for destruction. They had once destroyed me, thirty years

earlier. The head of the Greek goddess Medusa flaunted a fierce mane of snakes instead of tresses, and to look upon her face to face was to die. Yet there we were, Medusa and I, linked together in Riverdale, New York, and her frightening energies were available, so it seemed, to me. And then there were the scarab beetles. Symbols of rebirth, for they lay their eggs in dung, in seemingly dead and used-up matter, yet out of this comes the forms of new life. (Life out of excreta . . . Do you remember the obsession of my madness?) Khepri, the Egyptian god, appeared as a scarab, or with a scarab face, for he was the god of life's transformations. And it is a sacred symbol also for the American Indians.

Yet another dream was of an egg. Simple, primordial. White, unblemished. Again the container of new life. Luminous, it lay there for me to eat, to assimilate into my own blood like a sacrament to replenish me. Inside was a wonderful chocolate substance, luscious and creamy with the richest butter-milk of existence. And then yet again, I dreamed one night of a precious golden box, numinous, its delicately-lacquered lid lying opened. Inside lay a moist wad of leaf, thick and dark green, offering itself, enticing me to eat it. The fertile stuff of life. Of new life.

Another time, I dreamed I went with a dark-haired, dusky woman to a White Mass — the antithesis of a Black Mass. The tabernacle was dressed in the whitest of white cloth, and inside, I knew, lay the heart of the god of all gods. Everything, outside the sanctuary as within it, was speckled with blood. It was sanctifying blood. The choir sang *Kadosh, Kadosh, Kadosh* in Hebrew, which means *Holy, Holy, Holy,* with the sweetness of harmony in thirds. In the history of European music, harmony in thirds developed in the Renaissance, that is in the 'Rebirth', after the time called the 'Dark' Ages: it was the harmony of a world newly revealed and a new world of discovery. So too was I discovering a personal New World of my own in the historical New World.

Snakes and scarabs, chocolate Easter egg, lacquered golden box, white mass blessing a New World, all messengers of life which the next decade fulfilled. So many new friends; but also professional recognition: I was 'a composer of real stature' said the New York Times; and my work for you, the *Holocaust Requiem,* performed under the baton of Lukas Foss in that great Gothic St. John's Cathedral, a huge ribcage for a caring heart, was nominated for the Pulitzer Prize. The test of this work is the great effect it has had on survivors who were in the camps themselves. Jerry Jacobs was in Auschwitz like yourself (as well as five other camps!), and had buried his pain — until he heard my oratorio. It was the centerpiece of the Kristallnacht commemoration in 1988, at the Tilles Center in Long Island, also with Lukas Foss conducting. You remember how I formed masses of sound by having the children's choir chant names of the camp victims, with your own name highlighted? In that performance, children filed out into the aisles as they sang, holding lighted candles in their hands. Ah, if tears could change the world! Perhaps even the impenetrable God also shed a tear that evening. After that experience, Jerry Jacobs set up his 'Interfaith Concerts of Remembrance', in the first of which my *Requiem* — your *Requiem* — was the main event. As in Canterbury Cathedral, Christians and Jews collaborated in mourning.

You know, don't you, that I have a post-psychotic wariness of what came to be called *romantic* a century and a half ago: the passion which can destroy if it is not harnessed, or which declines into sentimentality and nostalgia for a past removed from everyday reality. The partnership Miriam and I have developed is both romantic and everyday: romantic it is, in the style of Chopin and George Sands, or Robert and Clara Schumann, but also down to earth. Romance and reality? Only a few weeks after we met, I took Miriam in reality to the unreal Queen's garden party at Buckingham Palace, where I was being honored for services to music, a week before the wedding of Prince Charles and Diana. The palace gardens and its guests milling past pastel flamingos, secluded by a wall from the hurly-burly of Victoria Station, dreamed for an afternoon of the once vigorous myth of royal divinity, with all its pomp and pageantry representing the heavens on earth, its crown of the stars, its sceptred orb of this globe. Here was *romantic* in decay, necromantic, nostalgia for the corpses of tradition. For my American lady, you can imagine, this was the stuff of fantasy, a status fantasy, a film-set where women compete in outrageous hats.

Romantic? I write Miriam music which she performs everywhere, from London to Hong Kong, from Bombay to Bangkok, from Prague to Jerusalem, from New York to St. Petersburg. The whole world is cut open for us, like an orange peeled, by the courses of the luxury cruise ships on which Miriam gives classical recitals or is music direc-tor. We were engaged on the *Sagafjord* at Bar Harbor in Maine, on its way to the St. Lawrence and Montreal. We usually cross the Atlantic between our two homes in Lon-don and New York on the elegant Queen Elizabeth II. We have crossed the Indian Ocean on the *Rotterdam,* through the Suez Canal to Cairo, Ismir, Athens, Haifa. We sail the Caribbean regularly to St. Thomas, Martinique, St. Maarten, Barbados . . . The *Crown Odyssey* to Cartagena, through the Panama Canal, to Costa Rica and Mexico; across the Pacific, Hawai, Samoa, Fiji, to New Zealand: or into the Arctic Apocalypse of the North Cape, where a midnight sun swallows up the nights, while Miriam plays piano dressed in white like an angelic apparition.

We could make a fascinating volume of vignettes of people we meet on the ships. Dmitri Shostakovitch — the year before he died — whom Miriam advised to sit in the balcony of the Queen Elizabeth II Theater, the better to hear her recital. (Maxim his son we took to dinner in Hong Kong: and Miriam has played under his baton in New York.) The weeks on the *Rotterdam* with Teddy Kollek, the *shalom*- making Mayor of *Yir-shalom,* city of peace, Jerusalem: sunning himself on the pool deck as the Egyp-tian premier Mubarak was sailing his yacht below on the Suez Canal. Rusty Schweikhart in the next cabin to ours, the first man ever to walk in space: a mystical experience, he told us, like a rebirth out of the Earth's belly, the mother-

sphere rotating beneath him in all her giant gravity. Rusty
was one of the three astronauts on the failed Apollo 13
moon flight: after an explosion in the main rocket, they
climbed into the command module to travel the three days
back to earth in darkness and bitter cold to conserve electricity, while the whole world watched them on television . . . Or Bill Bronk, a top NASA astronomer, whose
ancestors gave their name to the Bronx. A succession of
writers, actors and actresses: Cornel Wilde on the *Royal
Odyssey,* an old man now, no longer the romantic Chopin or the muscular movie he-man, delighted by Miriam's
playing. Or Virginia Mayo — you remember she was
Danny Kaye's dreamgirl in *The Secret Life of Walter Mitty?*
I shared with that legend the 'creative writing' class
onboard, and she was still beautiful. Terence Stamp the
actor, who was born a few blocks from where I was, in
the East End of London — he who ravished an entire bourgeois family, one by one, in Pasolini's film 'Teorema', taking homosexuality out of the closet with all its cobwebbed
guilt. Lynn Redgrave. Tony Warren who created *Corona-
tion Street,* Jeffrey Archer. Charles Strauss, the composer
of *Annie.* Anthony Newley of *Stop the World I want to
get off . . .*

There is another side to Miriam's work which is dear
to me: she plays for the chronically sick and the elderly in
many nursing homes, and has had a US Government
grant for this work. Music penetrates through and behind the disorders of the mind, a healing power revered
in many cultures. I experienced that myself, remember?
Miriam plays not only for the organized institutions, but
also for the 'bag-ladies' from the shadow-world of the
homeless, the destroyed women who wander the streets
of Manhattan carrying their belongings in bags, the remnants of their lives. I remember them in the basement of
the Times Square Hotel, gathered off the streets by the
Franciscan Sisters on a Tuesday, hovering in strange pos-
tures against the walls, sullenly, as far as they could from
each other and from the upright piano as if it were a light
hurting their eyes or challenging them out of their pri-

vate worlds. As Miriam played — and also talked to them, asking them to bring their memories to the music, they thawed, they drew closer to the piano and to each other, and at the end could not leave Miriam alone. A token handful of the needy: for New York has emptied its mental asylums and, as in the Middle Ages of Europe, the mentally sick wander through the city's unfriendly streets.

Ditukam, I can't tell you how rich a new life I owe to Miriam. You could have chosen her for me yourself. Perhaps you did.

And we have been back to your own Czechoslovakia. Prague, a few months after the 'Velvet Revolution', with introductions to the young men from the Civic Forum who first began the march from the Charles Bridge to Wenceslas Square, introductions even to Havel himself, now improbably President in the Hradjany Castle. And of course your ghost haunted me there, as it did in New York. Many times.

I am getting angry at your ghosts, I have to repeat. I do need to be free of you at last. I glimpse the electric eyes of an eight-year old girl, eager, spellbound among the stones of the old square, the *Staromeska.* I see her, holding the crabbed hand of her skullcapped grandfather, even on the stairway of the austere *Stone House* where Miriam is playing. My Miriam. My new wife. You've got some nerve! They're not very tactful, your ghosts. They don't choose the right time or place. And now I'm looking at a teenage specter who is fingering that silk scarf which was your sixteenth birthday present. She is peering impishly around the free-standing pillars in the *Naprikape,* which are now plastered with posters telling the truth about the Communist years. I catch glimpses of her from the inside of the shop where I am buying Miriam some jewelry. I watch spring bursting and spilling from her eyes onto the stones and pillars of the Prague street. Just as it bursts from your eyes in the teenage photo I have of you, also wearing that silk scarf . . .

Perhaps it's not so surprising that your ghosts should appear in Prague, in the country where you grew up, or in New York, where you lived for years. But in Moscow? In the Great Hall of the Conservatory, no less. Once, during a break in the rehearsal of my *Holocaust Requiem* — or is it, after all, *your* Requiem? — you were at the top of the magnificent marble stairway. Again, you were at the back of the orchestra itself, the Moscow Philharmonic, standing next to the timpani, while the adult choir were rehearsing the final *Kaddish* prayer for the dead. The third time you were up in the balcony by the oval portraits of the Great Composers, your head was bobbing up and down beneath Beethoven's. Beethoven continued to frown into the hall while Miriam played the piano solo in his Choral Fantasy: but at least you had the good grace not to show up during that time. Although I half expected you to.

As I did elsewhere in Moscow, along the potholed streets, in front of the peeling pastel paints on the walls, in and out of the stalls and the old men and women in the cold of all hours selling anything they can, including their household possessions: or I thought I'd see you at the luxurious Danilovsky Monastery, at the dinner after my concert, impish among all those dignitaries, sticking your finger into the cheese or caviar, the way you used to lick the jam. And I thought you would haunt my other concerts too, where my *Requiem* wasn't played, the one at the smaller Philharmonic Hall in St. Petersburg, the one later at the Composers' Union in Moscow, in both of which Miriam figured so largely. Ah, you'd have had some nerve!

But of course you were there to haunt me at the Nazi camp Terezin near Prague even in May 1995. How could you not be? Your hair glinting in the morning sunlight, in and out of the endless rows of stones in the cemetery, even peering at me, sad-eyed, through the wreaths which the ambassadors of each nation laid as a commemoration, half a century after the camp's liberation. And then in the courtyard of the Little Fortress, surrounded by the cells which had been Gestapo torture chambers, you were there on the podium with the orchestra and choirs and soloists, there in front of the angle of wall against which prisoners had been shot. Your ghost among all the other ghosts. The ghosts of the dead, of the tortured and of the murdered. And the living ghosts of the survivors. One lady was amazed to hear something she had written as a child prisoner, fifty years before, now set to my music. My *Holocaust Requiem* was a Kaddish for Terezin, as well as for you especially; and now the ghosts of Terezin, dead and alive, were there in the very place they had suffered and died, and my music was being played and sung for them as it was for you.

Were you ever going to cease to haunt me, my darling?

But I finally understood. Well, really, deep down, I always had. And you were reminding me of what I'd always known. I'd even written you about it myself, remember, about your being two persons for me. Two persons, and hence two ghosts. Your two ghosts. The one which wanders into my mourning for you, as the ghosts of the dead always haunt the bereaved who loved them living. The ghost which must learn to disappear at the right time, to bow itself out as the sunlit seeds of new life take root, grow in brilliance and make it invisible. I am sure there must be some school for ghosts to achieve this gracefully.

The other ghost is the symbol of suffering and surviving, and in particular of Auschwitz. This is the ghost I recognized in the Great Hall of the Conservatory. When I think it roams through buildings, in and out of pillars and balconies, I am mistaken. This ghost of yours, my love, searches only through my musical architecture itself, among the bricks and stones of sounds, in and out of the arches of harmonic tones, as it did in Canterbury Cathedral or St. John the Divine in New York, as it will in Tel-Aviv and Prague and Washington and Los Angeles and London and Berlin and Sydney, and wherever else this *Kaddish-Requiem* is performed, searching always for the same thing, for the meaning of so much pain and cruelty. Because music is not merely a game of plasmic forms in plasmic skins: it penetrates into the very nucleus of the cosmos. And your ghost searches for the insight, the transfiguration, and finally the peace which music promises.

And therefore I yearn, my dear one, that this music will swell and rise from so many cities into the atmosphere itself and into all its secret recesses of silence, the silence where music is at home after all words have faltered and failed; that its sound waves will pattern and paint the air like the phosphorescent wings of night-moths; this music which is so insubstantial but has the substance of our lives locked up within it; music which carries us with it even while it swallows up our souls, which bears all our sorrows and all the anguish of time into timeless zones, mingling with the incense from ancient altars which propitiated the anger of gods, purging the black smoke from the Auschwitz chimneys and all its shame: I yearn for this music to reach you, you whom I loved, and soothe your pain as it soothes my own, and finally to lay your ghost. Music, which makes us mad in order to heal us.

Chronology

1944: (May) Dita taken to Auschwitz. All her family are gassed except her father.
1944: (May) Ronald wins scholarship to Oxford and goes up in September.

1945: (February) Dita liberated by Russians, after a month's forced march westwards out of Auschwitz.

1946: Dita and her father emigrate from Kosice in Czechoslovakia first to Palestine (Haifa) and then to USA. (California, New York).

1950: Prefrontal leucotomy performed on Ronald in St. Andrew's Hospital, Northampton.

1944: 2000 tons of bombs on Berlin; 1000 V-2 rockets on Britain; D-Day landings in Normandy (June); German officers attempt to assassinate Hitler; US forces enter Germany near Trier; Red Army occupies Hungary, besiege Budapest.
1945: Hitler's suicide Apr. 30; Germany capitulates May 7; US drops atomic bombs on Hiroshima (Aug. 6) and Nagasaki (Aug. 9); Japan surrenders Aug. 14.
1946: UN holds first session in London, Jan. 7; verdict of Nuremberg War Crimes Tribunal — death sentence on Ribbentrop, Goering and 10 other Nazis.
1950: Britain recognizes Israel; West Germany joins Council of Europe.

1960: Dita and Ronald meet in London, and begin to live together. Dita comes to London from Lugano where Riverside Records (of whom she is a director) has an office. Riverside Records, founded by Bill Grauer and Oran Keepnews, a leading US promoter of jazz records, are setting up another office in London. Dita is also visiting Daniel, whose sister is her friend in New York. [Daniel was sent from Czechoslovakia as a child to England, his parents died in the camps. He would commit suicide 25 years later.] In this way Dita meets the members of CHOFA (chosen family) and even begins therapy sessions with Kay, who is the community's founder and inspiration. The members are sharing several separate apartments, although meeting together regularly.

1963: Dita and Ronald married within the community CHOFA, which in this year had moved to a group of large houses in Surrey, converted into a single communal complex of private and communal space.

1969: Ronald and Dita make their first trip to Australia, and round the world.

1960: Former Gestapo Chief Adolf Eichman arrested by Israeli agents; John F. Kennedy elected President of the United States; the President of West Germany, Konrad Adenauer visits the United States; the US nuclear submarine *Triton* circumnavigates the globe under water; William L. Shirer publishes *The Rise and Fall of the Third Reich;* neo-Nazi political groups banned in Germany.

Between 1944 and 1960, some 200,000 leucotomies performed in Europe and North America, using the so-called standard leucotomy developed by two American surgeons at Georgetown University, Freeman and Watts. But the number of operations declined dramatically by 1960, because of the ghastly after-effects.

1963: Nuclear test ban is signed by US, USSR, and Great Britain; 200,000 'Freedom Marchers', blacks and whites, descend on Washington; President Kennedy assassinated in Dallas, Texas.

1969: Neil Armstrong steps onto the moon from Apollo 11 module.

1980: Dita's father dies of colon cancer. In June, ovarian cancer diagnosed in Dita; growth removed surgically, further diagnosis reveals spread of cancer; chemical treatments follow
1981: (February) Dita dies.
1981: (May) Ronald meets Miriam in New York

1982-4: Ronald composes *Holocaust Requiem (Kaddish for Terezin)* in memory of Dita.
1986: (June) *Holocaust Requiem (Kaddish for Terezin)* premièred at Canterbury Cathedral in England under the auspices of the B'nai Brith, the United Nations, and the German Government.
1988: US première of *Holocaust Requiem (Kaddish for Terezin)* in Tillis Center, Long Island. Brooklyn Philharmonic conducted by Lukas Foss.
1990: Manhattan première of *Holocaust Requiem (Kaddish for Terezin):* Lukas Foss directing Brooklyn Philharmonic, Ron Silver as Narrator. Nominated for the Pulitzer Prize.

1980: Iran-Iraq War; Israel opens embassy in Cairo; Soviet cosmonauts end 185 days in space; Ronald Reagan elected president of US.

1981: Israeli air-raid destroys Iraq atomic reactor; 8 ex-Nazi guards convicted in W. Germany; death of Albert Speer, architect of Nazi concentration camps; President Sadat assassinated.
1982: Israelis invade Lebanon; blamed 'indirectly' for Sabra and Shatila massacre.
1986: Gorbachev offers plan to eliminate all nuclear arms by the year 2000; Pope John Paul II's unprecedented pontifical visit to Rome's central Synagogue.

1988: Arab uprising in Israel begins; Reagan signs agreement with Gorbachev on arms control and human rights.

1990: Neo-Nazis disrupt Leipzig rally, march in Dresden, celebrate Hitler's birthday; German Parliament apologizes for Holocaust, bans Nazi Party; Germany re-unified, Berliners cross border for May Day.

1992: Historic performance of *Holocaust Requiem (Kaddish for Terezin)* in the Great Hall of the Moscow Conservatory, first official Russian recognition of specifically Jewish suffering in the Nazi Holocaust: Moscow Philharmonic conducted by Spiegelman, Bel Kaufman as Narrator: video, and CD by Delos.

1995: May 21-3. Three-day commemoration of the liberation of the Terezin (Theresienstadt) Nazi camp, in the presence of the President of the Czech Parliament, Vaclav Havel, the ambassadors and consuls of many countries, and many of the camp's survivors from all over the world. Performance of the *Holocaust Requiem* on the morning of May 21 in the Little Fortress courtyard by the Czech Radio Symphony orchestra and the State Opera Chorus, conducted by Vladimir Valek.

1992: Memorial at former Nazi camp at Sachsenhausen destroyed by arson; Holocaust Museum opened at Wannsee 50 years after Hitler's 'Final Solution' Conference there; Schwammberger, former overseer of Polish Camps (including Auschwitz) sentenced for war crimes; secret talks begin in Norway, leading to limited Israel-PLO agreement on the West Bank: Clinton elected President of the US.

1995: Fifty years after the unconditional surrender of Nazi Germany in 1945, most European countries, the US and many other countries worldwide commemorated the end of World War II in Europe. Special photographic and art exhibitions were arranged, television documentaries were shown, radio programs were broadcast, books were published, and commemorative services were attended by Royalty, Heads of State, and ambassadors in London, Paris, Washington and elsewhere.